Return to the Drum

Teaching Among the Dene in Canada's North

To Carolyne,

Hope you enjoy these Northern stories,

Best Wishes,
Miggs
Feb 2002.

Miggs Wynne Morris

Canadian Cataloguing in Publication Data
Morris, Miggs Wynne, 1938-
Return to the drum

ISBN 1-896300-31-6

1. Morris, Miggs Wynne, 1938- 2. Déline (N.W.T.)—Biography.
3. Teachers—Northwest Territoris—Déline—Biography. I. Title.
FC4199.D44Z49 2000 971.9303'092 C00-910690-1
F1100.5.D44M67 2000

Editor: Eva Radford
Map: Wendy Johnson, Johnson Cartographics
Interior lineart: Robert Nichols
Cover and interior photographs: Miggs Wynne Morris (unless otherwise stated)

Front cover photos: *top:* This picture of the fireweed was taken at Déline at 11:30 PM in July 1995. *middle:* Fort Franklin drummers, 1966. *bottom:* Ice fishing on Great Bear Lake, 1966.

NeWest Press acknowledges the support of the Canada Council for the Arts and the Alberta Foundation for the Arts for our publishing program. We also acknowledge the financial support of the Government of Canada through the Book Publishing Industry Development Program (BPIDP) for our publishing activities.

NeWest Press
201-8540-109 Street
Edmonton, Alberta T6G 1E6
(780) 432-9427
www.newestpress.com

1 2 3 4 5 04 03 02 01 00

PRINTED AND BOUND IN CANADA

This book is dedicated to my former students
and friends at Déline (Fort Franklin), NWT,
with respect, admiration and affection.

A portion of the proceeds from the sale of this book will go towards a scholarship fund established to assist Sahtuot'ine students from Déline with their post-secondary studies.

ACKNOWLEDGEMENTS

Although writing is often a solitary process, *Return to the Drum* would not have been possible without the involvement of many people who provided support, encouragement and information along the way. To all those listed below and others too numerous to mention, I wish to express my heartfelt gratitude.

First of all, I must thank the people of Fort Franklin/Déline who shared their lives and their friendship with me in the 1960s and then again in 1995. In writing *Return to the Drum* I hope that I have conveyed my deep admiration and sincere affection for these people who are true survivors and whose spirit is indelibly imprinted on my heart.

A special word of thanks to George and Doreen Cleary (now of Yellowknife) who reassured me about returning to Déline in 1995 and arranged for my accommodations, also to Gary Juniper and Cheryl Cleary with whom I stayed in Yellowknife, and to John Baton (now deceased) and his wife, Cec for allowing me to stay with them in Déline that summer. Thanks also to the many Déline residents who filled my notebooks with answers that led to more questions as they shared their perspectives on the changes in Déline. Special thanks to Jimmy Tutcho and Morris Neyelle for allowing me to quote them on the sensitive issues of children's behaviour and alcoholism.

I am particularly indebted to Chuck Bloomquist and René Fumoleau, OMI, both long time residents of Déline and the North. Chuck deserves special appreciation for being so patient and prompt in answering my many questions and verifying numerous details. My friendship with René goes back to those years when he was the priest in Déline in the sixties. He has been a strong advocate in my writing this book. Thanks also to René for allowing me to retell and expand upon our earlier discussions of Treaty 11 by incorporating information from his authoritative work, *As Long As This Land Shall Last*.

Although I look back fondly at many of my non-Dene friends in Déline in the sixties, I also wish to express my gratitude for the advice and friendship of Helen Chan, the nurse in charge, who features prominently in the first chapters of the book.

Sincere appreciation to Mark Kearney, who was one of the first people to support me in the early stages of writing this book as well as providing me with professional advice; and to Elaine Barrie, Cheryl Cleary, Maureen Hyatt, Valorie Tkaczuk, and Carol Robinson-Todd for providing valuable feedback on my manuscript. It has also been very gratifying to receive enthusiastic support for the book from my relatives and friends in Wales and England.

NeWest Press also deserves my appreciation for having the courage to support my vision of this book. I am extremely grateful to Ruth Linka and staff who handled the design, production and publicity so capably, and to Eva Radford, for her gentle guidance and excellent editing skills. Together, they have transformed my manuscript into a much better book.

And lastly, words cannot adequately express my gratitude to my good friend Alison Ogilvie without whose ongoing encouragement, support and patience, this book would never have been completed.

Mahsi cho to you all.

Table of Contents

PREFACE

It was as if the elders were saying:

> *As a people we have always faced challenges. When we lived on the land, every day was a struggle just to survive: being on the edge of starvation when the caribou could not be found for food, clothing, and shelter; times when the fish or rabbits were scarce; times when our families were decimated by death and disease; the intrusion of strangers who changed our lives in so many ways; and always the endless bitter, biting cold, except for a few brief summer months. Dealing with those hardships was our way of life and ultimately we overcame them and survived and believed that life was good. Now we have new hardships and challenges and we shall overcome these too, and even though some will not be able to make the journey, we will survive as a people.*
>
> —From *Return to the Drum*, "The End of a Journey"

Return to the Drum takes the readers on two deeply personal journeys—mine and that of the Sahtuot'ine of Great Bear Lake in the Northwest Territories.

My journey began in 1965 when I arrived at Fort Franklin, a young and naive Welsh teacher who found herself in a isolated northern community of two hundred and fifty Indians, four hundred dogs, one skidoo and nine whites. No radio, no television, no phones, no newspapers, only outdated magazines flown in with the mail and an occasional passenger on the one small plane a month—weather permitting. I entered a world of hunters and trappers, of caribou, fish and moose, of lice and outside latrines, of little English and a whole lot of Slavey, of skilled craftswomen and men, and of delightful, fun-loving students.

It was a time of transition for the Sahtuotíine as the people went from being nomadic hunters and trappers to living a more sedentary existence in the small community where their children were to attend school. Their story, as told in *Return to the Drum*, begins in the mid-1700s before the arrival of the Euro-Canadians. The book touches on the more than two hundred years of profound changes they have undergone—their struggles and their triumphs—as the outside world has encroached upon them.

I left Fort Franklin in 1968 and, other than a brief stay in the summer of 1969, more than twenty-five years were to pass before I was able to visit my former students and friends again, in the summer of 1995. As memories of the time I had spent with these proud and capable people sprang to life during the writing of the early chapters of this book, I felt an increasing need to revisit Fort Franklin, now called Déline again, its original Dene name, and so made plans to return. However, my excitement was tainted with trepidation for what I might find. I had read and heard about the devastating changes that had occurred there, especially in the 1970s and 1980s, when the outside world—both real and televised—had trampled the village, where the Sahtuot'ine, in their confusion, pain and sorrow, had lost much of what they held dear and feared for their future. But I need not have worried. To large extent the people of Déline were back in charge of their lives. I also enjoyed my return visit immensely as I met again many of my former students and old friends.

I did not return in 1995 with the intention of writing about my visit. I thought my book was finished. Once there, however, I realized that I had to continue. Although Déline is a unique community in many respects, *Return to the Drum*, by focusing on one small group of people, sheds light on the concerns, the struggles and the successes of First Nations people across Canada.

The story of the people of Déline is a story of hope, of overcoming insurmountable odds, of laughter and tears, and, for me, a story of love.

Author's notes:

1. Place names used in Part I reflect those commonly used in the 1960s. However, traditional names are used primarily in the Prologue and Chapter 7. Aboriginal names that have come into common usage in recent years are reflected in Part II.
2. The terms Indians, Natives, Aboriginal people, Dene, and First Nations have been used interchangeably; however, Indians and Natives were used more in the first part of the book as was the custom in the 1960s, with Dene coming into greater use in Part II, reflecting its common usage in the western Arctic since that time. First Nations was used sparingly, as the people of Déline in 1995 tended to see that term pertaining more to aboriginal people in southern Canada rather than to themselves.
3. Speech patterns depicted in the book reflect the way children spoke in the 1960s, where English was seldom used in their homes. It does not reflect the speech of children in the 1990s.

Northwest Territories
Denendeh
Area of map
CANADA
Beaufort Sea
Tuktoyaktuk
Aklavik
Inuvik
Paulatuk
Victoria Island
Fort McPherson
Tsiigehtchic (Arctic Red River)
Dehcho (Mackenzie River)
K'áhbamitúé (Colville Lake)
Kugluktuk (Coppermine)
Rádeli Kó (Fort Good Hope)
NUNAVUT
Smith Arm
Arctic Circle
Sahtú (Great Bear Lake)
Echo Bay (Port Radium)
Norman Wells
Déline (Fort Franklin)
Keith Arm
Tulit'a (Fort Norman)
Sahtú Dé (Bear R.)
YUKON
NORTHWEST TERRITORIES
Ekati
Diavik
Diamond Mines
Wrigley
Wha Ti (Lac la Martre)
Edzo
Bèhcho Kó (Rae)
Yellowknife
Fort Simpson
Lútselk'e (Snowdrift)
Nahanni Butte
Fort Providence
Tucho (Great Slave Lake)
Fort Liard
Fort Resolution
Liard River
Hay River
Slave River
Fort Smith
BRITISH COLUMBIA
SASK.
0 100 200 km
Hay River
ALBERTA

PROLOGUE

A summer day in the year known as 1765 to the Europeans

The small birchbark canoe wended its way through the calm waters of the channel between the shoreline and the extensive sheet of ice that covered the large lake known as Sahtu. Paddling the canoe that he and his father had recently built, the young man glanced down at the results from his day of hunting. Four ducks, a fat goose and three ptarmigan, now mottled brown as the snows had long since disappeared, lay at the bottom of his canoe, proof that he had used his bow and arrows well. His father would be pleased that he was at last, in his tenth summer, showing the benefit of all his lessons, and his mother would be glad of the tasty fresh meat.

The day was still warm, with only a slight breeze blowing off the lake ice. He looked towards his destination where some thirty tall tipis stood in a loose cluster along the western shore of Sahtu. Each tipi was made from about eight to ten long spruce poles covered by hides of moose or caribou, or birchbark and branches. As he came closer he could recognize several of the adults strolling between the tipis, and the voices of children at play carried clearly across the water. The youth smiled. He had enjoyed a quiet day of hunting on his own but he was glad to be heading back home towards his family and friends.

He loved this time of year when many families gathered at the place they called *Déline*, "where the waters flow," for a few weeks of fun and feasting and giving thanks to the Creator for having helped them survive yet another winter. The People of Bear Lake, or the *Sahtuot'ine* as they called themselves, had travelled hundreds of kilometres through the tundra forests surrounding Sahtu to come together at this location near where the river exited the lake and the fish were plentiful.

For most of the year, small family clusters scattered throughout this vast land rarely met with others, except when several families joined together to hunt for caribou from the large migrating herd. They lived in small temporary dwellings made from willow and spruce that could be erected quickly when they moved seasonally to follow the migrating caribou. Life was good when food and shelter were abundant, but sometimes, when the caribou did not come close, and the deep snows made it difficult to run down a moose, and the fish had disappeared, as they usually did during the coldest months of the year, sometimes life became tenuous. Winters were long and dark and very cold and the people looked forward to the summer gathering at Déline.

The youth pulled his canoe onto the sandy beach and was immediately thronged by many children eager to see his catch. His younger brother, already down by the lake getting water in a birch bag for his mother, helped him carry his bow and remaining arrows. They headed through the summer encampment towards their tipi and the youth nodded proudly at the words of praise from some of the elders as they eyed his catch. As the boys approached their summer home, the youth could see his mother cleaning the fish caught by his father in the long net of woven strips of willow bark placed near the edge of the ice towards the river. Some of the fish would be boiled and eaten in the next day or two; the rest would be dried for future use on rods erected over smoking fires inside the tipi. The smoke also helped keep the mosquitoes away at night, although they were less numerous by the lake than in the bush.

His mother smiled when he handed her his catch. She told him there would be a drum dance that night, the first one held since their arrival a few days earlier. He was pleased. The night before he had attended a handgame, where two teams of men competed against each other in a complicated guessing game. He wished he could have joined in but he was not yet old enough, and so he had to stand with the women who loudly cheered on the players for many hours into the night. But he hadn't minded too much as he reveled in the pounding of the drums that added to the excitement of the game. As his mother began to pluck and clean the birds, he wandered happily through the camp.

Oh, this was such a good time of year with its abundance of trout, whitefish, herring and grayling, an occasional caribou or moose, fresh fowl as he had caught today, and an assortment of berries from the surrounding shrubs, picked by the women and young girls. Not having to spend hours in the daily chores so necessary to survival in the bush, people could just sit together and tell stories about the events of the past year and join in the Dene games. It was also a time for parents to arrange suitable marriage partners for the young men and women. Soon it will be my turn, thought the youth, but he was glad not to be the subject of discussion for a few more years.

Soon, the aroma from the roasting ducks cooking on wooden spits over the fire made him feel hungry and reminded him that he had eaten but a few pieces of dried moose meat since leaving early in the morning. Eating wild fowl and fresh fish would make a nice change from the diet of dried caribou, moose and fish of the past weeks. A handful of berries, washed down by a brew of herb tea, would complete the feast.

That night, the sounds of drums carried from the direction of a large fire just beyond the tipis. Drawn towards the drumming, all the people came together. A small group of men stood around the fire, warming the round, flat drums until the caribou hide reached a certain pitch when struck by a wooden stick. He loved the sound of the drums. His father had made a small one and carried it around in the bush, so that they might give thanks to the Creator each time an animal provided them with food. But the sound of one drum was nothing compared to several beaten in unison and accompanied by the high-pitched singing of the men.

Several elders, recognized as having strong medicine power, began to walk slowly in a big circle around the fire, beating the drums and singing the sacred prayer songs passed down from generation to generation, while the people followed in prayer. The elders gave thanks to the Creator for helping the Sahtuot'ine survive the long, harsh winter and for bringing them together to this place called Déline to feast well and enjoy each other's company. They gave thanks for the rich land on which they could roam freely and for the medicine power that helped them survive. Then they gave thanks to all the animals for giving themselves to the people to provide food and clothing and other necessities of life. And finally, they asked the Creator to help the Sahtuot'ine again during the coming year.

Once the prayer songs had ended, the social drum dances began. The youth, entranced by the pulsating of the drums and the primordial voices of the drummers, joined in the circle with the others as they danced for many hours to the ancient songs. He didn't notice the sun dropping briefly below the horizon only to begin a new day a few minutes later, another step in the circle of life. The circular drum, symbolic of the heartbeat of the people, was as integral to the lives of the Sahtuot'ine as was the setting and rising of the sun and the coming of each season.

As the youth headed home, his mind still filled with the power of the drummers, he knew in his heart that his turn with the drums would come and he, too, one day, would lead the dances, sing the sacred songs, and watch all his people celebrate in the goodness and fullness of life in this land.

The church, mission and new nursing station at Fort Franklin, Northwest Territories, as seen from an approaching plane in 1965.

CHAPTER ONE

THE BEGINNING: AUGUST 31, 1965

How small and insignificant the village seemed, on that last day of August 1965, perched on the edge of the vastness of Great Bear Lake in the Northwest Territories. Claire and I, the two new schoolteachers, had been flying for several hours since leaving Inuvik that morning and were now on our last leg, flying from Fort Norman on the Mackenzie River to our new jobs at Fort Franklin.

"See that white dot ahead to the left?" yelled the bush pilot, as we strained to hear him above the high drone of the plane's engine. "That's the church at Fort Franklin."

There was no mistaking what Dirk Hadler was referring to. Minuscule though it was, the tiny white triangle stood out clearly from the dreary, dark-hued landscape of merging muskeg, lakes and pine trees, made more forbidding by the low, grey ceiling of dense nimbus clouds.

"That's a very special church. It's built in the shape of an Indian tipi and the white aluminum tiles reflect the light. It's become a great beacon for Franklin." Dirk was our pilot that August day and knew the area well.

The changing pitch of the engine indicated that the sturdy six-seater Beaver aircraft had already begun its slow descent. Before long we could see the miniature houses and larger buildings, a small island of habitation surrounded on one side by hundreds of miles of uninterrupted northern forests, lakes and muskeg, and on the other by Great Bear Lake—known locally as *Sahtu*—one of the largest lakes in the world. I felt a moment of trepidation. This is where I was to spend a whole year with no outside contact.

As we flew lower and closer to the village, curiosity in what lay below replaced my uneasiness. Two rows of log cabins, stretching along a narrow dirt road, were surrounded by several more grey shacks and a few larger, colourful buildings.

"That red and white building on the left is the Hudson's Bay post," Dirk continued. "The large pink building is the new nursing station which will be opening soon, and the yellow building ahead of you is your school and," as he banked to the right, "below us is the duplex building where you two will be living."

A glimpse was all Claire and I were allowed. Dirk then continued his arc up and around to the right, taking us again beyond the western extremity of the small huddle of buildings, before turning and straightening out to land on the lake alongside the village. As the dark waters loomed towards us, we saw about two dozen people standing at the water's edge, all eyes watching our arrival. Others were hurrying towards the lake as the single-engine float plane landed gracefully on its pontoons and pulled up to a small wooden landing dock.

My nervousness, tinged with anticipation, returned. A sea of dark faces watched as we waited for Dirk, assisted by two young men, to secure the plane to the dock. Encumbered by our many suitcases and bags, Claire and I clambered down onto the wooden platform. No one smiled. No one greeted us. No one offered to help. We were just watched.

"Hey!" I heard Claire yell confidently behind me. "Would some of you kids like to help us with our bags?" I noticed a slight movement from a group of girls near the front of the crowd and several hands went up to hide their smiles as they pushed and egged each other on. But no one moved to help. Most of the boys, in their uniform-like black and red jackets and army caps, just stood there stone faced.

"Here, let me help you with your bags and show you where you're going." Finally, someone had emerged from the back of the crowd to rescue us. "You must be the new teachers. I'm Helen Chan, the nurse." In a louder voice she added, "Walter! Morris! Come and help carry these bags. These are the new teachers," and two of the black and red jackets stepped forward, each grabbing a bag.

After waving goodbye to Dirk—he had already told us that he could not stay this time but would be back to check on us in a couple of weeks—we followed our rescuers as best as we could. Stumbling over the uneven muddy ruts, I turned one last time to watch the tiny Beaver fade from sight and sound—my last link with the outside world.

As Claire and I tried to take in our new surroundings, Helen and the boys led us to a small cabin, filled from floor to ceiling with hundreds of boxes, with little extra room left for us and our luggage.

"Find a couple of boxes to sit on. The coffee is almost ready," said Helen. We thanked the boys for their help as Helen shooed them on their way. "This is just temporary," she explained. "These are supplies for the new nursing station which is almost ready. Then I can move in. Much better than this small shack."

"The pilot pointed out the nursing station to us as we flew over," Claire volunteered. "It looks very impressive compared to the other buildings."

I suddenly felt a sense of nausea that comes with being overly tired. It had been a long and noisy seven-hour trip from Inuvik, with stops at Fort Good Hope, Norman Wells and Fort Norman on the Mackenzie River. If I could only close my eyes for a few minutes, I felt sure that I'd be able to cope with all of this. So I leaned back, sipped my welcoming coffee, and listened to Helen and Claire chatting away as my mind drifted back and forth from their conversation to my own thoughts.

"I'm from Ontario and have long since had an interest in teaching in the North," replied Claire in her deep booming voice, in response to Helen's questions. Claire at some five-feet-five, with short black hair, was solidly built. "I've done a lot of hunting and fishing especially in the Gatineau Hills in Quebec. I also thought it would be interesting to work with Native people," she added.

Claire Barnabe and I had first met at the teachers' orientation course arranged for all teachers new to the Mackenzie District of the Northwest Territories—the NWT—by the federal Department of Northern Affairs and Natural Resources. During those four days spent at Fort Smith we received many lectures, mostly on the topic of being sensitive to the culture of the Indians and Inuit (or Eskimos, as they were then called). We had also been given dozens of tips on how to survive in the North, which, we were assured, were especially necessary for those of us destined for the more isolated settlements. It was there that Claire and I had discovered that we were both going to teach in a four-room school at Fort Franklin. I recall little else about those four days, for the memories that have travelled through thirty years began with the airplane ride from Fort Norman.

Sitting in that stuffy little plane with conversation kept to a minimum by the loud noise of the powerful single engine, my eyes had drifted aimlessly over the unfamiliar, forbidding scene below. It was easy to let my mind wander back to a day in May when I had been in the middle of teaching a grade nine geography class at the high school in Langley, British Columbia.

The vice-principal had arrived at my door with a telegram in hand, my long-awaited telegram confirming that I had been accepted to teach at the Fort Franklin Federal Day School in the Northwest Territories. I was very excited although I had no idea where Fort Franklin was. Nor did any of the other teachers. I soon located Franklin District marked in big bold letters across Canada's northern islands. Fort Franklin must be up there somewhere, I thought to myself, and was pleased that I would, therefore, be teaching in a small Inuit community, which is what I had requested.

It wasn't that I had particularly strong feelings about whether I taught Indians or Inuit. As I had explained during my interview in Vancouver, a friend of mine had invited me over to see slides of a friend of hers. She had just returned from two years of nursing in the Inuit village of Tuktoyaktuk on the Arctic Ocean, near the mouth of the Mackenzie River. I was immediately enthralled by the scenes she showed and the tales she told, and I decided then and there that this was a part of Canada I must see.

Soon after, an advertisement appeared in the *Vancouver Sun* inviting people who were interested in "Teaching in Canada's North" to apply to such and such an address. My letter was dispatched with speed and a reply soon arrived inviting me to an interview one Saturday morning at one of Vancouver's largest hotels.

Dressed in my best interview clothes, I approached the front desk of this large edifice and announced, with an enthusiastic smile, "Good morning! I have an interview with Miss Jones at 10 AM."

"And your surname is?" as the receptionist perused her list.

"Morris." I was about to add "Miggs Morris" when the receptionist replied, "Ah, yes Miss Morris, ten o'clock. Miss Jones is waiting for you in the lounge. Go through that open door behind you and you'll find her sitting in there."

"Thank-you."

The usually busy, large room was now silent and dark, illuminated by only two sidelights shining on one of the tables. Miss Jones, a tall, slim middle-aged woman in a navy and white suit, got up to greet me with a warm smile and extended hand. She pointed to a chair and asked if I'd like a cup of coffee. We talked briefly about the beautiful March weather we were having. Recognizing my British accent, she asked if I had been in Canada for long and so we chatted as she proceeded to make me feel comfortable.

"Now tell me about your past working experiences," said Miss Jones.

I told her about my previous four years of teaching in Wales and my almost two years in British Columbia. This was much more pleasant and relaxing than interviews I had been through in Britain, I thought to myself, as I responded to her few questions. I certainly couldn't see myself being interviewed in Britain sitting in the corner of a restaurant lounge like this. But I had now lived in Canada long enough to know that things tended to be much more casual here.

"Tell me more about your experiences in the restaurant and hotel business," she requested, in response to my mentioning briefly that I had worked in these areas. Even though I was slightly puzzled by her question I remembered the nurse from Tuktoyaktuk saying that you had to be extremely versatile to be able to survive in the North. I surmised that experiences such as these would lend credence to my flexibility.

So I told her about the restaurants where I had waited on tables and the hotels where I had been a chambermaid—all summer jobs that I had thoroughly enjoyed and had helped me pay my way through university. Even after I had started teaching I had continued my summer jobs so that I could afford to buy myself a car and do some hitch-hiking on the European continent.

Miss Jones stood up. My enjoyable interview was at an end. I stood up too. "Well, Miss Morris, you certainly have a most varied and interesting background. Although you are a little short on restaurant experience, you are clearly a person who learns quickly, is willing to take initiative when needed, and who obviously has excellent personnel skills." Extending her hand and giving me a warm smile she added, "I am delighted to offer you the position of head waitress."

I was stunned. Pardon? Head waitress? But I want to teach up North. Confusion, horror and disappointment flooded my mind in quick succession. What time was it? Would the interviewing team from the North still want to meet with me or was I too late?

Clearly the personnel skills in which Miss Jones had expressed so much confidence a few minutes earlier suddenly disappeared as I blurted out, "But I don't want to work here. I came for an interview for a teaching job." I felt sick and couldn't believe that such a mix-up could happen. I uttered a hasty, "I'm sorry," and rushed back towards the receptionist's desk in utter panic. Poor Miss Jones. She was probably just as confused as I was by this sudden turn of events.

Puffed up like an angry cat I descended on the receptionist and spat out: "I've been in the wrong interview. That interview was for a hotel job and I want to teach in the Northwest Territories. I must now have missed my chances for going North."

Dismayed, she quickly scanned her lists and exclaimed, "Oh, good heavens! There is a Miss Morris scheduled for a 10 AM appointment with another Miss Jones from the Department of Northern Affairs. What a coincidence! I'm very sorry." She picked up the phone, and, as the number rang, added, "I'll explain the situation to this Miss Jones and that the error is mine."

"It's all right," she said, replacing the receiver with obvious relief, though not as great as was mine when I heard her say, "Miss Jones understands what happened and she can see you straight away." She gave me directions for my new interview room on the seventeenth floor.

Feeling somewhat calmer, though still anxious, I stepped off the elevator and was greeted by the hearty laughter of the other Miss Jones, a much larger lady, leaning against a nearby door frame. I started to apologize but she cut me off with "Listen, Miss Morris, anyone who can teach and land herself a job as head waitress of this hotel is exactly the kind of person we need up North. You're hired!" and then we sat down and talked about the experiences that had resulted in the hotel job offer. And yes, we did talk about school and teaching up North, too.

Now, two months later, I continued the geography class with my grade nine students in Langley but my eyes and mind kept drifting back to the unfurled map of Canada hanging on the blackboard. I had been given twenty-four hours to decide whether to accept or reject the teaching position. Franklin District, teaching Inuit students, sounded exciting, but what a huge area of the map it covered. Where exactly was this Fort Franklin?

And then I found it. The tiny words on the map leapt at me. FORT FRANKLIN. Nowhere near the Franklin District. But there it was, clearly marked, much further south, on the shores of Great Bear Lake, north of Yellowknife and Great Slave Lake. Indian country. I felt a momentary pang of disappointment that I would not be living in an Inuit community. But then again, what difference did it make teaching Inuit or Indians? After all, my preference for teaching Inuit children was only based on the few slides I'd seen and the fact that people always seemed to talk about the Inuit in glowing terms, whereas Indians were frequently described in negative and disparaging terms.

This Fort Franklin was in the far North and it certainly seemed very isolated. Strange how I kept coming back to the thought of being isolated and the fascination that held for me. It didn't spring from a wish to escape from the kind of life I lived in British Columbia for I had thoroughly enjoyed my two years on the

West Coast. But there was a sense of excitement, a sense of adventure at the thought of testing oneself in what could be a strange environment, a fascination tinged with fear that somehow only made it all the more alluring.

There was little need for a lot of soul searching. My answer was an unqualified "Yes" on my acceptance telegram.

"Mi-ggs! Mi-ggs! Wake up. Helen has supper ready for us, then we're going to take a walk around the village." Claire's booming voice brought me back to the present.

"Oh, I'm sorry Helen, I guess I dozed off. Mmm! Something smells good," and realized, as I stood up, that I was ravenous. We hadn't eaten all day.

"It's just macaroni and cheese," said Helen. "I don't have much food until I unpack the boxes. The bread is from the Hudson's Bay store. It's very expensive because it's flown in. I usually make my own but everything is packed. I hope it's OK." Claire and I both grunted our assents. Obviously I wasn't the only hungry person. Misunderstanding the reason for our enthusiasm for the meal Helen added, "You have lots of macaroni and cheese in your rations. By the way your rations are already here. The barge brought them in with the rest of your luggage. But you can eat with me until you unpack them," was Helen's kind offer.

These were the rations that would feed us for the whole year. The Department of Northern Affairs had strongly recommended we purchase this bulk order through them. Soon after receiving my teaching contract, a long list of possible food items had arrived from which I made my selection. The items would then be shipped to me by barge from the Edmonton supplier. However, as I was to discover later, when unpacking the dozens of boxes of canned and boxed food, there seemed to be little resemblance between my order and what actually arrived. When I bemoaned the fact that I had received only four cans of mushrooms, which I loved, but had twenty-four very large bottles of ketchup, which I rarely used, Helen's explanation was, "Nutritionists make sure you have a balanced diet."

Now outside the whitewashed cabin, the three of us walked across the muddy rutted road towards our duplex. As we stood looking down this road—the main street, Helen informed us—I was aware of a freshness in the air, almost a sharp nip, tinged with the pleasant odour of wood burning. In response to my comments, Helen replied, "Every cabin has a wood-burning stove which provides heat and it's what the Indians cook on."

"Is that what we have?" inquired Claire with a degree of panic in her voice. Claire loved to cook.

"No," laughed Helen. "You have propane gas. White people have all those conveniences as well as running water, a flush toilet and electrical heating. But that's only for whites, not Indians."

"How many people are there here?" I asked.

"About two hundred and fifty Indians, nine whites, including us three, and four hundred dogs." Helen replied.

I greeted our one-storey, white and green duplex with a mixture of disappointment and relief: disappointment that it was so modern, so ordinary. I had felt sure that we would be living in log cabins not in some building that was right out of southern Canada, yet I was also relieved to notice the fridge, stove, flush toilet and bathtub. Roughing it only went so far! Claire and I each had a bachelor apartment, comprising a kitchen, small dining room area, living room with sofa bed, and a separate bathroom. We shared the washing and drying facilities and a large storage room for our rations. It seemed like a good arrangement.

But we didn't linger long. We were both eager to walk through the village. In answer to our questions, Helen explained that she was originally from Hong Kong. She had spent some ten years in Vancouver before coming north to Franklin where she had been for a year. Helen's petite five-foot-two frame was attired in a check shirt, navy jeans, and padded Chinese jacket. However, it was her mukluks, although now inserted into a pair of rubber boots for walking around the village, that caught my fancy. Helen informed us that the locally crafted legging boots, made from moose hide and wool stroud, trimmed with wolverine fur and beautifully decorated with beaded flower patterns, had been made by one of the local women. That will be my first purchase, I thought to myself.

Brandishing an axe handle in her hand Helen stated, "First thing you learn when you walk through the village is that you must always carry a big stick. There are lots of stray dogs in the village and they can be very dangerous when they're hungry."

We had now reached a large, pink, two-storey rectangular building. Even from our brief glimpse of Fort Franklin from the air we knew that this was the new $250,000 nursing station and clearly the largest and most imposing building in the village.

"There are no doctors in these small villages," Helen explained. "Nurses have to do everything. Up until now the nursing station was that small hut where I now live, my home and nursing station, with no room for sick people. This will be much better. Now people can stay here when they're sick instead of leaving their families and having to fly to Inuvik." She waved at some of the men still working on the outside of the building. "I can move in next week and then I'm going to have a party for Indians and whites. Everyone will be invited."

Close by, the white tipi-shaped church, which we had seen from the air, stood tall and proud. It was even more impressive from ground level. Helen led us up the imposing flight of wooden stairs and through the main double-door entrance. A hint of incense hung in the cool, damp air inside. The bright sun shone through several stained glass windows on to rows of gleaming Varathaned pews. A statue of the Virgin Mary garbed in the familiar pale blue veil and a cross of Christ guarded by six tall candles on the simple altar radiated warmth and tranquillity. I felt like staying for a few minutes, but not this time. There was still so much to see. Much later I was to realize how unique this church was, but for us, at that time, it just seemed so fitting in this small Indian village.

"What's the building next to the church?" inquired Claire, "the mission?"

"Yes," replied Helen, "and I'll take you there on our way back and introduce you to Father Fumoleau. He's originally from France but has been at Franklin for years. He's very nice."

We continued down the main street, no more than a strip of dirt the width of a narrow lane, edged on both sides by stubbly, scrawny grass and two rows of small log cabins, most of which looked quite old and dilapidated. The pungent odour of fish and some other smells I couldn't quite place blended with the smell of wood smoke. Outside one cabin a couple of small children played near several scrawny and ragged looking dogs, tethered to a pole—cute little chubby kids, one clad only in a T-shirt and no underpants, and the other in only a large diaper, despite the cool air.

"I keep telling people not to let their kids play near dogs," said Helen, as she proceeded to walk up to the children and shoo them away from the gaunt animals. "When the dogs are hungry and little kids play with them, the dogs sometimes attack them. You should see the bites I've had to stitch up, even bites on faces. But they never listen."

Helen then turned towards an elderly couple just entering a nearby cabin. "*Gonezo*," she said brightly, "How's George doing? You giving him my medicine? Good," she added, responding to their nods.

"Do most people speak English?" I inquired.

"No, very few do. Most of the women don't speak any English or know just a few words but several of the men speak quite good English. They learn it from working on the barges and at the fishing camps in the summer."

"And the kids?" I continued.

"Only when they go to school."

About half way through the village two young girls approached us. "Come here Laura, Agnes," Helen called to them. "These are the new teachers," and she introduced us to them.

The girls were about eight years old. Laura was slightly taller and wore a navy jacket and dark blue jeans. She had a white hair band through her below-the-shoulder-length, straight black hair. Agnes had on a blue and red striped top and red jeans. Both wore rubber boots. Claire and I tried to engage them in a conversation and started asking them questions, but they only smiled and giggled shyly at us behind their raised hands.

We had now almost reached the other end of the village. "That's the Hudson's Bay store." Our guide pointed out a one-storey building, painted white with red trim. I would eventually come to realize that this was typical of the approximately four dozen or so legendary Hudson's Bay posts dotted across the North. The building looked small when one considered that this was the only shopping outlet in the village and that supplies had to be stored there from one annual barge to another. "Pete and Liz live next door in the other red and white small house. Liz teaches at the school and Pete is the manager of the store. They're very nice. By the way, we're invited there for dinner this evening."

Turning slightly to her left she added, "And over there is the only other white family here, Forrest and Minnie. They're missionaries from Alberta. They're very nice, too, but don't have much to do with the other white people," a statement which did not surprise me since their little log cabin was indistinguishable from any of the Indians' dwellings.

It was certainly reassuring to hear that all the whites were so "nice" considering how few there were of us and how we would have to get on together for the next ten months. But Helen was correct in her assessment, and it wasn't until much later that I fully appreciated how fortunate I was that first year to be among people whose company I enjoyed and, more importantly, who respected the Native people and were committed to assisting them wherever possible.

"I'll just take you a little further before we head back," said Helen. Following a dusty, winding pathway, we climbed up a slight incline. At the top of this low hill we stopped and turned to look back towards the village that lay slightly below us. Forty or so grey, weathered, log and plank cabins, interspersed by flashes of colour representing the three edifices of government, church and commerce, stretched haphazardly from east to west for about a kilometre along the shore of Great Bear Lake.

Overhead, a whitish haze from the smoke that drifted upwards from the log cabins hung heavily, suspended between the warmth of the land on this late summer day and the chilling Arctic air overhead. Narrow pathways radiated like spider webs through sparse grass from the main artery to the cabins lying further back. Sounds of dogs barking and children laughing in play carried clearly up the hill. Young people scurried from building to building and older folk ambled along.

The sun, still high in the sky, streaked across the lake, suddenly shimmering, as a boat hummed across its waters. It came to stop at the landing dock onto which we had stepped a mere two hours ago. These were the sights and sounds of a life I was about to enter, my new home, and, much to my surprise, I already felt a small sense of belonging.

I looked beyond the village. To the south lay Keith Arm at the western end of Great Bear Lake, a lake that extended more than three hundred kilometres to the east, the largest single lake in Canada and almost five times the size of Prince Edward Island. Six kilometres to the south of the village, the waters of this vast lake disgorged into Bear River where they began their rapid descent westwards, meeting the mighty Mackenzie River some hundred and forty kilometres away at Fort Norman. Beyond, the flat southern shoreline of the lake was broken by a single low mountain. How often I would glance towards that distant mountain during the long winter months when in mid-December the sun rose to its east, barely skimmed the summit, and disappeared to the west about half an hour later, having completed its lunchtime journey, for Fort Franklin lay just ninety kilometres south of the Arctic Circle.

To the east stretched endless miles of dark-hued black and white spruce with some tamarack and jack pine, interspersed with poplars and a few birches. Few trees had trunks of more twenty centimetres in diameter and most took a hundred years to grow to a height of some three metres, for we were close to the northern limits of tree growth.

Behind the village where the shores sloped gradually upwards, the surrounding area for about two kilometres north of Franklin had been completely cleared of trees. During the past fifteen years, villagers who needed the wood to support their daily existence had decimated these slopes; and each year it became necessary for the Indians to travel further inland to access an adequate supply.

"Those trees used to reach right down to the village," Helen broke through my silent thoughts. "Everyone needs wood—for the wood stove to cook on and for heat, so getting wood is a job people have to do every day." As if on cue an elderly woman dressed in a dark-coloured, calf-length dress and red jacket similar to that worn by young Agnes, her long black hair enclosed in a paisley head scarf, appeared nearby carrying a huge bundle of twigs and short branches. Helen said a few words to her, and she smiled and nodded at us before continuing on her way back home. "Old Louisa has no husband or sons so she often gets wood for herself," added Helen.

"We'll just go a little further," volunteered our guide, as we continued walking through a ground cover of short berry bushes already turning red and gold with the impending arrival of autumn. Helen informed us that berries were a mainstay of the Indians' summer diet and, sure enough, the nearby bushes had been stripped clean of any fruit.

"Next time I'll take you to the ski hill and the Little Lake," said Helen.

"Ski hill?" I inquired curiously. I had brought my cross-country skis with me but certainly not downhill skis.

"Yes, we have our own little ski hill. There's quite an escarpment along the side of the Little Lake and Pete carved out a run for us on one of the steepest slopes. We use our cross-country skis so it's a bit tricky, but lots of fun."

"And the Little Lake you mentioned?" asked Claire.

"That's where the planes arrive during freeze-up and break-up when they can't land on the big lake. Well, we better go back. It's getting late."

"And getting cold," I added, as I buttoned up my jacket, "but I guess I better not start complaining about that, had I?"

"No, it gets really cold once September arrives and the days get shorter. Soon the ice will form along the lake shore and by late November the whole bay will be frozen." I didn't want to think too much about that yet.

So on this cool evening in late August of 1965 I stood and surveyed my new home, and at that moment, although I had enjoyed our walk through the village and felt a sense of excitement at embarking upon this new adventure, I recognized just how different an environment it was from anywhere I had lived. The village, so small and far from anywhere else, seemed strange and daunting, which only heightened its sense of isolation. Little did I know, as we descended into the village that evening, that I would end up spending more than three years in Franklin, three of the happiest and most interesting and memorable years of my life.

top: Four young boys peer out of a school window at Fort Franklin Federal Day School, Northwest Territories, September 1965.

bottom: Kids play in the school yard at recess.

CHAPTER TWO

SEPTEMBER

Today is the first day of school. Today I will meet my students.

My principal, Joe Matters, originally from Prince Edward Island, had already told me I would be teaching approximately twenty-two students in grades four and five. He wasn't sure of the exact number as this would depend on how many children returned from the bush where several families had been living during the summer months.

All four classes and Joe's office were located on the first floor of the school. The upstairs had been fitted out as an apartment with the traditional maple furniture found in all government houses across the North. This is where Joe currently lived although he was anticipating moving soon into a new two-storey building being constructed next door to our duplex.

I had spent time in my class during the long Labour Day weekend, looking through whatever teaching materials were available—not much—and doing some planning on how I would approach the first few days, until I had a better handle on my students' abilities.

Claire was to teach grade one and the beginners class. These were the six-year-old students that began school speaking no English. Liz had the next two grades, and Joe taught grades six, seven and eight. After that, those few students wishing to continue their education had to leave for the residential high schools at Yellowknife, Fort Smith or Inuvik.

I immediately liked the location of my room. All along the south side a wall of windows looked out onto the lake and, because of its southern exposure, it was the classroom that received the most sunlight throughout the year. The desks were already placed with their backs towards the windows and I left them that way so that I might glance out periodically, over the heads of my students, and observe the daily world of Franklin as it continued outside.

The second bell rang. The first bell had rung half an hour before as an alarm clock for the village as few people had watches or clocks. With this second bell the students silently entered the classroom and sat at their desks, their eyes downcast, and stealing only occasional glances at me.

"Good morning! I'm Miss Morris, your new teacher," I began. Looking around the room I added, "I think I saw some of you meeting our plane the other day. Thank you Walter and Morris," as I recognized the familiar faces, "for helping us with our bags." They slunk even lower into their desk seats.

I continued, sharing a little of my background as I referred to a world map on the blackboard. I pointed to Wales where I was born and had lived for twenty-five years before immigrating to Canada in 1963. Covering the long distance with a sweep of my hand, I showed them how far I had travelled by ship, all the way from Liverpool, England, to Quebec City. Then how I had crossed this vast and wonderful country by train, arriving in Abbotsford, British Columbia, five days later. Finally, after two years there I had decided to come and teach in the North.

I ended my monologue feeling rather unnerved by the apparent lack of response from my audience. No one had moved nor looked directly at me, and other than my voice, the silence had been broken only by an occasional coughing spasm and the sound of dogs barking outside. So, to fill the void, I continued.

"Well, before I can teach you anything, I need to know what you have already learned at school. I'm now going to pass around some exercises for you to do in math. Then I would like you to read some stories and answer a few questions on the stories. Don't worry if you can't answer everything. This is only to give me an idea of what you know."

By now I was walking around the class handing out the sheets I had prepared and run off during the weekend. "Please make sure you put your names at the top of each page." I had already placed a pencil on each desk. Quickly, each student began to work at the task at hand, some with more enthusiasm than others, but they all seemed pleased to be engaged with the papers in front of them.

I looked around at the sea of long, dark hair in front of me, long hair for both boys and girls. Then I noticed a tall boy at the back of the room with his head down sleeping on his desk. I walked towards him, not sure if I should wake him or not since I had never had a student sleep in my class before. I stood by his side looking rather puzzled when one of the girls nearby volunteered, "George come home from bush last night. Better you let him sleep." So I did.

"Thank you for telling me that. And what's your name?"

"Judy. Judy Tutcho." Then she went on with her work.

By now I had grown aware of an increasingly unpleasant odour in the room. It was so strong that I began to feel nauseated. I tried to figure out what it was. I didn't want to ask the students so I left them to their work and knocked on Joe's classroom next door.

"Joe, there's a terrible smell in my class."

What kind of a smell?"

"Like a mixture of smoke and sweat."

Joe grinned. "That's exactly what it is." He continued, "Did you notice how all the children are wearing moose hide slippers and mukluks?" I nodded. "The moose hide is smoked to preserve it before it's made into clothing. You're smelling that and the sweaty feet inside."

"But I didn't smell it when the students came in this morning."

"It gets stronger as the feet get warmer. Sorry, Miggs, that's a smell you had better get used to very quickly!" and, with a grin, he turned around and went back to his own class.

I'll never get used to this, I said to myself. I have an awfully fussy nose. But I did. It was a bit rough that first morning but within a few days I had ceased to notice it. In fact, before long I came to love the distinctly smoky moose hide odour.

Most of the children continued to work steadily. Some had finished and had taken out a book from their desk. Some read, others looked at the pictures. I could also see that some children had barely written a thing, even though they looked as if they were busy. A couple of children doodled all around their sheets, mainly animal pictures that showed great promise. But there was no restlessness, no giggling or talking amongst themselves as they waited. How polite and well-behaved were my new students!

The bell rang for recess and the children filed out quietly after I dismissed them. I decided to follow and was joined outside by Claire, coffee cup in hand.

"I have twenty-seven children, eleven of which are in my beginners class," Claire announced. "Eleven that speak no English at all and the rest know very little. And to top it off," her exasperation growing, "I have found absolutely no programs to follow, no curriculum, nothing. How am I supposed to teach these children? And remember, Helen told us that they only speak Slavey at home since that's all most of their parents speak. This is going to be fun." Since most of my children apparently spoke some English, my task seemed much easier than poor Claire's.

We stood a little away from the children and Claire, having temporarily forgotten her tirade of a few moments before, began pointing out some of her students by name. What cute little kids she had, laughing and giggling, as they played together on the gravel surrounding the school—no real school yard here. My kids were mostly huddled together in small clumps, chatting away and stealing many furtive glances towards Claire and me, the obvious source of much of their discussion.

We shared a few more of our morning's observations and then the bell rang again and it was time to return to class. The fresh outside air had been most welcoming and I longed for it again a few minutes after being back in my aromatic room.

And so the school year began.

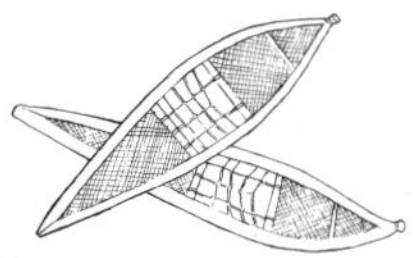

It wasn't long before I knew all the children by name and began to have a sense of their individual personalities. Much of their initial silence and reticence had disappeared. Instead, my eager and pleasant students often depicted a delightful sense of humour and for the most part worked hard. They ranged in age from nine to sixteen, George being the oldest.

George's parents had sent him to school at this late age so that he could learn to read. Joe put him in my class since all of his students read quite well. (I'm sorry to say that my success with George was limited since he soon took off again for the bush with his father once the autumn trapping season began.) Judy Tutcho seemed to have the best command of English in the class and was not afraid to speak out. Jane, Judy's best friend and George's sister, was quieter than Judy but an equally competent student. Evelyn, with her gruff manner, was always willing to help with the younger children, as were Irene and Georgina.

Peter, a grade four student and one of the shortest boys in my room, always held his own with the older boys with his impish smile and great sense of fun. Jimmy was a tall, slim boy with an appealing smile and infectious chuckle. His left arm was totally paralysed and his right arm had only partial mobility, the result of polio as an infant. But he never let this affliction get in his way and participated in whatever the rest of the boys were doing, often with considerable difficulty. Morris, another good-looking boy, was quiet and able. Walter, two years older than his brother Peter, was more studious than most of the boys and performed well in school. Francis, a handsome lean boy was less enthusiastic about school work than most of his friends and often looked rather sullen. However, occasionally when something amused him, his face broke out into the most beautiful of smiles.

On the whole, the girls were much more timid than the boys and rarely said very much, nor did they show much enthusiasm for school work, although they seemed to enjoy being in the class and participated well in many of our less academic ventures such as when I played my guitar and sang songs with them. However, other than Judy and Jane and a couple of other girls who became excellent students, most of them had little interest in learning, and why, from their perspective, did they need to? They saw themselves getting married and starting a family within a very few years, as had their mothers and grandmothers for generations. On the other hand, many of the boys clearly enjoyed being at school and worked hard.

By now, most of the children in grades four and five could read and write up to about a grade two or three level, some very haltingly and some quite well, and I was soon able to plan work activities to help them progress. I had been provided with Alberta's Curriculum Guidelines which outlined not only what we were to teach but also how we were to instruct our students, a notion that was quite alien to my British educational training and experience, where teachers were expected to plan their own curricula and teaching methods. Accompanying manuals and textbooks were also provided. I became increasingly frustrated as I attempted to follow southern guidelines that were clearly inappropriate and unrealistic for my students.

Most of the topics bore little relevance to their experiences. Furthermore, given their unfamiliarity with English until they came to school, how could they be expected to learn a new language and learn to read in this strange language at the same pace as southern students? So it wasn't long before I began to modify the curriculum and design my own lesson plans. I still wanted to introduce them to concepts, places and ideas that were beyond their limited world but they needed to be taught in a way that linked this information to their own experiences and interests. My newly designed curriculum didn't always work but I considered it to be much more meaningful and appropriate for my students than what I was supposed to teach.

Earlier that month, when I was still dutifully trying to follow Alberta's Curriculum Guidelines, I attempted to teach the students about the life cycle in the manner described in the manuals.

"The cows eat the grass and this turns into manure. This manure fertilizes the soil, which helps the grass grow. Then the cows eat this grass."

The students, with furrowed brows, were clearly trying to follow my neat blackboard drawings of cows, grass and arrows depicting the life cycle. I had just completed my diagram of a cow standing in the grass with a little pile beneath its rear-end when suddenly I heard, "Oh, you mean shit, Miss," and there was Peter grinning from ear to ear with his new-found understanding.

"Yes, Peter. You're right, only when we talk about cows we call it manure," and I continued with my lesson.

Shortly afterwards Francis broke his ruler and I heard him exclaim, "Shi.....manure!" And so I guess I was responsible for adding a new swear word to their vocabulary.

Another time, I decided to read "Bambi" to my students. They loved being read to, especially fairy tales, myths and legends. I had just finished reading "Beauty and the Beast" and decided to move on to "Bambi," since I had recently received a beautifully illustrated version from a friend.

Well into the story, with the kids hanging on every word, I suddenly began to feel uncomfortable. Here I was, in a society that depended on hunting animals for much of their food, yet these children, like any in the South, were clearly siding with Bambi and his mother against the hunter. What was I doing to them? Perhaps I should stop reading. But since we were close to the end, I finished the story and then followed up with the kind of discussion we often had.

"How did you feel when Bambi's mother was killed by the hunter?" I began.

"Sad," they responded in unison.

"Would you have been upset if Bambi had been killed?" All heads nodded.

"Why? Aren't Bambi and his mother just deer, just caribou?"

A hesitant "Ye...es" followed.

"You said that the hunter was very mean when he wanted to kill Bambi's mother." Heads nodded again and I continued, "Are your fathers and brothers mean when they kill caribou?"

"NO!" It was more of a gasp than a word.

"Why not? What is the difference?" For several moments there was silence. I waited. I had become much better at waiting.

Then slowly a few children raised their hands.

"It not the same." This was Walter. "When our fathers shoot caribou it because we need it for food."

"And for making clothes and tents," added one of the girls.

Now the understanding came and more hands went up. "It not bad to kill caribou when we use it," said another boy. "The caribou happy we kill them when they know we not waste them."

"This hunter not like our fathers. He want to kill Bambi's mother and put antlers on wall. He not respect this deer."

Throwing out those questions had been gamble but I felt I was beginning to know the kids well enough to be assured that they would be able to reason out the difference, even if it was difficult for them to articulate these complex thoughts in English. And they did.

Not long after school began, I had my first Northern encounter with the bane of many schoolchildren and their parents: lice. One day, as I leaned over one of my students helping him with his work, to my horror I saw creatures scrambling blithely from strand to strand in his long hair. I managed to control myself from yelling out the dreaded word "LICE!" Then, with gritted teeth, I moved slowly up the rows and checked more heads from a distance. Sure enough, lice were visible in almost every head of hair, if you peered long enough. What was I to do about this?

Fortunately, or unfortunately, depending on how one looks at these things, I wasn't quite as horrified as were some friends to whom I've since relayed this story. I also had lice as a child. Shortly after the end of World War II, my mother, much to her chagrin, realized that her dear little daughter was infested. They were discovered during the summer holidays when I was about eight years old. I had complained about an itchy head for days, or maybe weeks. My mother kept assuring me that it was due to the sand in my hair as I spent most of my days playing on the beach. Then one day she finally checked my head and was appalled to see that my hair was alive with lice. She couldn't believe it. Not her daughter! It had to be due to "The Evacuees." (During the latter stages of the war many children had been sent away from London and other large cities that were being repeatedly bombed, to live in Wales and other more isolated parts of Britain.) For several evenings that summer, my head was subjected to a fierce fine-tooth combing as I squirmed on a chair, my long blonde hair spread over sheets of newspaper on the table. Then my hair was washed in vinegar to "kill the nits too."

I didn't say anything about the lice to my students that day. I needed time to plan my attack. First of all I didn't have much vinegar in my rations so I visited Helen, now settled into her large, new nursing station. I wasn't expecting her to be upset about my problem but I was rather surprised at her total dismissal of my concerns.

"Oh, everyone always has lice when they come back to school in September after being in the bush most of the summer. As soon as we have a nice day, I will visit every house with a strong disinfectant and clean houses, blankets, clothing, everything and everyone."

I was horrified. "Don't the people mind?" I asked.

"Miggs. People here are just like people in villages in China. They don't know about lice or germs. They don't understand, so I just tell them it has to happen and do it. It's for their own good. Then no more lice till next autumn."

"What about the kids?"

"I do them too. But if you want to wash their hair in vinegar maybe they'll like that better than my strong disinfectant treatment."

That evening I talked to Claire and asked if her kids had lice. "They probably do but I haven't looked that closely." Her classroom didn't get the sunlight that mine did.

The next day I broached the subject, rather tentatively, with my students. Did they know what lice were? What were their reactions to having lice? Yes, they knew what lice were and some said that they didn't really like having them as it made their heads itch, but most of the kids didn't seem too concerned.

I decided to share that I also had lice as a child and how my mother had got rid of them, mainly, by washing my hair in vinegar, which also had the nice side effect of leaving one's hair looking very silky. Then I invited those who would like to have their hair washed in vinegar over to my duplex that evening. Several children had already dropped by to visit Claire and me in the evenings, mostly younger children. That evening several of my students—all girls—arrived in a rather subdued gang.

And so the hair washing sessions began, followed by hot chocolate and a "tour" of our building. The kids were amazed at the amount of rations we had stored on the shelves made especially for this purpose. So had I been earlier on when it had taken me two whole days to stack my year's supply of food. Could one person possibly eat that much in a year? The kids then decided that Claire and I had to be very rich as we had almost as much food on our shelves as did the Hudson's Bay store, and they weren't far off—at least, about the amount of food.

The evening turned out to be a success and we really enjoyed the company of the kids who were much more talkative than they were in school. The next day I dug out the microscope, retrieved from the back of a classroom cupboard, and showed them one of the lice, a victim from the previous evening, under the microscope. Boy! Did that cause a panic when they saw the louse magnified twenty times. Now they all wanted their hair washed. So that evening, having obtained more vinegar from Helen, Claire and I were busily at it again as several more students arrived. However, I still wasn't sure if it was the lice treatment or their curiosity at seeing our duplex and our gigantic amount of food that had really brought them.

A few days later one of the boys asked if I would cut his hair. His father used to cut it but he had lost his clippers. I didn't take his request too seriously but when I mentioned it to Helen that evening she thought it a good idea. "The man who usually cuts everyone's hair has already left for the bush so you would be doing the kids a favour," said Helen as she handed me a pair of hand-operated clippers and a professional-looking pair of scissors and comb. The next day I told the kids that anyone wanting his or her hair cut could stay after school. Much better to perform this operation in my classroom, I thought, since the linoleum floors would be easier to clean than my carpet.

Only two boys stayed behind that day, two boys who had not joined in the vinegar treatment. To this day I can see the lice scampering ahead of the shears and up the back of each boy's head. I did a lot of teeth gritting in those days. However, I must have passed the test, as the remainder of the boys stayed behind the next day and were even joined by two older brothers who were not in school. Occasionally even some of the kids' fathers came. And thus, for a while, I became the village barber.

As for the lice? Perhaps it was due to Helen's delousing campaign of the houses, or because people had discovered the magic of vinegar, or just because I had become immune to them, but I never noticed another louse in three years.

"Good morning, people," I began one Monday morning in my usual manner. Much to my surprise I was greeted by stony silence. This is odd, I thought. By now, towards the end of September, the kids were opening up and becoming quite chatty.

"What's the matter? Is something wrong?" I inquired.

After a few seconds, Judy, with arms crossed and a scowl on her face, solemnly stated, "You bring storm to Franklin."

"Pardon?"

"This afternoon we have big storm and it your fault," Peter added.

I looked over their heads and out of the windows at the searing blue sky with not a cloud in sight, a beautiful day. What were they talking about and what was this about it being my fault?

"How am I going to make it storm today? It certainly doesn't look as if it's going to. It's a beautiful day." Was I trying to convince myself that it was going to stay that way? I'm not sure I liked being seen as someone who could produce storms, and even less so since I didn't understand what was going on.

"You kill big bird yesterday," Francis volunteered.

"A raven." The accusations were coming quickly now.

"It bad luck to kill that bird. It will make storm come," Judy repeated.

Now I knew what they were talking about. Yesterday, Helen, Claire and I had gone along the path towards the Little Lake. It was a beautiful Sunday, cold, crisp and sunny. Autumn at its best. Helen had brought her .22 rifle and had let us use it. As a child I had done a bit of hunting with my father, mostly for rabbits. Sometimes, when the annual funfair arrived in our town, he would pay for me to shoot round after round at moving targets since I was, apparently, pretty good. Then he took great delight, as did I, in bragging about "his little Annie Oakley" to friends.

For a while, Helen, Claire and I took turns shooting at branches and other inanimate objects. Then, I spied a raven sitting at the top of a tree a good distance away. Pointing to it, I boasted, "Let me see if I can hit that raven."

"It's much too far," replied Claire. "It must be at least sixty yards away and about thirty feet up." This was the one area near Franklin where the trees grew tall.

The bird sat there, obligingly, as we discussed it's future. It sat there long enough for me to reload the .22, long enough for me to take aim, and long enough for me to shoot it.

"You hit it!" was Claire's astonished comment as we watched the bird fall. I ran through the bushes and lofted my dead prey with one hand and rifle in the other, feeling very proud of myself. Here I was in the land of hunters and I had already claimed my first kill.

With the bird slung nonchalantly over the rifle on my shoulder we returned to the village. We passed an older couple and I generously offered them my prize. They declined. So did the next Indian family in the first house we stopped at. I was quite disappointed. I would have liked them to accept my gift. No doubt they were too polite to take it from me, I thought.

Next came the house of missionaries, Forrest and Minnie. Since I didn't fancy eating my kill I offered the bird to them and they accepted. When we told them about the Indians' reluctance, Forrest explained that the Indians did not eat raven and, in fact, considered it bad luck to shoot a raven. What a disappointment. Instead of being the great white heroine, I had blown a local taboo. Still, our afternoon's adventure had been enjoyable and I promptly forgot the incident—until I faced my accusers the next morning.

"Oh, the raven," I repeated to my students. "Yes, I'm sorry I killed that bird. I didn't know it was a bad thing to do. I certainly won't do it again. Are there any other birds I shouldn't kill?"

"No," replied Jimmy, "better you shoot ptarmigan, geese or ducks. They good to eat, but not black birds like raven."

"Even though you sorry we still have storm this afternoon," Francis persisted.

Now that was stretching things, I thought, as I looked again at the unchanged clear, blue sky. But I said nothing and went on with the morning's work.

The storm arrived later in the afternoon.

The clouds rolled in soon after lunch and by mid-afternoon the snow was falling heavily. By the time the school day ended the wind had picked up considerably. The lake lashed the shoreline with good-sized waves and all my students looked at me. They didn't say anything, but there was no doubt at all in their minds that I was responsible for this change in the weather.

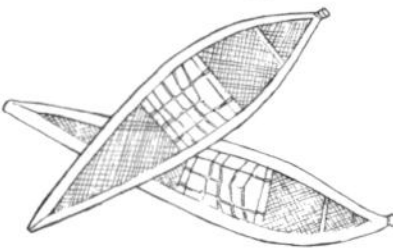

Several days later Joe Matters popped in to see me just as I was leaving my class. "Oh, Miggs. I forgot to tell you that you have to run the Bingo tomorrow night. The community club uses the school in the evenings to hold movies in my class and Bingo in yours. Tomorrow night is Bingo night."

"OK, Joe, but why me?"

"It's a sort of tradition that whoever has your room runs the Bingo. I run the movies next door because my room is much darker." Now I finally understood why I had been favoured with the best and brightest room in the school and this was the price I would have to pay.

Joe showed me where the numbered sheets, small plastic markers and a miniature Bingo tumbler were kept in one of my cupboards. "Only the women play," added Joe. "It's a good excuse for them to get together and have some fun," and with that he left.

My experience with Bingo had been very limited. It wasn't a favourite game of mine but my mother had once persuaded me to accompany her for a few months to local Bingo games run by a Catholic priest called Father Murphy. It can't be too difficult, I said to myself, as I tried to recall those games back in Wales.

Bingo night arrived and I smiled and nodded at the women as they received their sheets and plastic chips then sat down at the kids' desks. This was my first opportunity to meet several adults and I was very curious to see how things would work out since most of the women spoke no English. Many arrived with babies or young children in tow so we carried in more desks from Joe's room, but people still overflowed into the hallway. Bingo night was obviously very popular with the women.

Coloured headscarves covered their long, straight, black hair and they all wore what I had now come to realize was the "official dress" for women and young girls: calf-length print dresses over woollen or rayon stockings and moose hide mukluks or slippers which they had made themselves. The colour and design of their jackets had been dictated by this or last year's shipment to the Hudson's Bay post. Ordering supplies was obviously a fairly unsophisticated job, as designs were limited to either red or light blue nylon jackets for the girls and women, black and red wool and nylon for the boys and young men, and a more subdued design of black nylon, with a draw string around the waist, for the older men.

Dense cigarette smoke and the low murmur of Slavey, frequently interrupted by hacking coughs and wailing babies, soon filled the classroom.

"This will be interesting," I thought, and, determined to do a good job, I began.

"Hello, I'm Miggs Morris and many of your children are in my class. A great bunch of kids." Several women nodded their heads and smiled back at me though few had understood what I had said. "Well, let's get started."

I pressed the lever of my miniature Bingo machine and continued the tradition. "Under the B, seven." A sea of headscarves looked down and found the seven in what seemed to be an amazingly short time given that most of the women had several sheets each. I spun again. "Under the N, twenty-five. Twenty-five," I repeated. Hey, this was going well. Nothing to it.

I spun again. Ah, one of my favourites. "Under the B, Kelly's Eye, number one," and some murmuring was heard. "Number one. Kelly's Eye," I repeated. A few minutes later this was followed by, "Under the I, Legs Eleven." Oh, I was in fine form now, as some of Father Murphy's more creative expressions came back to me. The muttering became louder as sheets began to fill. Just then one of the younger women, whom I had briefly met before, came up to me.

"Hi Sarah," I said and looked at her expectantly.

"Teacher," she began, "the women can't understand you. They only know numbers. They don't know this Kelly's Eye or something about Legs. You just say 'B two' or 'G thirty'," as she pointed to my master sheet. She returned to her seat, leaving me feeling rather deflated. And I thought I'd been doing so well. I took her advice and the rest of the evening went by smoothly, quickly and enjoyably.

Movie nights were held in Joe's classroom, with Joe in charge. A whole year's shipment of fifty movies, ordered by the community club, arrived by barge every summer. Joe usually showed two or three movies each week in September and October, rather than spreading them across the year. "Some of the men are reluctant to leave the village to go trapping in the bush until they've seen several movies." Almost all were in black and white and most were old, old by date of production and old by use. The celluloid frequently snapped during a showing on our 16mm classroom projector.

Joe's class was packed tighter than the proverbial can of sardines that first movie night and every following movie night, I soon discovered. Men, women, children and babies sat on the floor and on the desks, packing the room from wall to wall. Others stood in the doorway. All were attired in their customary jackets and caps or headscarves.

The room was soon engulfed in a haze of dense smoke accompanied by the continuous coughing of adults and crying from babies. Claire, Helen and I sat squashed on desks near the back of the room. So much for fire regulations, I thought, as I estimated there to be close to a hundred people in that regular sized classroom.

An arm near the doorway turned off the lights. Crackling music burst forth in the middle of the movie title and credits. We were to see a Western and every eye, except for those of the still crying babies, stared at the desert-like scenery of the southwestern United States. Four cowboys rode their horses mercilessly across the screen, coming to a sudden stop next to a tall Saguaro cactus.

"Howdy partners!" Now that was a voice I knew, as a very young John Wayne greeted his men.

The story unfolded. Wayne's cattle had been rustled and Indians were the prime suspects. A number of cowboys were dispatched to hide among the boulders along the boundary of the ranch to wait for the offenders. The camera zeroed in on two of the cowboys lying in wait. Suddenly three Indians, bare except for their loincloths, painted faces and a feather in each headband, appeared behind them.

There was a loud gasp from the classroom audience. With bows and arrows at the ready the braves crept up behind the cowboys and the audience in this crowded room went crazy. Above all the unintelligible but clearly agitated sounds I heard several people scream "Watch out!" The cowboys on the screen must have heard them because at that instant they rolled over onto their backs firing quickly and killing all three Indians. The audience cheered!

In my naiveté I had expected the local Indians to support the screen Indians. Instead they had clearly supported the cowboys. But then why not? The Indians of Fort Franklin bore no resemblance to those screen Indians in dress, in habitat, or in their murderous, treacherous ways.

Over the next several months I came to realize that although westerns were big favourites with the audience, most favoured of all were the few Elvis Presley movies we had. The fact they were in colour added to their popularity. Because colour movies were far more expensive to rent for a whole year than were the old black and white ones, we had very few. But we treasured them all. After all radio and television had not yet come to this little corner of the world.

September was coming to an end and the days were rapidly drawing shorter. Each day I gazed out of my classroom windows at the lake in all its moods, some days so calm, so utterly still, a pale shade of milky blue merging with the haze crystals overhead.

At other times, particularly as the autumn weather changed with the onset of winter, the lake transformed itself into an angry rough sea, its towering waves smashing into the shoreline, spewing forth its icy waters, transforming the tall grasses and small bushes along the shoreline into cascades of glittering jewels. Time and time again those frozen shoreline displays appeared and disappeared.

Then one day they stayed. Water along the edges of the lake crusted over. The beginning of the miracle of winter had begun, the time of the year when northern life begins its real journey. Summer and early autumn seemed but a rehearsal for the serious business that lay ahead for the next nine months. It was almost as if, with the first settling of snow on the land and ice on the lake, a calm and quiet understanding of the rightful nature of things had begun to unfold.

I had learned so much in this one short month. Each new day revealed unique facets of the life of the people of Fort Franklin, as well as the various demands living in the North made on a person from elsewhere. I was totally enchanted by my new life. Roll on October!

Fort Franklin's well-known church—a beacon from afar—and John Tutcho's dog team.

CHAPTER THREE

A WAY OF LIFE

Evening visits from the children were becoming more frequent. Everything in the duplex intrigued them. The flush toilet was a huge success and came into considerable use. Competition among some of the girls to wash our dinner dishes became quite fierce. The clothes washer and drier that Claire and I shared were fascinating. But the numerous pairs of clean underwear I owned were the most amazing of all.

"I only got two underwears," said one of the girls. "I wear one. I wash other."

Claire and I sometimes felt quite guilty with what, in the children's eyes, appeared to be our wealth of clothing and food, although to anyone else it was obvious that neither Claire nor I placed a high priority on our wardrobe, preferring to wear the same few casual items repeatedly. Whenever we offered the children some of our clothes and food, they declined. They made it very clear that they were not there to beg and scrounge, only to enjoy the opportunity of trying out all these new gadgets and dressing up in our clothes. However, a cup of hot chocolate and a few cookies were always gratefully received. It was only after I had visited some of their homes that I began to understand their interest in what we took for granted.

There were no roads between Franklin and any of the other settlements, and distances between the communities were measured in hundreds of kilometres, with Fort Norman, at a hundred and forty kilometres, being the closest. The nearest railway was almost a thousand kilometres away. For two months during the summer, when Great Bear Lake was finally free of ice, several barges brought in most of the following year's supply of goods—everything from safety pins to sewage pipes.

During the rest of the year, small single-engine airplanes, either a ten-passenger de Havilland Otter or a six-seater Beaver, brought us our long-awaited mail, supplies, and passengers. These regularly scheduled planes usually arrived once a month, subject to local weather conditions. Between those flights government planes occasionally descended on us, usually from Inuvik. The sound of an airplane—our only link with the outside world—was indeed welcome. How quickly our ears pricked up whenever we heard a pilot flying over the village, announcing his arrival before landing. During that first year when flights were rare, many village people hurried down to meet each plane in anticipation of seeing a relative or friend or receiving mail, or just to make contact with the world outside for a short while.

Twice a year planes were unable to land on the lake, each time for a period of about six weeks. "Freeze up" arrived in October with a skim of thin ice. Fortunately, the ice on the Little Lake became solid enough for planes to land on long before that was possible on the vast Great Bear Lake. Flights, again, came to a halt at "break up" in the late spring when the melting ice became too unstable for planes to land on.

Cars or trucks of any kind were nonexistent. Father Fumoleau owned the only snowmobile, old and battered, one of the first to have ever been produced.[1] A government-owned autoboggan, a kind of larger snowmobile covered by a canvas and acrylic cabin for the driver's protection, was under the jurisdiction of the power plant operator.

Dog team was the commonest mode of transportation. Every family owned six to eight dogs—mostly a mixture of wolf and husky—strong dogs when well fed, with thick fur to withstand the northern cold. Dogs and their sleds were in constant use for at least eight months of the year. I soon came to the conclusion that there was no more pleasant way to travel than in a dog sled, provided that you were well wrapped. Snuggled in a sleeping bag and listening to the pat, pat, pat of the dogs' feet and the swishing of the sled's runners on the glistening, hard-packed snow, accompanied by the jingle of harness bells and the driver's occasional loud commands of "Gee" or "Haw" to his dogs, was just sheer delight, even at -30°C.

We had no phones, not even local ones, no television nor radio, except for a couple of short wave radios, used mainly for emergency contact with Inuvik. Our only newspapers and journals were those sent by relatives and friends, long since outdated, but still eagerly devoured. So, by most people's standards we were indeed isolated. But once I had become involved in school and community activities, except on rare occasions, I never gave it much thought. There existed but two worlds: ours was that of Franklin and the Bear Lake People, the *Sahtuot'ine* (Sah-too-ot-in-eh), and somewhere out there, far in distance and in mind, lay the vast Outside.

Of the forty or so cabins that were the year-round Sahtuot'ine homes, only a few newer dwellings could be accurately described as log cabins, the older ones being little more than shacks. Rectangular, one-storey buildings, approximately five by eight metres (sixteen by twenty-five feet), comprised nothing more than one large room with temporary dividers of plywood or curtains separating the two or three tiny bedrooms from the living room cum dining room cum kitchen. The wood stove, made from a forty-five-gallon oil drum, was placed prominently in the centre of each dwelling. As the only source of heat for warmth and cooking, this was the most essential household item. Wooden floors were swept bare.

Furniture was sparse and usually comprised a Formica table and a few chairs ordered through an Eaton's catalogue and shipped in by barge, as had been, many years before, an old, well-worn couch and perhaps an old armchair. A makeshift sink area and a small cupboard for storing a few dishes, some cutlery, pots and pans, along with bags of flour, tea, coffee, sugar, baking powder and a few other essential items, designated the kitchen.

A recently installed electric generator provided electricity for the government, church and Bay buildings, as well as for the school janitor's house, but there was insufficient power for the Sahtuot'ine cabins to be hooked up. One summer, a fortuitous error by someone in Northern Affairs resulted in the shipment of a dozen tall streetlights. It was decided that installing them would be more economical than shipping them back to Inuvik. So, although the houses remained dimly lit by their oil or gas lamps, stretches of the dirt road were well illuminated.

The peoples' cabins had no running water, no flush toilets, no insulation and no heat, other than that provided by the wood stove. Outhouses, located some twenty metres away from their homes, were no joy to visit in the middle of the night in most of the year's sub-zero temperatures. When one of the new streetlights was installed too close to an outhouse, thus compromising a family's privacy, it wasn't long before a .22 rifle shattered the bulb!

Consider for a moment the steps involved in brewing a hot cup of tea, much treasured by the Sahtuot'ine. First of all the men, usually the young men of the family, hitched up the toboggan and a team of six to eight dogs a couple of times a week and rode off to the distant surrounding woods, returning a few hours later with a large supply of logs, all cut by axe or swede saw—few could afford a chain saw. The wood was then sawed and chopped into smaller logs for the wood stove.

For many months of the year, the children, whose job it was to carry pails of lake water back to the houses, had to chop through the ice which quickly formed over the hole after each visit. The tea, sugar and powdered milk would already have been purchased from the Hudson's Bay store at about triple the cost in the South. (Freight on items brought in by the barge during the summer months was expensive by southern standards, but the cost of items flown in later on in the year was astronomical. For example, a head of lettuce cost five dollars and a cabbage, ten dollars.) Yet, despite all the effort required just to boil a pot of water for tea, most of the children and their threadbare clothes were clean and neat when they arrived at school. And I rarely visited a home that wasn't swept clean and tidy.

Although the Sahtuot'ine purchased many food items from the Hudson's Bay store, they were, to a large extent, self-sufficient at a subsistence level for most of their food. Fish such as trout, grayling, whitefish and fresh water herring were always abundant in the lake, although not always easy to catch, particularly through six or seven feet of lake ice. Caribou and, to a lesser extent, moose were hunted with rifles by men when they were out trapping. Bannock, a round, flat loaf cooked in a frying pan on the stove top, supplemented the game and fish.

Later on in the spring, when the caribou migration paths took the animals close to Great Bear Lake, a large community hunt filled the communal village freezer with frozen legs, shoulders, ribs and other parts of the caribou carcasses. One morning each week, while supplies lasted, villagers gathered around the freezer and then carried home on one shoulder or tucked under an arm, a large hunk of frozen meat, to be hacked up into pieces for boiling in a pot on the wood stove. Although these provisions were for the use of the Sahtuot'ine, caribou, fish and moose soon became a staple part of my diet when I discovered that some people were most willing to exchange some of this real meat for our rations. They enjoyed the variety provided by macaroni and cheese and ketchup, which were their big favourites. Moose steaks and trout were mine.

Up until the building of a Roman Catholic mission, a trading post, and a government day school in Franklin in the early 1950s, a scant ten to fifteen years before my arrival, most Sahtuot'ine families had lived in tents in the bush for much of the year. They roamed around Great Bear Lake in search of game, stopping for a while when they had a plentiful supply of caribou, moving on to known fishing areas at other times. Similarly their trap lines, extending over large but specified areas, were moved to different locations from time to time so as not to deplete the game in any one area.[2]

They worked hard to feed themselves and their dogs, often rising at six in the morning and working well into the evenings. A constant supply of wood needed to be cut and hauled. The men hunted ducks, ptarmigan and rabbits as well as moose and caribou, which then had to be prepared into food and clothing, mostly by the women, both for their immediate consumption and to carry them through the trapping season. Fish nets or fish hooks, set in lakes and rivers, had to be checked daily.

Hundreds of kilometres were covered on foot, by dog-team and by canoe when checking their traps and procuring adequate supplies of food. Then further long distances had to be covered to take the furs to the trading posts. It was a harsh and strenuous life especially in such severe temperatures. Sickness was never far away, repeatedly causing the deaths of many young children in each family.

But the Sahtuot'ine enjoyed living on the land. That is where they felt at home. All obstacles could be overcome as long as they had the freedom to wander, the strength of their beliefs, and an abundant source of food. They considered themselves wealthy if supplies of fat, dry meat, fish and berries were plentiful and provided them with a varied and healthy diet. They lived according to their own laws and culture. People helped one another and when sickness and starvation struck from time to time there were always others better off who were willing to share their food and warmth with the less fortunate. Elders were held in great respect and were listened to. Children learned all they needed to know in adult life by assisting their parents with the family chores from a very early age, and they learned their laws and values from the stories and legends told and retold by their grandparents.

In many ways it might be considered a lonely life as each family traversed its own area, seldom meeting other families. But when they did meet, several days were spent in visiting and feasting and sharing the news about babies born or those who had died or where caribou or a moose had been spotted. This was the way news travelled. During the summer months, larger groupings of Sahtuot'ine came together to enjoy the feasting and drum dancing, to update the news, arrange marriages, relax and just have fun after the hard toil of winter. Such a gathering place—called *Déline* (Dell-in-eh) since ancient times—was located on Keith Arm at the western end of Great Bear Lake, near the source of the Bear River. This was known to have been a favourite meeting place for hundreds of years because of its reliable and abundant supply of fish.

Beginning in the 1950s the federal government introduced new game laws, set up game wardens' offices, and introduced closed seasons for game, which only aggravated a situation already made difficult for the trappers by declining fur prices. Soon after, having ignored the earlier plight of the Indians—or *Dene* (Den-eh), as the people collectively called themselves—several other government policies afforded some support for these people, although some of them proved to be a mixed blessing. Health and education services were introduced and all Native people received the same Social Assistance benefits, such as Old Age Pensions and Family Allowances, as did all Canadians.

To enable their children to attend the new federal day school, parents had to build permanent dwellings clustered around the school, mission and Bay store, thus resulting in several changes to their former way of life. While the bush still played a major role in the Sahtuot'ine's lives, the women and children stayed behind in the village while the men, old and young, departed in mid-autumn with their dog teams and their toboggans, laden with all the trapping and living supplies required for the next three months. As before, the winter was spent in setting traps, snares and deadfalls, checking the extensive trap lines, cleaning the furs of mink, marten, wolverine, foxes, and, occasionally other animals, and just surviving in temperatures that were continually below -20°C. However, these and all other chores were now completed without the assistance and company of women.

At Christmas and New Year the men left their traplines and returned to be with their families in the village for about two weeks before heading back to the bush again. Furs were sold to the Hudson's Bay store, and with only one store to sell to they were at the mercy of the Bay manager's generosity and his need to balance his books. Prices had already begun to decline by the mid-sixties and were to drop much further with the ensuing hue and cry against trapping in southern Canada and Europe in later years.

The discomfort that I now feel towards the use of leg traps did not exist in the minds of most southerners living in Franklin in those days. I know I gave no more thought to these trapped fur creatures than I give now to the animals slaughtered for food in the South. If we did think about it at all, we knew that no animal, once immobilized, would suffer for long in those very low temperatures. Instead, we admired a way of life where people lived and worked for months in, what were to us, incredibly harsh conditions in order to obtain an income from fur trapping and other seasonal occupations, so essential to their survival and their dignity.

After another short break back in the village in the early spring months—one could hardly refer to the weather as spring-like—to sell their furs at the Bay, the men again returned to the bush, this time to trap beaver and muskrat.

Previously, people had traded their furs for food, clothing and other necessities. Increasingly, people living in the village required a more reliable source of cash income, but as money from trapping decreased additional forms of seasonal employment for the men were required. A few women also supplemented their family income by making clothing and crafts. During the summer months, once the ice had broken up, some of the men worked on the NTCL barges, hauling freight on the Mackenzie River, as well as up Bear River. Several men also took up their annual seasonal profession as guides at the five large fishing lodges dotted around Great Bear Lake. Fishermen flew in for a week or two, at a cost of thousands of dollars, to these luxurious northern lodges, owned by outfitters from Canada and the United States and renowned for their excellent lake trout fishing. Towards the end of the summer and early autumn, many of the men of Franklin engaged in construction projects in the village using materials brought in by barges, either building houses for themselves or erecting small government buildings. As the days shortened and winter's free-fall of temperatures returned, the cyclic pattern of life began again.

Although the sums of money made by the Sahtuot'ine from their seasonal employment were not large, nor consistent from year to year, most of the people were able to maintain a considerable degree of economic independence, with the addition of Social Assistance benefits. In 1965 only one person in the village, an elderly widow, received welfare. And, whenever possible, just as they had done in the old days when one family's hunting or trapping was poor, people still attempted to support each other in these times of rapid economic change.

In many ways Franklin was a unique community. Isolated for much of the year and visited by few outsiders, the effects of incoming southern society had not yet afflicted Franklin as was the case in many Dene communities in less isolated parts of the Northwest Territories and especially along the Mackenzie River. There, where changes had been extremely rapid and southern influence, to a large extent, negative and detrimental, evidence of immense social upheaval was already apparent. In many of these communities, excessive drinking, drug addiction, physical and sexual abuse—symptomatic of social disintegration—were becoming increasingly common as people lost touch with their spiritual and traditional roots. They could not adjust quickly enough to the demands thrust upon them by all the changes or to the lack of economic opportunities available in this new world.

However, with few exceptions, there was little excessive drinking in Franklin and drugs had not yet found their way there. Similarly, episodes of physical and sexual abuse remained infrequent. Instead, most of the Sahtuot'ine were capable, independent and self-reliant, still able to maintain their dignity and take pride in themselves and their accomplishments as they lived and worked in a manner that was, for the most part, an extension of their traditional ways.

Was I not appalled by the poverty in which these people lived, their substandard housing that lacked basic necessities such as heat, light and running water, things that other Canadians, including me, took for granted? For a long time I didn't question why things were as they were. I just accepted that this was the way the Sahtuot'ine lived. I was more interested in the viability of the people—how well they coped with their circumstances—and in their immensely different culture and life style. Over time I did begin to wonder about their impoverished conditions as they struggled to eke out an existence, but the actions I took were quite minimal. I remember thinking that too much had already been done "to" and "for" these people, with the best of intentions, but often with detrimental results. I willingly supported and took action on their behalf when they asked me to, as occurred in my third year, but I did not see it as my place to initiate too many things outside the realm of the classroom.

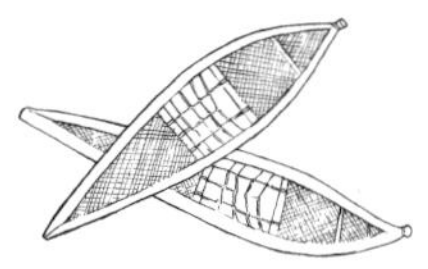

It was late in October. My students and I were into a comfortable routine at school. Most seemed to enjoy coming to class and showed a considerable willingness to learn. I was pleased with how things were progressing. Only Lucas (not his real name) worried me. Although at times he seemed happy and vivacious, I didn't seem able to establish a good relationship with him. Unlike the other students, he was often rude and defiant, clearly challenging me. I was bothered.

I talked to Helen about him. Why was he so unlike the other children? She informed me that his father had more contact with southerners than most people in the village. As such, he had easier access to liquor and at those times the parties often ended in violence. Helen told me how it had been necessary for her to intervene on several occasions and then provide medical attention to various family members, beaten up in the ensuing melee.

One day, an argument erupted in my class between Lucas and one of the other boys. In a flash, Lucas whipped out a stiletto-like knife with a six-inch blade, thrusting it close to the other boy's neck and yelling threats in words that needed no translation. I stared in disbelief at the scene.

I was terrified. I had never experienced anything like this before. Lucas seemed so wild and out of control. Realizing that I had to intervene before anyone was hurt, I walked slowly towards him, my heart pounding and a sick feeling in my stomach. From the recesses of my mind, I recalled hearing or reading somewhere that when you meet a wild animal your best chance is to remain calm. I didn't know if the same thing applied to a wild child but it seemed to make sense. So, as calmly as I could, while feeling anything but calm, and struggling to maintain a low, unemotional voice, I said, "Lucas. Give me the knife. Give me the knife before you hurt someone." I held out my left hand.

He turned his angry face towards me and spat out, "You bitch, you stay away from me."

Without overtly reacting to his comment, I continued walking slowly between the rows of desks towards him, hand outstretched and dimly aware of the silent, frightened faces watching me. I took a deep breath and again repeated as calmly as I could, "Lucas. Give me the knife."

He lunged forward as if to stab me but at the last moment he slammed the steel blade onto the palm of my outstretched left hand. I closed my fingers around the cold steel only to feel him begin to pull it out again. But by then I had a firm grip on his wrist with my right hand and as such he was unable to remove it.

We struggled briefly, but finally, with a flurry of more angry words, Lucas let go of the knife and stood there, body taut, his faced filled with emotion. He stared at me for a brief moment before lowering his gaze and dropping his arms to his side.

What was I to do now? I became aware once more of the other children still sitting motionless at their desks, watching us intently, horror written on their faces. And at the same moment, with a clarity that comes at such times, I heard the sound of barking dogs and the fleeting glimpse of young Paul standing on the back of his toboggan, racing past my window on his way to getting a load of wood, oblivious to what had just transpired in our classroom.

I told the students to get back to work then led Lucas from the room, now docile, as if all the air had been sucked out of him. I clutched the knife in my right hand and desperately wanted to do something to the ease the pain of my left hand. The small cut was only bleeding slightly—the knife must have been dull—but other than wrapping a handkerchief around it, it had to wait.

There are times when I still wonder if what I did next was the right thing to do. I felt it was then, and most times, in retrospect, thinking of the relationship that developed between Lucas and me afterwards, I think it probably was. Or maybe that would have happened anyway.

I took him into Joe's office, a small room containing only his desk, a filing cabinet and two chairs. As was customary for principals in those days, Joe had a strap, a wide leather belt, in the top drawer of his desk. I took it out and said, "Lucas, you can't threaten other kids with a knife. You shouldn't even bring it to school. And you shouldn't have attacked me with it." I had to make him realize the seriousness of his actions.

He just stood there, his face filled with loathing and anger. Or was it fear? He didn't say anything.

I continued. "Lucas. I am going to strap you three times on each hand and it will hurt, but you must realize that you can't threaten or hurt people with knives. Hold out your right hand." I raised my arm, stood on my toes and came down as hard as I could with my best badminton smash. To have done any less would have been self-defeating.

He cringed, ever so slightly, as he returned his hand again, palm upwards. I strapped him twice more on his right hand. He blinked several times but his mouth remained clamped. "Now hold out your left hand." He did so. The sound of the strap cracking across his hand was all I heard but the look in his eyes told me that he was in pain.

I stopped. "Lucas. I hurt you didn't I?" He looked down and nodded very slightly, then glanced back at me, clearly close to tears, as was I.

I went on, "I want you to try and understand what I am going to say. I shall never strap you again no matter what you do. I don't believe in beating up kids and that is what strapping is. I was just beating you. But I want you to remember that I can hurt you and that I am *choosing* not to strap you again. It isn't because I'm too weak but because I don't want to. I don't think it's a good thing to hurt kids or anyone else. Do you understand what I'm saying?" He nodded his head.

I let the strap slip to the floor and I reached out for this twelve-year-old waif and hugged him. He hugged me back. We stood there for several minutes, just leaning against each other, both crying silently. Finally, I handed him back his father's fishing knife and repeated, "Lucas. Please don't ever bring knives to school again. But even if you do, I won't strap you. I will take the knife away and you won't get it back. But I will not hurt you again like this."

I replaced the strap in Joe's desk drawer. It was not mine to throw into the lake in disgust.

I returned to my class and, as it was close to the end of the day, dismissed my very subdued students. Lucas stayed in Joe's office until they had all gone. Then I went home and cried again in the quiet of my cabin. What had I done? How much of what I had said to Lucas had he been able to understand?

Somehow I had felt that because of the violence in his family, he would not respect anyone less powerful than himself, and especially not a woman teacher, all of five foot three. But, I reasoned, if I showed him I was capable of hurting him with the strap but chose not to do so in the future no matter what he did, he would not see it as a weakness in me, but rather as a strength. I also hoped that it would give him the message that things didn't have to, shouldn't have to, be settled by force. It all seemed so logical—to me.

I agonized over my actions. How could I possibly expect Lucas, with his limited English let alone different cultural mores, to understand what I had just done? And what effect would this have on all my other students? Would they see me as a bully? Would they now be afraid of me? I felt terrible.

I heard a knock on my door. I didn't want to see anyone tonight so went to the door to send the children on their way. But when I saw several of the boys from my class standing outside in the cold I changed my mind and, endeavouring to hide my emotions, let them in. Last to enter, but for the first time, was Lucas.

"I'm having some hot chocolate. Would you like some too?" I tried to sound cheerful. They nodded and then we chatted as we usually did and as if nothing had happened that afternoon. Even Lucas joined in. But my mind was not fully on these incidental events. I wanted to talk to them about what had happened. I needed to be reassured that all was still well, not realizing that their mere presence here tonight was telling me that. And most of all I wanted to say something to Lucas, but I was sure they would clam up if I said anything. So I kept these thoughts and words to myself, difficult though it was, and concentrated on enjoying their company. They lingered for a while but left soon after finishing their hot chocolate. Perhaps they had seen more in my eyes than I had realized.

As I closed the front door behind them Lucas, the last to leave, turned back, flashed one of his beautiful smiles at me and said gruffly, "It OK. I understand," and then with a wild whoop, his open jacket flapping in the breeze, his arms spread wide, he leapt down the stairs and onto the backs of a couple of the boys.

I stayed in the doorway for many minutes watching him and the other boys disappear. But Lucas would not disappear from my life for a long time. From then on, even though schoolwork was never easy for him, he plodded away cheerfully and he continued visiting me in the evenings, sometimes with the other boys but increasingly, on his own. And much to my great relief I noticed no change in the other children's attitudes towards me.

CHAPTER FOUR

FALL ARRIVES

The weeks rolled by quickly. Now, in late October, the sun rose at morning recess and disappeared in the mid-afternoon, barely four hours later. Sundogs—parhelion—frequently appeared when the sun was still low in the morning sky: two small arcs on either side of the sun that shimmered like the ends of a rainbow. Keith Arm began to freeze with serious determination. The snow was here to stay and everyone revelled in this clean and bright earthly blanket.

Outside my classroom windows, an eighteen-foot aluminum boat danced and hummed speedily across the lake, as the men sped to check the fish nets they had suspended under the icy-cold waters. At other times I watched some of the women going into the bush to collect small toboggan loads of firewood. Or a hunter, off with his .22 or .410, returning a little while later with a bundle of good-tasting ptarmigan, the chameleon of the North, a small grey-brown mottled bird that turns white with the coming of snow.

Claire and I also indulged in some new-found pleasures. Sometimes on weekends we accompanied Liz, Pete, Helen and Joe to the ski-hill that Pete had carved on a steep slope near the Little Lake, where we launched ourselves down the run on our cross-country skis. Fortunately there weren't too many turns to navigate as we skied, time and time again, laughing and screaming at our many tumbles, none of us being very proficient, then dragging ourselves back up the hill for another turn, until we finally succumbed to exhaustion.

Near the top of the hill, Pete had also built a small lean-to from branches and twigs and covered the floor with interlaced spruce branches, as was the traditional way of erecting a small dwelling. We gathered there at the end of the short afternoon to watch the last moments of the setting sun and settle our weary bodies around a blazing log fire, sipping the strongest tea I had ever drunk—Indian style, said Pete—where handfuls of tea were thrown into a small pot of water to brew. It was so good and warmed the cockles of my heart, as my mother would say, not to mention my fingers and toes.

A little later, when Keith Arm had frozen solid, Liz introduced Claire and me to skiing behind the autoboggan. This was similar to water skiing, only on ice. A long rope was attached at one end to the autoboggan. At the other end of the rope was a two-foot stick that the skier held on to for dear life while being pulled on cross-country skis. It was great fun and we became quite good at it, carving large arcs as we swung from side to side, maintaining supple knees and ankles to absorb the bumps from the hard drifts of snow caused by the wind whistling across the ice. Occasionally, if we could persuade a third person to

drive, two of us attached ropes and learned to do some fancy weaving in and out.

I soon discovered the downfall to this activity. Gripping the stick tightly for too long caused the circulation in the arms to cease. I can still recall the excruciating agony of my frozen arms as they began to thaw out afterwards. Back in my duplex I dunked them in lukewarm water, having been told that hot water was not the thing to do. Then I wrapped them in towels and "hugged" my crossed limbs while prancing around the room in sheer agony as my blood circulation slowly returned. I wish I could say that I only went through that once and then learned my lesson. Unfortunately, because you don't feel your arms or any other part of your body freeze, I was to agonize through throbbing arms several more times over the years.

One bitterly cold Sunday morning, I trudged to the church through the packed-down snow, bundled up in my new parka, mukluks and mittens. Local women had made all of my outer garments. The parka, worn over a sweater and jeans, came down to just above my knees and was really two coats, a zippered outer coat of navy wind-proof nylon worn over a white duffle under-coat. A strip of wolverine fur edged the hood and bottom of my parka. My mukluks were of moose hide and red and navy stroud (a woollen material) and decorated with flower patterns of beads. To complete my new outfit I had purchased a large pair of moose hide mittens decorated with beads and fringes. The mittens, attached to each other by a long cord of braided moose hide, hung around the neck to ensure that the mittens were not lost when one took them off. Frozen bare hands became useless very quickly in these temperatures, creating a dangerous situation. I felt and looked like a real Northerner, or so I thought. And I felt assured that my new clothes would protect me from the serious winter yet to come. The thermometer placed outside the church read close to -40°C, yet the wolverine trim around my parka hood, unlike most other furs, was almost frost free despite my frozen breath.

I knew that the church would be nice and warm, partly because of the wood furnace lit early that morning by Father Fumoleau, and partly because the church would soon be filled with most of the village adults and many children. I found a place among all the women sitting on the right side of the church. As was the custom, the men occupied the left side.

Dressed in his vestments and accompanied by a couple of my students as altar boys, Father Fumoleau began Mass. I had met Father several times by now, a soft-spoken, slight man in his mid-thirties, or so I guessed, with a delightful sense of humour. Since leaving France as a young priest in 1953, he had spent seven years in Fort Good Hope, on the Mackenzie River, before coming to Fort Franklin in 1960.

He lived in the mission next door to the church, a very sparse building that,

Helen Chan (*left*), nurse-in-charge, and me in our winter attire.

despite its lack of warmth in terms of furniture was nearly always occupied by several children. They ran in to get out of the cold and to play for a while. And adults frequently dropped by to visit with Father. In a relatively short number of years Father had already learned the local north Slavey dialect and could converse with the Sahtuot'ine as well as deliver his Sunday sermons in Slavey. In fact, he had done more than just learn the language orally; he had studied it thoroughly and was developing a new orthography.

Father's affection and concern for his charges was obvious, even if understated. He also had a considerable understanding of these people who were caught between two cultures. He never seemed to thrust his religion on them but merely provided them with an opportunity to worship in the religion that most of them had adopted, at least, in a symbolic sense.

The Mass continued. The pleasant and familiar odour of incense was accompanied by the continuous sounds of deep coughing that often ended with a loud spitting of phlegm into the tin cans carried to church by many of the older people. Consumption and tuberculosis were never far away.

The people began to sing hymns that had been translated into Slavey and written in the syllabic script familiar throughout the North. Perhaps, because I was brought up in Wales, a country renowned for its music and song, I have to admit that the harsh, nasal, droning sounds from adults singing hymns at a very slow pace was not pleasant to my ears. Interesting, yes, but not musical. However, the Sahtuot'ine's enjoyment and devotion in singing these hymns could not be denied.

As the congregation filed out at the end of Mass into a cloud of freezing breath, people chatted with Father and to each other just as any group of churchgoers does at the end of a service. The extent of my participation was several smiles and utterances of "*Gonezo*" since it was indeed a beautifully sunny day, even if darned cold. I trudged home through the dazzling snow to my Sunday dinner of canned beef, canned potatoes and canned carrots, topped by my own homemade gravy.

One day a plane arrived bringing one of our few visitors to Franklin, a Mr. B., our school superintendent. Retired from a school board in southern Ontario, he had taken on another superintendency in the Territories. I welcomed him to my class and proceeded, not without some pride, to show him how well the children were progressing and how enthusiastic some of them were about learning. He spent a few minutes walking around the room and then stormed up to my desk. The silence was broken by a loud, "What are these children doing reading from these books?"

I wasn't sure why he seemed so angry and replied, "The children are doing very well, aren't they?" Several students, who even three months ago could barely read anything, were now reading simple books quite well.

"But these are not the readers they should be in!" he bellowed. "Where are the grade four and five readers that they should be reading?"

"Mr. B., very few of the children can read those books. Most of these children couldn't even speak English two or three years ago and only a handful of them could read beyond a grade three level in September. Now they are all reading, even if at various levels."

"I don't want to hear all your excuses. They should be reading the grade four and five readers, the ones prescribed by the Alberta curriculum," he stated emphatically in a loud voice. "And young lady," as he looked at my lesson plans, skimming quickly through several pages, "where do you make reference to the Alberta curriculum?"

"I don't," I replied, as I now felt myself getting upset in response to his belligerence. "There is very little in that curriculum that has any meaning to these children. I use what is important in their lives to teach them things."

He obviously wasn't listening to anything I said. "I am making notes in my book here," he bellowed, as he waved his little black book close to my face. In a threatening voice, his round face and large body glowering at me, he continued, "I shall be back and the next time I come, if you want to keep your job here, I want to see all these children in the correct grade four and five readers!" He stormed out of the class, leaving my students and me in an agitated state.

I later mentioned Mr. B.'s visit to Joe who replied, "Oh, he's new Miggs. He's only been in Inuvik a few months and this was his first visit to Franklin. He's a retired superintendent from the South and probably doesn't know anything about the North. You're doing a fine job with the kids so don't worry about him. He'll learn."

"Thanks, Joe. That makes me feel a bit better, but I'll have to come up with something to get him off my back the next time he returns, and, more importantly, off the kids' backs."

And in the spring he did return.

Joe had been notified that he would be visiting us one day, weather permitting. We heard the plane fly over the school and we knew he would have to land at the Little Lake, which meant at least half an hour before he arrived at the school. The children had come a long way in six months and by now several were working their way through the grade four and five readers. But these books were still beyond the ability of most children, so I had given them others that they could handle and enjoy reading.

When we heard the plane overhead I asked all the children to take out their readers and place them on their desks, open to pages such and such. I also made a few hurried notes in reference to the Alberta curriculum in my daybook. All very devious, I was quite aware, but sometimes such tactics are necessary when dealing with ignorant people with power. All I said to the children was, "Remember when Mr. B. came last time and how angry he got?" and they all nodded their heads well remembering him. "He was angry because we weren't using these nice new books so he'll be pleased to see them on your desks this time."

In he marched. No knock on the door. No "May I come in?" or "May I join you?" Just a quick "Good morning" to the class as he made his way towards me. In readiness for this occasion I had prepared exercises for the kids to work on, at their own levels, which only very slightly coincided with the stories they were "reading," so, now as I handed them out, I asked the children to get on with their work.

"Well, Miss Morris," as he looked into his black book. "I hope you've learned something since my last visit."

"Oh yes, Mr. B. I've learned a great deal—about life in a small northern community, about the children and their lives beyond school, about their pride and determination and sense of fun, about...," but by now he was walking around the room.

"I'm glad to see the children in the correct readers. You know, we must not give these children a second-class education just because they are Natives. They deserve the same education as any other child in Canada, so we mustn't short-change them."

"I agree, Mr. B.," having decided that I must remain calmer this time. "They do deserve the best education we can give them. But we must also realize that we have to go about teaching them in a different way, so as to make things meaningful to them. We have to use the context of what is familiar for them, at least to begin with, and the stories in these readers don't have much meaning for them."

"Nonsense! They have to learn about things that every Canadian learns about or they will always be stuck in these backwoods. Education will bring them into the mainstream of Canadian society. That is what they need. Once they forget their own language and old ways and learn how to speak, read and write in English they will be much better off."

I didn't want to keep arguing with him in front of the children but, even though I hadn't been in Franklin very long, I knew he was totally wrong. He displayed the same old superior "Colonial" attitude, a mentality born from a belief that if you had a white skin and a European (or Canadian) background, then you knew what was best for these "poor Natives—just make them more like us and they will be better off." But this was not the time for protracted debate, so I let it go with one more comment, which I expressed as brightly as I could.

"Considering that these children speak no English when they come to school at the age of six, they do wonderfully well. You can be assured, Mr. B., that they enjoy coming to school and they are receiving an education that will allow them to have choices in the future." I wanted to tell him that they would do a lot better if we didn't destroy their language and culture, the things that made them who they were, but these were ideas that I was just beginning to explore in my own mind and I lacked the courage to argue my case. I also did not want to say anything that might jeopardize my staying there. Instead I turned to safer ground. "Boys and girls, get out your math books and your handwriting and spelling books and show Mr. B. the great job you're doing."

He walked around and several times grunted at the children, which I took to be his way of giving them some positive feedback. Then he looked at his watch and headed for the door. "Much better, Miss Morris, much better. I'm glad to see you took my advice," and he left.

The kids just grinned at me and I smiled back at them. There was no need to say anything other than "Lunchtime!" and they put all their books back in their desks. Joe had the pleasure of entertaining Mr. B. for lunch, one of the duties which comes with being an administrator!

That evening Claire and I spent some time discussing Mr. B's visit. "I can't believe some of the things he said, and as a former superintendent, you would think he knew something about education and how children learn. And how can he think that ridiculing a people's language and culture will help them?"

"Forget about him, Miggs. He's just like most southern experts who come up North. They think they know it all and so never listen to what any northerner has to say."

I gave that statement and the events of the day much thought that evening. Did I consider myself to be an expert on northern education? I didn't think so. I really didn't believe that just because I had taught here for a few months that I had all the answers to educating Native people. But surely some things were self evident to anyone who was familiar with the basic principles of sound teaching. If you want someone to learn anything you have to start where they are at, and then help them grow and expand from there in small, meaningful steps. Furthermore, how can you expect people to have pride in themselves and the confidence to learn new ways, when others keep denigrating what is important to them? It would be several years before I realized that Mr. B.'s views were, in fact, very much in keeping with the paternalistic views of the Canadian establishment of those days towards Native people.

A year later, Mr. B. was back at our school. As I passed Claire's room I heard him say, "You mean these children don't speak English when they start school? Good heavens! Then you teachers do have a tough job on your hands."

Later that evening I asked Claire, "Hadn't you told him before that most of the kids speak no English when they come to school?"

"Of course I had," replied Claire, "each time he came here, but some people just take a long time to catch on."

November 14, 1965, was a big day in Franklin, the day the new nursing station received its official blessing. All the village people were invited to attend the open house. Father Fumoleau, in his best Sunday cassock and vestments, presided over the religious ceremony in the afternoon. Merle Pottinger, the nursing supervisor for the Mackenzie District, chartered a plane from Inuvik for this special occasion and brought a considerable amount of food with her for the feast that was to follow.

The Sahtuot'ine greeted the occasion with a mixture of awe at the size and modern appearance of the nursing station, and joy and relief at knowing that their health needs would be better met in their own village. No longer would they have to leave their families and fly to Inuvik every time they required medical care. It was also the first occasion for me to meet some of the children's parents in a casual situation—movies and Bingo games were serious business. Even though most of the men and older brothers had already departed for the bush, women, children, older siblings, and grandparents soon crowded the nursing station. This gave me an opportunity to chat with those who spoke some English and smile a lot at other folk, unless their children agreed to translate for us. It was all very enjoyable.

A few days later Theresa Baton became the proud mother of baby Erma, the first baby to be born at the nursing station. Laura Tutcho, Judy's sister and a student in Liz's class, had the dubious honour of being the first patient. However, her family was not too sorry about this as it gave them an opportunity to visit the nursing station quite frequently.

It was around this time that Father Fumoleau introduced me to northern Co-operatives. He explained that the concept of co-operatives was new in the North. They were started by James Houston, a Toronto-born artist who visited Baffin Island in the late 1950s where he gained a life-long fascination with Inuit soapstone carvings and artwork. Houston decided to assist the Inuit people of Cape Dorset in developing silk-screen prints of their designs. Houston's Co-operatives played three important roles: they promoted Inuit art in the South, provided competition for the Hudson's Bay Company and developed leadership skills in the local people.

Once Father Fumoleau became aware of these Inuit Co-operatives, he realized that the concept could be equally viable in Franklin, even if on a smaller scale. One of the mission outbuildings was converted into a small Co-op store. Now the local Co-op could provide some competition for the Bay by also selling mostly non-perishable items to the villagers. It also enabled Father to train the Sahtuot'ine in the skills necessary for them to operate a business of their own.

Furthermore, the Co-op purchased local handicrafts and then sold them to companies in the South.

When I arrived, the Co-op was already showing promise. Among the beautiful and carefully crafted items one could buy there were beaded moose hide jackets; felt appliquéd moose hide wall-hangings; moose hide mukluks and slippers of various designs trimmed with beaver, rabbit or wolf fur; bleached and decorated caribou skin mittens, a pair of which would be donated to Princess Alexandra during her Canadian visit in 1967; miniature versions of wooden and babiche (animal hide) snow shoes, fishing spears and scoops; and beautiful little dolls dressed in traditional fur and hide clothes. All were produced locally, and all provided additional income as well as employment for those involved in the Co-op store itself.

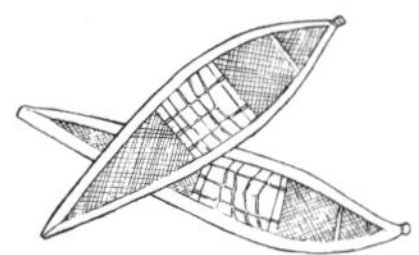

Then the pipes froze. No water. No flushing toilet. What were Claire and I to do? After all it was only November with most of the winter still ahead of us. We rushed over to see Joe and give him the bad news. Calm as always, Joe dug out a couple of blowtorches and we went back to our duplex. Joe quickly found the culprit. In the corner of the attic some of the insulation wrapped around the ninety-degree angle of the pipe had come undone, causing the water to freeze. He lit the blowtorch and waved it back and forth over the offending corner and before long we heard rushing water again. But my joy was short-lived when I saw my bathtub fill with backed up toilet effluence.

At this point Joe went to get William Sewi, our school custodian, and before long, with Claire and I feeling quite useless to do anything more than ply them with coffee, they restored our plumbing and my bathtub back to health. Thank goodness. It certainly left me with a renewed appreciation for the village people who managed to survive all the time without running water and had to use outhouses.

Adeline Vital leads a drum dance in Fort Franklin, 1966.

CHAPTER FIVE

WINTER SETS IN

"*Heh-ah—heh-ah—heh-yah-ha-ah-ha-ah-ha!*"

The men of the village were back from the bush for a short respite from trapping and to enjoy Christmas with their families. Our students had invited Claire and me to the drum dance, the first to be held since we had arrived. The dense night air caught at our throats as soon as we stepped outside our duplex, making breathing difficult. The alcohol thermometer outside the church registered around -50°C (-70°F).

Overhead, a panorama of northern lights, shimmering curtains in hues of mostly pink, lavender, pale orange and yellow, with occasional glimpses of ghostly green, danced in Arctic splendour. Nowhere else did I ever experience the intensity of colours and duration of displays as those above Fort Franklin. Despite reading that the northern lights are silent, I am still convinced that, at times such as that night, during their most splendid performances, rustling sounds accompany the successive waves of curtains dancing in the celestial breezes. Such was their performance that night, a portent of the ancient celebration in which we were about to take part.

Our mukluks crunched on the hard snow. Ice from our freezing breath even encrusted the wolverine fur on our parka hoods. We walked through the village not sure of our destination. But, just as the children had advised us, the beat of the drums led the way.

On opening the cabin door we were engulfed in a cloud of hot air that instantly turned to steam as it met the freezing outside air. My eyes were drawn to three young men in the centre of the crowded room—Dolphus, Paul and George. They were hunched over the pot-bellied stove, holding the flat drums by their babiche strings over the heat and beating them with wooden sticks until the tension and pitch of the caribou skin, stretched across one face of the circular drum, was judged to be just right.

People made room for Claire and me to squeeze in and sit on a tabletop. We waited with anticipation. Before long the prepared drums were handed over to three older men sitting on chairs to one side of the room. The beating of the drums began, tentatively at first, gathering speed, unison and volume. Then suddenly, as one, the men stood up. A crescendo of sound erupted from them. The steady beat of the drums reverberated throughout the cabin, accompanied by the full-throated, unison chanting of the three drummers. Their heads thrown back and features strained, perspiration poured down their intense faces. The chant reached a higher pitch, in partnership with the drums—a strong and steady heartbeat from some past, distant time, pulsating through my every bone.

"*Heh-ah—heh-ah—heh-yah-ha-ah-ha-ah-ha!*"

A few minutes into the chanting one of the women stepped forward, followed moments later by many women and men of all ages, as they began their single file shuffle around the stove. Someone beckoned for me to join in. A few young men joined the circle from time to time. Their fancier footsteps, weaving and bobbing movements were a contrast to the static, stoic bodies of the women, arms hanging limply by their sides.

And so began the dance, so understated compared to the fever-pitched drums and chanting, a drum dance that was to continue for some five hours. I was totally captivated by its power and primal beauty. The sounds were like none I had heard before. They were exciting and hypnotic and reached into the core of my being, compelling me to dance, to join the large single file line of men and women encircling the blazing wood stove. We shuffled in our mukluks in steady rhythm to the beat that went on and on and on.

Around the room, sitting on whatever furniture had been pushed to the sides, were older men and women and women with babies and young children, still wearing their jackets, their backs sticking to the ice-covered walls. The accumulation of sweat and breath had turned to ice upon contact with the uninsulated inside walls of the cabin. But those of us dancing around the hot stove at the centre of the room had soon removed or opened our parkas.

Later I came to learn about the importance of the drum to the Dene. George Blondin, a native of Fort Franklin, wrote about it in his book, *When the World Was New*:

> The tradition of the drum has been going on for many years, before the non-Dene came to our country. The old people tell me that the Creator gave our people medicine powers to help them survive the hardships of living. It was part of our spiritual beliefs, just as it was part of the beliefs of all native peoples of Canada. The Elders say our people could not have survived without this medicine.
>
> All people did not have the same kind of powers. Some individuals had very strong medicine power, and to them a drum song was given. The song came from the Creator and was given for a special purpose...
>
> Although our people had some songs just for fun and dancing, drum songs were different. They were for praying, healing, seeing the future, for thanksgiving, and for preaching and teaching. Drum songs came in two ways—through visions, or through a person's medicine. Life was so hard in the old days, and people depended on the drum for spiritual strength....
>
> Many songs were passed from generation to generation. That's why we know how to sing drum songs even now, although a lot of

us—especially the young—have forgotten where the songs came from and what their original purpose was. When the missionaries came, people started going to church and used new ways of praying, along with traditional songs.[1]

The Christmas season began early in December for us at the school. It was customary for the students to put on a concert for the village just before the holidays, to be held in Father Fumoleau's mission. So the planning and the practising began. Following our classroom discussion it was decided that some students would put on a short Nativity play and the rest would sing carols, accompanied by me on the guitar.

Everything went well until we came to the business of costumes. We needed enough for Mary and Joseph, the Angel Gabriel, the Three Wise Men and several shepherds. Where were we to obtain them? My grade four and five students came to the rescue. "Teacher you got lots of sheets and towels. Why we not use those?" Good idea, and all my tablecloths and curtains got thrown in, too. With the addition of a few items such as crowns made from construction paper, and a bushy wolverine tail used as a beard for Jimmy who played Joseph, these Indian children of the North were soon transformed into a group of authentically attired Middle Eastern people from biblical times.

The mission was packed on the night of the concert. Claire began the evening with her little kids performing a delightful Nativity play. Liz had her grade two and three students sing a few carols. Then half of the class depicted a scene where an angel greeted the shepherds as "they watched their flocks by night," and the other half gave a rendition of a smartly dressed Santa, eight little reindeer complete with homemade antlers and Rudolph "with his nose so bright."

Finally it was our turn. We began with some more carols and invited the audience to join in, without much success. But, undoubtedly in my mind, the stars of the show were my students in our Nativity play. With the opening of the "stage" curtains, the audience burst into delighted laughter and talking as they pointed at the children, resplendent in their brightly coloured costumes, before again becoming subdued and eager for the students' performance. The entire concert was indeed a big hit with the audience, and the kids and we teachers, too, were delighted with the evening.

Christmas began in earnest with midnight Mass at the church. It was attended by virtually everyone in the village. The church, Father Fumoleau, and the altar boys were all specially attired for this festive occasion.

During the holidays our small group of southerners celebrated Christmas together with several delicious feasts. Helen hosted our sumptuous Christmas dinner, complete with turkey and various kinds of vegetables, potatoes and seasonal trimmings. Liz and Pete, and Claire and I contributed too. It was amusing to see how items, secretly hoarded for months, suddenly appeared. Out came the linen tablecloths, (mine recently washed, starched and ironed after the concert), long tapered candles, Christmas crackers and paper hats, crystal wine glasses and quality wine brought in last summer and kept hidden especially for this occasion, brightly decorated Christmas trees and favourite Christmas music. For each of these parties, we all donned our best southern duds. Heavens! I even wore my red, woollen dress on Christmas day.

Many of our students also visited Claire and me during the holidays, proudly dressed in their new clothes purchased from the Bay and accompanied by new mukluks and mittens, sewn by their mothers and grandmothers. We chatted, played cards—even the younger kids were great rummy players—drank mugs of hot chocolate, baked and ate cookies and cakes, played lots of music—mostly country and western—as was their choice and to which the girls danced in southern style, and we sang songs with the guitar. Several adults also dropped by to wish us a Merry Christmas and they shared in a cup of tea, hot chocolate, or a glass of wine.

In the new year Father Fumoleau organized a games night in the mission for all the village children, young and old. There were many different games and contests for the children to participate in such as balloon bursting, ping-pong, ball blowing, and coin tossing. Even though all the kids tried hard, the losers always laughed and enjoyed themselves just as much as the winners. And as always, the audience of parents, uncles, aunts and grandparents, sitting around the large room, enjoyed watching all the activities, encouraging the children in these strange games and smiling, laughing and clapping at their efforts.

Our holidays were coming to an end. The trappers had sold all their rich assortment of furs—marten, mink, wolverine, white and red fox, even an occasional wolf—to Pete, in order to pay off past debts and to again outfit themselves for another three months of trapping in the bush. Another couple of drum dances were held in which we again gladly participated and then I was introduced to another long time Dene traditional game, the handgame.

In the handgame, also known as the stick gamble, two teams of equal numbers of men line up and face each other in a kneeling position. The tempo of the game is set by an accompanying group of men with their deafening drums and loud chanting. This intensifies in volume and speed as the game and the guessing progresses. The teams take turns at being the active players. The objective is for the members of the active team to fool the captain of the opposing team about which hands hide their tokens. Bets, often bullets, are placed in front of each active player.

The game begins when players on one team bend over jackets loosely draped over their hands in which the tokens are hidden. The men bob and weave in time to the drumbeat, then letting their jackets fall in front of their knees, they slowly raise themselves from the waist up holding their arms now in a folded and outstretched position. The single standing opponent, after several minutes of suspenseful hesitation, makes his guess with a flick of his thumb to either the right or left and all of the players' hands are opened to reveal which contain the hidden tokens. At that time, the intensity of players, drummers and audience is broken and replaced by laughter and jovial kidding of each other as bets are settled.

Daylight began to increase slightly with the coming of January. Since the end of November the only sun we had seen was at lunchtime when it put in a brief appearance behind the mountain due south of us, and by the twenty-first of December appeared for only half an hour. Much to my surprise, all these long hours of darkness didn't bother me. Maybe I was just too busy. Then again, it never seemed really dark when the stars and moon shone on the blanket of snow from the clear skies overhead. In fact, I recalled many cloudy days in September, prior to the arrival of snow that seemed to be far darker and more forbidding.

Most of the time the lake ice was covered by snow. But every now and then, after a huge storm, all the snow in Keith Arm blew away, leaving the ice bare. I loved to walk on it at those times and look down through the more than two metres of transparent black ice, all the way to the stones below. The Sahtuot'ine assured us that this was an extremely cold winter and that the ice was about as thick as they had ever seen it.

Every day, when there was enough light outside for me to glance out of my class, I watched people walking or driving their dogs and sleds across the lake ice towards their fish holes. They used a method that went back hundreds of years. Once the ice became solid enough in the late fall for people to walk on, several holes of about a foot in diameter were chiselled in a row through the ice. Then a stout rope, attached to a long pole, was slung under the ice between the holes until anywhere from fifty to a hundred metres separated the two end holes. To this rope a net was attached and pulled through from the one end hole to the other so that the net, weighted by stones, hung down under the ice. These two end holes were then enlarged and the ropes affixed in the ice and snow. The intervening holes soon froze.

Each day, the villagers checked their nets by re-chiselling the end holes and clearing the ice debris with a netted scoop. Then they pulled out the net and removed all the fish. Finally, the net was replaced by pulling it in the opposite direction from the hole at the other end. Most days, with a freezing wind blowing steadily across the ice, handling the icy, wet net was a bitterly cold, but very necessary, task. Fish provided an important contribution to the family diet as well as to each family's seven or eight sled dogs which required, on average, about seven herring each a day.

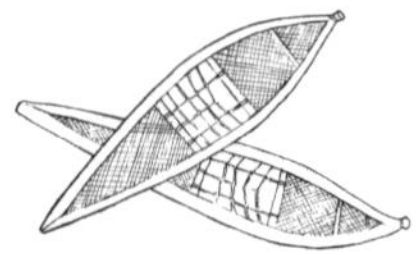

"Nurse! You come. Come now." One of the children from Liz's class was standing in Helen's doorway. "My mother want you come."

"Tell your mother I'll be there in a few minutes," replied Helen. "I'll get my medical kit." Turning to me she added, "Will you come with me Miggs? They've been drinking again and I'm always afraid to go on my own when that happens."

"Sure." I grabbed my parka and hauled on my mukluks. "Does this happen often?" I inquired as we rushed through the village.

"There's always a fair bit of drinking home brew when the men come back from the bush at Christmas time and on a few other special occasions during the year, but for most families that's it, and there is seldom any violence attached to those parties. But for those few families who have worked a lot with white people and have easy access to hard liquor, the drinking and the violence can get pretty bad at times. Here we are."

Without knocking on the door of the log cabin, Helen marched straight into the main room where we were accosted by loud yelling and the stench of stale blood and alcohol. My eyes soon adjusted to the dimly-lit room and I took in the scene before me. A youth of some nineteen or twenty years old towered over an older man who lay cowering on the floor, his face a bloody mess. On a dilapidated couch nearby, a frail-looking woman sat hunched over, her body heaving slightly from her sobbing and moaning, while three younger children, including the young girl who had come to the nursing station, huddled together watching the scene in front of them. Beyond them lay a huge chunk of raw caribou melting slowly from the warmth of the pot-bellied stove.

I turned back to the centre of the room and my eyes were drawn to the pointed toe of a shiny black shoe and, incongruously and inappropriately, at that moment, I recalled that such shoes were the height of fashion in the South. But this shoe was relentlessly and indiscriminately kicking the face and body lying on the floor while a stream of English and Slavey obscenities emerged from the youth.

"Stop it! Stop!" Helen yelled as she stepped up to the youth and grabbed his arm, trying to pull him away from his father. I was terrified for her, terrified that the youth would now attack Helen. He seemed so out of control in his drunkenness.

Instead he turned to look at Helen and yelled, "He beat up my mother and started hitting the kids when they tried to stop him." Much to my surprise, even though his speech was slurred, he was reasonably coherent. With one last vicious kick at his father he let Helen, who was barely up to his chest, lead him a few feet away from the moaning body. "He's always like this when he gets too much to drink, then when my mother tries to take the booze away from him he beats her up. It's time someone beat him up so that he knows how it feels. No!" he blurted, as Helen knelt to check his father, "First you see how my mother is." Helen hesitated. "I won't kick him again, the son of a bitch."

It only took Helen seconds to verify that his mother had a large contusion across the left side of her face, but the woman was more frightened than hurt. Helen turned her attention back to the father. "He needs some stitches in his face," she said in her nurse-like manner. Then turning to the youth, she added, "Help me get him to the nursing station. Grab his arm and pull him up."

"Better to let him just die here. He's no good."

Ignoring the outburst, Helen started tugging on an arm and, still protesting, the youth grabbed the other arm of the bulky parka. With difficulty they got him up. He half-opened his swollen eyes and Helen informed him that he was going to the nursing station. He tried to struggle but had no strength left. His legs buckled as his body sagged but Helen and the youth now had a good hold of him. I opened the cabin door, gave one last glance back at the mother and children, still sobbing quietly, and, carrying Helen's medical kit, followed the trio.

The youth kept talking. "It's a good thing I was home, but what happens when I'm in Edmonton? My brothers and sisters are too young to handle him. And if they get in his way when he's mad he beats them up too. But I have to go back to work on the next sched," and the next scheduled flight was due in a few days' time.

After she had washed the father's face and given him about a dozen stitches from his left eye down across his cheek, she checked his upper body, but there was little damage except for a few developing bruises. "It's a good job he had a heavy parka on," Helen said. "He'd better stay here tonight. Come and get him in the morning." The youth just nodded his head and left.

Later I asked Helen, "How could he do that? How could he kick his father so viciously?"

"A lot of it is guilt, Miggs. He's trying to make something better of his own life by working down South because he doesn't want to be a trapper like many of the other boys. Family and home are very important to these people and the South can be a strange and alien world for them, so when they get lonely and their thoughts turn to home they worry about their families. And in J's case, he feels guilty because he's not here to protect his family when his father gets like this, nor can he afford to fly home very often."

Helen got up and walked towards the kitchen to put on the kettle.

"Then why don't they just stay up here?" I asked, following her. I got out the mugs, sugar and milk.

"It's not that simple, Miggs. Most young people are very satisfied to stay in Franklin and become trappers like their fathers and grandfathers before them. But they know that there's another world out there, another world where everyone is very rich, by their standards. It's thrown in their faces by every white person who comes North. Just look at how we live up here compared to the Indians.

"Some young people want a chance to become something else, to be teachers, nurses, engineers or work in construction. For some of the girls they just want to get away. Life can be very hard on the women here and they grow old before their time, like Chinese women." Helen paused, her mind, suddenly thousands of miles away. Then she continued, "They want something better for themselves and so when a white man comes to Franklin and wants to sleep with a young girl, she might go along with him, seeing that as her ticket out of here. But it hardly ever lasts. A few young people have survived in the South, but very few."

We had talked about some of these things before but never with quite the same intensity as Helen showed this evening. The kettle boiled. Helen poured the water into the teapot and carried it back to where we had been sitting.

"It's also hard for the parents to understand why the young people want to leave when so many bad things happen to them in the South. Their families are everything to them. That's the way it has always been. So when their kids move down South it's like a slap in the face to the parents, as if their kids are rejecting them."

We drank our tea and talked for a while about other village matters. I stood up. "It's late. I should go. Will you be OK now?"

"Oh, he'll sleep well until the morning and tomorrow he'll feel badly for everything and it won't happen again for a while—until the next time. Adults can get very mixed up when they have too much to do with white people up here."

As I walked back to my duplex I couldn't stop thinking about what I had witnessed tonight and all that Helen had said. I kept seeing the shiny black shoe repeatedly kicking the slumped body with its bleeding, battered face, and the mother looking so old and tired and frightened, even though she was probably still in her early forties.

And the young children, what would happen to them growing up in a home with so much violence? I thought of the son returning to Edmonton, and of the two other young people I had met in the village who had returned to live in Franklin after several years spent in the South. One young woman had become quite friendly with me but she poured out an incredible amount of bitterness and hatred towards white people in general when she had too much to drink.

Tonight I had been exposed to a side of life in Franklin I had not witnessed before and it bothered me, both in terms of the specific incident and the discussion afterwards with Helen. Up until now Franklin had seemed almost idyllic, but after what had been revealed to me tonight I felt as if another layer of an onion had been peeled away and a more disturbing view of Sahtuot'ine life had emerged. I was beginning to realize, even from this brief exposure, that solutions to these complex problems would not come easily for these people caught between two cultures.

"Claire, do you have any heat? Does your stove work?" I yelled heading down the short passageway between our two apartments.

"Yes, why?" as she went over and tried her gas stove.

"Well, mine doesn't."

"Oh, that's no problem. Your first tank of propane has just run out. Here, I'll show you how to switch over to the other tank. Mine went about a month ago." Claire always seemed to know much more about these kinds of things than I did. "It's from all my years of cottaging in the Gatineau," she explained when I mentioned that to her.

I thanked her and returned to my side and turned on the stovetop. There was still no sound of gas flowing. I returned to tell Claire.

"We'd better get Joe," was her sage advice and I heartily agreed since my side was already getting colder as my heat was also dependent on propane. Joe came and investigated. His solution was to fetch William. He checked the controls then tapped the tanks and pronounced knowingly, "They both empty." Now what was I to do for the remainder of the winter?

"I'll go and radio Inuvik," said Joe. "They'll have to fly in another tank for you. Why don't you stay with Helen since your place will soon be too cold."

A small plane arrived the next day and a new tank replaced one of the empty ones. I was relieved. As we watched the plane fly overhead, I asked Joe, "What did that little trip cost?"

"About four hundred dollars of taxpayers' money."

"And what did the propane tank itself cost?"

"Just a few dollars," Joe replied. An expensive mistake.

I invited Joe in for a cup of coffee and turned on the stovetop. Nothing happened. We went out again and checked the connection and it was fine. We tapped both tanks again as William had done. They both sounded the same. Both empty. I couldn't believe it. "You mean, they didn't even check the tank in Inuvik before flying it down here?" I exclaimed in disbelief.

"I guess not," replied Joe as he headed off again to radio Inuvik to send me in another tank.

And at the cost of another four hundred dollars my full tank arrived the next day. It was reassuring to know that the government took such good care of its employees in emergencies but it would have cost less than forty dollars had anyone bothered to check the original tank before shipping it to Franklin. It was my first experience of recognizing how careless government people can be when dealing with "just taxpayers' money." Ouch!

One Saturday Helen came rushing into the duplex, "Miggs! Miggs! How would you like to come to Inuvik with me? I have two very sick patients and I can't get a signal through to Inuvik to come and pick them up."

"Sure! That would be great. How are we getting there?"

"J.C. hasn't left yet, so he'll take us to Norman Wells where we can catch the PWA flight. But we must leave now." J.C. was a Pacific Western Airlines pilot who had brought in a fresh store of supplies for the nursing station. I had met J.C. the night before when Helen had invited me over for dinner and to help her entertain him. Claire and I were often called upon to assist both Joe and Helen who, periodically, had government or construction people stay with them. We usually enjoyed the free meal, the after dinner card playing, and the change of company.

"Quick, Miggs. Pack a bag. There won't be enough daylight for us to get back today." Helen left to get her patients ready for the journey. I checked to see if Claire was back in her duplex but she had gone visiting in the village. It took me all of three minutes before I followed Helen and we all clambered into the Otter. J.C. invited me to sit up front with him, while Helen and her patients, a girl from Liz's class, and an older woman, sat just behind us in the cabin.

I was very excited about going to Inuvik. This was the first time I had been away from Franklin in almost six months. As I looked down from the banking plane at the small village that was now my home, I recalled with a smile, my mixed emotions upon arriving last August. I really had been quite nervous and now I wondered why. How much I had learned and enjoyed these past six months.

Deep in my thoughts, I realized that Helen was leaning between us and yelling, "J.C.! There's smoke coming from the back of the plane."

"Miggs, go check the luggage and the heater back there," J.C. ordered. A small heater provided the cabin with some much-needed additional heat. I approached the back to see the sleeping bags and other pieces of luggage thrown in beside the heater. But of more importance were the unwelcome flames racing up two wires that protruded from the heater. Instinctively, I grabbed the wires before the flames could return back into the heater and then extinguished them with my mittens. I returned to the front and reported back to J.C.

"Hmmm," he replied, "I'd better go and double check. Take over."

I felt my heart take a mighty leap. "What do you mean 'take over'?" I yelled back.

"You told me last night that you've done quite a bit of flying in BC. The controls are the same in this plane even if it is a little bigger." I started protesting. After all, I had only flown my friend Alan's small Cessna in the air for brief stints and under his guidance.

J.C. rose from his seat and repeated, "Just keep it in the air. I'll be back in a minute, but I have to double-check the back," and he was gone. And here was I seated at the wheel of a ten-passenger Otter with instructions to keep it up in the air. I was terrified. However, there was nothing else to do but pull back gently on the stick to bring the Otter's nose up slightly and then, keeping my eye on the indicators ahead of me, turn the "wheel" slightly to left or right to keep the wings on an even keel. As I was about to discover, the bigger the plane the slower the reaction to any move the pilot makes. So the plane kept bobbing up and down, and swinging from side to side, as I kept over-correcting. Sweat was pouring down my grim face and aching back when J.C. returned, in what seemed like hours later, though he assured me it had only been a few minutes.

"Don't ever do that again to me," I yelled at him as he took over the controls.

"Hey Miggs. You did fine. A bit bumpy perhaps, but we're still in the air and on course," he said, grinning.

I was just beginning to relax and enjoy the flight again when I felt a tap on my shoulder. It was Helen. "Oh no, not more smoke," I said, panic rising.

"No Miggs. It's not that. But we're all feeling very sick. Do you have any sick bags up front?"

J.C. pointed to my right side where I found a small bunch of brown paper bags. I handed one to Helen, and she immediately started retching. Then I helped the two passengers who soon followed suit. Obviously motion sickness. Well, it hadn't been that bumpy a ride, had it? I thought to myself. I collected all the sick bags and wrapped them tightly in a large green garbage bag. I returned to my seat with mixed feelings—embarrassment over exaggerating my flying prowess the night before, pride in keeping the plane safely in the air, and guilt over causing the two sick people further discomfort.

We arrived in Norman Wells in time for us to catch the daily Yellowknife/Inuvik PWA flight. It did, however, occur to me that J.C. could have reimbursed my fare given that I had spent most of the flight as copilot and stewardess!

I saw very little of Inuvik on that trip as the days were considerably shorter than ours, being some five hundred kilometres north of the Arctic Circle. Helen took me to visit one of her friends who was also originally from Hong Kong, and he made us a wonderful Chinese meal that evening.

We returned the next day and, although I had very much enjoyed my brief sojourn, I was delighted to be back home again.

Georgina and I admire a huge lake trout. Such trout attract many tourists to the sports-fishing lodges around Great Bear Lake.

CHAPTER SIX

THE SUN RETURNS

The annual teacher's convention in Inuvik served many purposes. A comprehensive program, including a series of sessions on northern educational issues, had been arranged. It was also a chance for those who had taught in the North for a few years to become reacquainted with other teachers and their families and for us newcomers to see another part of the Arctic.

Located on the eastern side of the Mackenzie Delta just south of the Arctic coast, Inuvik, a town of over a thousand people, is virtually treeless, with only the shortest and scrubbiest of ancient trees struggling to grow along small creeks. Walking around the town necessitated bobbing under and over the Utilidors, an above-ground, enclosed, insulated water and sewage system that criss-crossed the town. Similar in construction to the church at Franklin, Inuvik's white-tiled church had been built in the shape of an igloo, out of respect for its larger Inuit population. For much of each winter, beautiful, large ice sculptures surrounded the church.

We visited the imposing and, to my mind, rather forbidding and sterile student residences and school facilities, operated by the Roman Catholic or the Anglican churches. It was to Inuvik, as well as to Yellowknife, Fort Smith, and Frobisher Bay (Iqaluit), that Native and non-Native adolescents came for their secondary school education. The students were taught all subjects, including religion, in English. Speaking their own language was forbidden. I had talked to some of my older students in Franklin about going to Inuvik and they seemed quite eager to go to one of the larger towns. However, the reality was that only a handful ever stayed long enough to obtain their high school diploma as many became very homesick and confused, and returned to Franklin as soon as possible.

We had enjoyed our few days' break in Inuvik, the interesting sessions we had attended and meeting many other northerners but it was still good to fly over Franklin and feel that sense of familiarity again.

I seemed to be spending more and more of my free time at the nursing station with Helen, and also with Eleanor Hitzeroth, another nurse from Inuvik, who had been sent to assist Helen. Originally from Germany, Eleanor had worked for a while as a nurse in La Ronge, Saskatchewan, before coming to the Arctic. We usually played cards in the evenings, even occasionally attempting to stay up all night in canasta marathons, canasta being the preferred game for a while. Sometimes it was just the three of us and sometimes Claire joined us. Eleanor also loved to cook and bake which suited me just fine.

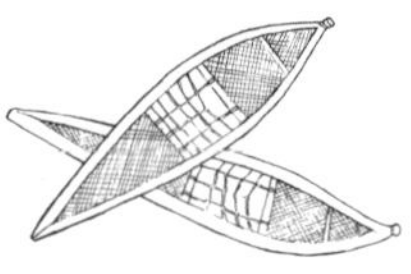

"Miggs, I want to ask you a favour," Helen asked during one of our evening card sessions. "You know how the Indians sometimes make their own home brew, well I've decided to make some too, in a big garbage pail." Home brew was a form of cheap home-made beer that varied depending on the mix of ingredients of yeast, molasses, sugar, dried currants or raisins. It required fermentation in warm surroundings for several days. I had only sampled it once but once was enough, as it tasted terrible. Helen seemed determined to give this a try which surprised and amused us since Helen drank very little of anything alcoholic.

"The problem is," she continued, "I really don't want to make it in the nursing station because the Indians will find out about it from the woman who cleans for me, and that could be rather embarrassing. So, could I leave it at your place to ferment?"

"Sure," said I obligingly. "I can put it at the back of my clothes closet." Several days went by. I stirred it periodically and Helen came over frequently to check on it. At last she proclaimed that the brew was ready and that we four should have a party that evening at my place.

I don't recall drinking a lot—I still thought it tasted awful—but perhaps I did because I woke up in the middle of the night with a gnawing stomach ache, sweating profusely and an overwhelming urge to vomit. In fact I ended up spending the rest of the night with my head in the toilet. Feeling close to death and almost wishing for its relief, I staggered out of bed the next morning, got dressed and went to school.

Joe took one look at me. "You look terrible, Miggs. Are you sick?"

Very ashamedly I explained the reason for my demise. "Go home and sleep it off. I'll send in some of my older students to look after your kids."

"No," I announced loudly, and with a sanctimonious tone, added, "Never let it be said that I failed to do my duty because I was too hung-over. Thank you, Joe, but I shall be fine," and with that I marched into my class and attempted to teach my students, totally oblivious of their strange expressions and secret smiles. Suddenly, overcome by an overwhelming urge to vomit again, I ran out of the class and barely made it to the washroom.

I suppose one of my kids must have let Joe know about this sudden turn of events and this time he ordered me home. "And only come back this afternoon if you really feel better."

"I don't want to feel better. I'm never going to feel better. I just want to die." And with that last dramatic flurry, I left. I didn't have far to go, merely some two hundred yards, but I stumbled twice in the snow, dragged myself up, reached the duplex and put myself to bed.

Some time later, Helen and Eleanor arrived. They had heard about my sorry state—news travelled quickly through the village—although they couldn't quite understand it since they felt fine, as did Claire, and they said that I hadn't drunk much either. "Perhaps it was due to the headstands you insisted on practising last night!" said Eleanor. Anyway, they were most sympathetic and Helen had even brought some medicine to settle my stomach. Grateful, and willing to try anything to ease this very unpleasant feeling, I gulped down a large spoonful of the medicine and immediately spat it back out. They had filled the bottle with the vile-tasting home brew! How could they? And, oh, did they enjoy themselves, one short and dark, the other tall and blonde, laughing so unkindly at my plight.

"Well, you know what they say about 'The hair of the dog that bit you'."

"Out!" I yelled. "Out! How could you do this to me?" As they left I could still hear them laughing. I eventually went back to sleep. I don't believe I made it back to school that afternoon and it was certainly several days before I, too, could enjoy a laugh about "the medicine." Needless to say I never touched home brew again.

"Dora Gully is back," said Helen one day.

"Dora who?" I inquired.

"Dora Gully. Remember, I told you about this older Indian lady who went to Edmonton to get her nursing assistant certificate."

Of course! Now it was coming back to me. Dora used to help Helen at the old nursing station. All her children had grown up and she wanted to do something useful for her people. In her fifties, Dora had insisted on learning to read and write and Helen had helped her. She had been in Edmonton since last spring. Knowing that few older women in Franklin spoke any English, let alone read or wrote it, this was a tremendous achievement and I was looking forward to meeting Dora.

As it turned out I saw very little of her because she was always out of the nursing station on home visits. However, I heard about Dora from my kids: "She always talk about germ. We must do this because of germ. We have to do that because germ bad thing. That all she ever talk about." I tried to reassure them that Dora was right and that germs were very harmful to us but the kids made it clear that they were sick of hearing about "germ."

When I later mentioned their comments to Helen she explained, "It's partly that and it's partly because Dora has bettered herself, risen above the other Indians, as it were, and some resent that."

"But she's doing it to help them and wouldn't they rather have one of their own people helping them than you or me?"

"It's not that simple, Miggs. Some people think it's a good idea, but others just resent her. They feel she's just become too 'white' since she's been down South. After all, she is the first older woman to assume what is usually considered to be a 'white person's role.' After a while they will come to appreciate her help, but for now, she has to put up with some rejection. Changes like this take time, but it also makes it difficult for young people who want to get ahead yet don't want to be ostracized by their friends and relatives."

As I became more familiar with the Sahtuot'ine ways I also wondered if their resentment was, in part, because they were very private people. Minding one's own business seemed to be a cardinal rule and rarely did one person interfere or give advice to another. Most of all they disliked bossiness. They put up with it from white people because that is what they had come to expect, but not from among their own. In time, Dora's work was appreciated and she did become a good role model for others.

The school year was rapidly coming to an end. I had long since renewed my contract for another year. There was still so much to learn and experience in this unique corner of the world. As the sunlit days grew longer and warmer, life in the village took on a new vigor. Ice around the lakeshores began to break up and float planes again arrived and took off from the open waters of the Little Lake.

One day, one of the boys came running into the school after lunchtime, yelling, "Dolphus! He stuck on ice." We immediately knew what had happened. Daily, huge blocks of ice broke off the perimeter of the main body of ice and, pushed by the easterly winds, drifted westwards and then away from Franklin. Joe had warned all the children about staying off the ice floes but in vain. Jumping from floe to floe had become a new spring game especially for the younger and adolescent boys.

It appeared that Dolphus and his friend, ignoring Joe's advice, had decided that they could make their way back to school by jumping from one ice floe to another. Unfortunately, a sudden easterly gust of wind had pushed Dolphus' floe further than anticipated and he was unable to make it back to the shore. So there he was, drifting alongside the village. No one appeared too worried. In fact, as we teachers walked along the shore giving him words of encouragement and looking for someone to rescue him with a canoe, the villagers who joined us clearly enjoyed the spectacle and made no move to rescue poor Dolphus. "He climb to shore at end of village where lake ends," was all the sympathy he received. And that is what he eventually did, none the worse for his adventure, only very embarrassed at being the focus of so much attention.

The Sahtuot'ine handled the ice "break up" in many interesting ways. Fishing nets, located under the more solid ice some distance away, still had to be checked daily. By now the ice had begun to "candle," a term used for when the ice melts slowly leaving a very rough, sharp edged, brittle surface that cuts the dogs' paws to the point of bleeding when they walked on it. Consequently, their paws were fitted with small caribou or moose hide booties.

In order to cross the twenty to fifty-metre leads of open water between shore and ice, the dogs and a long, wide sled were piled into a boat and paddled across. On reaching solid ice, the dogs were then harnessed to the sled and the boat was lashed on top of it. Once the nets had been checked and the catch dumped into the boat, the whole process was reversed when it came time to cross the lead again and return to the village.

We welcomed these longer and warmer days, although the breeze blowing off all those hundreds of square miles of ice still had a keen nip to it. Small colourful flowers sprang to life all over the tundra and the leaves of small bushes and birch and poplar trees unfurled. The skies became alive with birds of all kinds, most especially ducks, geese and swans returning North, fat from wintering on Prairie grain. How I loved to listen to their many different kinds of honking sounds and to watch them fly across the searing blue, wide open skies, especially the swans and Canada geese, in their symmetrical chevron-like formation—confirmation that spring had indeed arrived.

Strolling through the village you might pass a woman cleaning fish to dry on poles over a smoldering fire, or a man attaching a new canvas to his leaky canoe or else fixing its broken ribs. You might come across a group of women sitting on the grass and basking in the sun, near one of the cabins, or under the tipi poles, drinking tea, smoking a cigarette or pipe, and enjoying a cheerful gossip and many good laughs, just as they used to in the old days when families gathered together in the summer to socialize after the long, hard winter of living apart. And always there were children of all ages playing and laughing in small groups, oblivious to everything else. Not even the sea of oozing mud throughout the village could mar our joy. The mud was the result of the permafrost, never far from the surface of the land, melting from the warmth of the sun.

Picnicking days had arrived too. Many times on the weekends or sunlit evenings a bunch of us would go up to the ski hill, or sit on rocks along the lake shore, or walk into the bush just a short distance away from the village for a picnic of tea, coffee and cookies, or bannock or dried meat. How enjoyable it was just to sit around talking, basking our faces in the sun, or singing a few songs with my guitar. All very pleasant and relaxing.

We tried our hand at canoeing, occasionally borrowing an eighteen-footer. More frequently, we used a small rat canoe, much shorter and narrower and used for meandering through the shallower waters and reeds where the muskrats lived. Again, Helen produced her .410 shotgun and .22 rifle and we shot a few muskrats. Occasionally, we hunted for ducks from the shoreline, but we enjoyed this less since it meant wading into icy cold water up to one's thighs, *sans* socks, boots and jeans, to retrieve the catch.

Softball fever erupted and every evening, no, every night, since by June it was never really dark, many young people and older children played a version of softball in the space between the village proper and the school. Others took their boats, sleds and dogs, and followed the shoreline on the ice until they came across a small stream entering the lake. There, trapped by the main block of ice, fish teemed in great abundance, and the young people returned home again in the early hours of the morning with a boatload of fish.

I have never experienced such easy fishing. Cast in. Fish out. Sometimes we lit a fire and cooked the fish on the hot stones and enjoyed a scrumptious meal by the lake. Other times we sat on a boat-load of fresh fish all the way home and cooked a breakfast of fried grayling or whitefish, before going to bed at around 7 AM. Although we teachers restricted our midnight activities to weekends, the kids paid no such attention to the days and often arrived at school late and in a very sleepy state. Teaching anything of substance was becoming futile, but who could blame them?

"Nurse! You fix my daughter!" A man carried his screaming daughter up the stairs of the nursing station, followed by his weeping wife. Helen and I rushed from the living room and the cause of the young child's anguish was immediately obvious, as a huge chunk of her right cheek hung down in a flap. The father placed the child on the examination bed. "A dog bite her. I tell her not to play with them but she not listen."

I was appalled at the extent of the bite and her ripped flap of skin. But after bathing her face—there was less blood than I would have expected—Helen gave the child a local anaesthetic and set to sewing the flap back in place. "She's going to be OK," Helen reassured the worried parents. "It was a clean bite. She's young so she'll heal well."

"*Mahsi. Mahsi*," replied her parents gratefully and with obvious relief.

"I'll give her some medicine and keep her here overnight," said Helen. "You come and get her in the morning," she added, as she gave the young girl a tetanus shot.

Yet again I was impressed with Helen's skills in a wide variety of situations, but what happened when she required additional treatment? "I call Inuvik on the radio and hope that the plane arrives in time and sometimes it doesn't. It used to happen often when I worked out of that old building and I lost a couple of patients. It's so much better now with this new nursing station since I can perform many of the smaller operations, like this one."

A short while later, after the little girl's parents had left and she was fast asleep with the help of Helen's sedatives, I turned to Helen. "The people may not like many of the changes that we southerners have brought to their lives but I'm sure they must be very grateful to have capable nurses like you and facilities like these in Franklin."

"But they wouldn't need my skills nearly as often if they kept their kids away from those dogs in the spring when they get little exercise and almost no food," she replied, with obvious frustration.

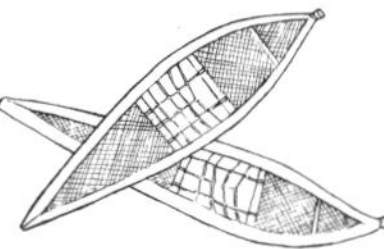

June the twenty-first, the longest day of the year. Pete had arranged for an Otter to come to Franklin and fly a bunch of us, at a reasonable cost, to Norman Wells. It was a beautifully clear, calm, warm evening with few clouds to be seen. We arrived at Norman Wells around 11:30 PM and sat quietly for a short while watching the sun disappear behind the dark and distant silhouette of the Mackenzie Mountains.

Then we clambered back into the plane and flew towards Fort Good Hope which lay virtually on the Arctic Circle. We climbed to a height of some two thousand feet to retrieve the sun again, and just in time to see it descend closer and closer to the horizon but never quite disappear from sight. Instead, after reaching its nadir at midnight, it continued on an upward curve, a golden pendulum, travelling slowly through a darkening sky, its path mirrored in the hundreds of lakes below. It was truly spectacular and a fitting conclusion to my first year in the North.

I departed for the British Isles and Europe a few days later. The ice in Keith Arm had all disappeared, but, as I flew over the bay on that first day of July I could see that most of Great Bear Lake, a lake that could have easily swallowed Wales twice over, was still blanketed by thick ice.

My thoughts turned to those questions that had intrigued me for a while. Where had the Sahtuot'ine come from and how long had they lived in this area? What had their life been like before they had experienced contact with the white man? I had been told that Fort Franklin was named after an English sea captain who, in order to winter here in the early eighteen hundreds, had built a stone fort of several buildings near the Little Lake. I also knew that Scottish fur traders and French missionaries had once lived in this area. Who were these people and how did they come to be here, so far from home? And perhaps most importantly, what impact had they all had on the aboriginal people of Great Bear Lake? How different, or even similar, were the lives of the Sahtuot'ine that I had come to know from those of their pre-contact ancestors? Clearly many of the customs and attitudes I had witnessed during this past year in Franklin were rooted in those of a long and distant history.

CHAPTER SEVEN

THE SAHTUOT'INE: AN HISTORICAL BACKGROUND

According to archaeologists, waves of aboriginal people migrated across the Rocky Mountains from the west and entered the Dehcho (Mackenzie River) valley thousands of years ago. Most of these people continued their long journey far to the south. Some wandered further east into the basins of Sahtu (Great Bear Lake) and Tucho (Great Slave Lake). There, in these low-lying rocky lands covered mainly with spruce, some deciduous trees, shrubs and lichen, and in the hundreds of small lakes and areas of muskeg, they found an abundance of food resources.

In the centuries before the first white man came to the shores of Sahtu in 1799, about a thousand aboriginal people lived in the vicinity of this vast lake. Although affiliated with four larger tribes, these people called themselves the *Sahtuot'ine* (Sa-too-ot-in-eh), the "People of Bear Lake," or the *Dene* (Den-eh), meaning "The People." They believed they had been placed on this land by the Creator, who had also provided them with all the resources necessary for their survival.[1]

The Sahtuot'ine were nomadic hunters who followed the seasonal migrations of the caribou over hundreds of kilometres around Sahtu. On the edge of the Barren Lands, long fences of rocks and branches were built into V-shape corrals with snares inside. The caribou were enticed into the corrals and caught by the snares and they were then killed with relative ease with spears or bows and arrows. Sometimes, the caribou were chased in canoes through narrow channels where they were then speared.

The Dene also hunted moose and snared fur-bearing animals such as hares. Fish, too, was an important element in their diet, as were numerous kinds of berries and roots available during the summer months. Sometimes the food resources in an area could only support a few families but, at other times when they came together to hunt caribou, there might be more than a dozen families living together. This was done partly to provide protection for the women and children left behind by the hunting men, and partly to share in the group's success, since the survival of less able members often depended on their being able to share in the spoils of the better hunters. They had a wealth of knowledge about all these animals and most especially about the caribou. Not only were the Dene familiar with the animals' migratory paths and their habits, they also knew when hides and meat were at their prime. There was little waste as virtually every part of each animal was used.

Guided by the stars, sun and wind patterns on snowdrifts, the Sahtuot'ine

trudged hundreds of kilometres through the deep snow. Women carried or hauled their family's meagre possessions on small sleds made from caribou skin and wood, as dogs had not yet been introduced. Birch-bark canoes were often used in summer. Larger canoes transported families and their possessions along the larger lakes and rivers; smaller ones were used for hunting and checking fish nets.

Even though temperatures for more than half of the year were always well below -20°C, the constant travelling meant that dwellings varied from simple lean-to shelters made from the surrounding bushes to small spruce-bush lodges, heated only by wood fires. Tipis were also constructed from long spruce poles covered by either caribou hides or branches and bark. These larger shelters were preferred when several groups came together for longer periods, such as for the group caribou hunts and when the people spent the short summer months together, relaxing, feasting, and playing Dene games at Déline, at the western end of Sahtu.

Normally, days began very early and there was little time for anything but those tasks necessary for survival. Since their existence depended primarily upon the success of the hunt, every other aspect of daily life, at least during the hunting season, revolved around this activity. Thus the men spent most of their days hunting, and setting and checking snares and fishnets. Men and boys were also responsible for procuring sufficient quantities of wood, using only a stone axe.

Though the men's roles were pivotal, women's work was just as indispensable. Because the men had to be free to follow game at a moment's notice, it was the women and older girls who carried all family belongings when travelling. They also erected the tipis or spruce lodges, laid the floor covering of spruce boughs, and maintained a fire. Since the ability to light a fire was crucial to the survival of the Dene, everyone carried a small bag of flint and dry moss or other kindling material with which to start a fire. Using the fur of the animals the men had caught, women made and mended all of the family's warm clothing and bedding. In addition to all the packing or hauling, the sewing and cooking for immediate and future consumption, the women looked after and carried their infants. Girls were usually given in marriage at an early age, sometimes before puberty, since marriage between members of different bands was also a way of establishing important ties, as was the practice of adoption and exchanges of children between groups.

The Sahtuot'ine had a strong sense of family, and children, especially boys, were highly valued. Children were expected to assist their parents in the daily chores from a very early age. Respected grandparents and elders played an important role in educating the young people in traditional Dene skills and values and

The remains of an early tipi located at the eastern end of Sahtu (Great Bear Lake).

helped out with the lighter daily family routines. Grandparents also used stories and legends to teach children about their history. Cooperation, respect for personal autonomy, and a willingness to share freely with others were considered crucial values in Sahtuot'ine society. The only leadership roles were those pertaining to the hunt.

The Sahtuot'ine were a highly spiritual people and virtually every act in their lives had some supernatural implications. They believed in a good spirit called *Nehwesine*, Creator of the Earth and everything on it. However, as is usual for a people whose lives are dependent upon hunting, they had a rich and sacred body of knowledge and traditions related to all the animals in their world. The Dene believed that, thousands of years ago, the animals and even the elements had been endowed with human characteristics that enabled them to react and reason like human beings and even communicate with the people.

Most religious behaviour for the Sahtuot'ine, therefore, lay, not in defining and controlling interpersonal human behaviour, but rather in attempting to placate and influence the animals and elements. Over time, the people developed certain rites for the hunting, killing and disposing of each animal. Similarly, many taboos and prohibitions were related to every event of significance in their lives.

Medicine power, also referred to as *ik'o* (ing-kho), was at the centre of traditional Sahtuot'ine beliefs. *Ik'o* allowed the people to communicate with the animals and the Sahtuot'ine believed that no hunter could survive without it. Although each individual could exert various degrees of control over the animals and elements through *ik'o*, the medicine man or shaman was believed to have a greater degree of medicine power and so enjoyed closer intimacy with the supernatural world. Such men were considered to be extraordinary seers or prophets. Since the Sahtuot'ine, like other Dene, attributed sickness and death to unknown forces and wrongful deeds, medicine men were also called upon to cure the sick by using herbs and roots, and extracting the effects of the evil deed from their patients' bodies.

One of the most powerful medicine men in Dene early history was Yamoria, the Lawmaker. He travelled extensively among the Dene bringing them together and teaching them how to live according to the medicine laws he established. Yamoria's laws taught people how to behave with one another: to share whatever they had with others; to love each other and never harm another in word or deed; to respect everyone, especially elders and strangers; to work hard and be happy with what the Creator had bestowed upon them; to pray with the drum and feed the fire to honour the spirit world. These are the laws that have guided the Sahtuot'ine for countless generations.

Every aspect of Sahtuot'ine life demonstrated a subtle and effective adjustment to severe environmental pressures. As hunters of wandering and migratory animals, they had to be free to follow the game, especially caribou. When the caribou failed to arrive in the Sahtu region, they searched for fish, hares and other resources. Their minimal material culture allowed for easy migration from one place to another. Their loose social organization enabled them to maintain this mobility since their ties to band and tribe were flexible and their choice of habitat was seasonally regulated. Everything the Sahtuot'ine required to satisfy their material, social and religious needs was available in the Sahtu region, provided they had sufficient *mobility* to use these widely distributed resources of a seasonal and migratory nature, and the ability to *adapt* to the availability of these fluctuating resources.

All elements—the people, land, animals, plants, social customs, individual initiative and spiritual beliefs—had been woven into a strong fabric. Is it any wonder that the land on which they lived for thousands of years was so sacred to the Sahtuot'ine since it provided them with life itself and affected every aspect of their existence? But changes were on their way. Newcomers were about to arrive at Sahtu and they would eventually create a state of disequilibrium, conflict and stress unlike anything the Sahtuot'ine had previously experienced.

The appearance of Duncan Livingston, a trader with the North West Company, at the western end of Sahtu in 1799 might have surprised the Sahtuot'ine camped there, but the arrival of the white man and his fur trade into the region was scarcely unheralded. During the previous three decades, traders of both the North West and Hudson's Bay companies had pushed closer to Sahtu, erecting trading posts as they went, in their relentless search for more furs, especially beaver.

A few years after Livingston had erected an outpost at Keith Arm, Alexander McKenzie, nephew of the renowned Scottish explorer Alexander Mackenzie, arrived in October 1804 and rebuilt the remains of Livingston's house. He noticed a few Dene located near the site they called Déline and encouraged them and others from around the lake to bring their furs and meat to the post. Over the next ten years several other traders occupied this post which had now become known as Bear Lake Castle. When the North West Company was absorbed into the more powerful Hudson's Bay Company in 1821, many smaller posts, including Bear Lake Castle, were closed, leaving trading posts at Fort Good Hope and Fort Norman, on the Dehcho (Mackenzie River).

With the coming of these first traders to this region, unfamiliar diseases against which they had no immunity spread swiftly and cruelly through the Sahtuot'ine as they succumbed to the likes of consumption, influenza, smallpox, measles and scarlet fever. With little understanding of preventative medicine and limited protection from the elements, they were helpless to fight this new enemy. Even the simple care of remaining warm and inactive was impossible. The hunter was often faced with the choice of taking time to recover from sickness or dying of starvation along with his family; it is likely that as many died from starvation as did from the actual diseases themselves. Nor was the medicine power of the shamans any help to the sufferers of these unfamiliar diseases.

After recovering, many of the Sahtuot'ine continued their former way of life but others were unable to cope and they gathered around the forts where food and other material goods were offered by the traders. To encourage the Sahtuot'ine to bring furs to the forts, the traders made it known that tools and trinkets would be available in exchange for furs. Trinkets such as beads and rings were designed to arouse the Dene's curiosity, but the advantages of small tools and utensils such as knives, awls, fire-steels, flints, soap, matches, needles, hatchets, and brass and copper kettles, as well as foods such as tea and sugar, were more appreciated by them. Before long a variety of furs were brought to the posts.

The effects of alcohol in this region were short-lived since, after 1826, the Hudson's Bay Company did not allow rum to be brought in. However, tobacco, whether chewed or smoked, was used as an enticement to obtain furs and tied many an addicted Dene to the trader.

The muzzle-loading musket was also introduced at this time. Traders, needing the Dene to hunt for food for them, soon realized that this would happen only after they had obtained sufficient supplies, especially of caribou, for their own families. At first, changes from old ways of hunting with bows and arrows and snares came slowly. Progressively, however, during this first half of the nineteenth century, more and more of the Sahtuot'ine came to replace their aboriginal weapons with guns. While these first guns were not very efficient, less skill was required in hunting and this often led to shortages of game around the forts where large groups of people congregated.

For a while, since the aboriginal Sahtuot'ine remained primarily hunters, trapping only to acquire what they considered necessary for their own survival, the traders often expressed dissatisfaction with the number of furs brought in and referred to the Dene as lazy. However, the Dene simply recognized the dangers of devoting too much time to trapping when food resources were in short supply as the possibility of starvation was always a real consideration to them. When the traders began advancing credit to the Sahtuot'ine for the goods they wanted, this resultant debt had to be repaid by more and more furs.

In time, this arrangement became suited to both the traders and the Dene. The traders not only needed the furs, they also depended on the Sahtuot'ine to prepare the skins required for their own clothing and a constant supply of moccasins, since only the Dene women could produce these. They also required a steady source of dried meat, also prepared by the women. For their part, the

Sahtuot'ine were able to incorporate more trapping into their economy with relative ease, enabling them to benefit from the new goods which the traders exchanged for furs.

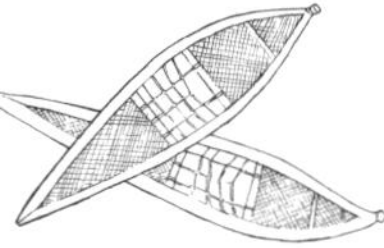

A number of European explorers were next to arrive at Sahtu, intent on finding the Northwest Passage to the Orient with its legendary wealth of silks and spices. Although most explorations involved trying to navigate through the ice and islands north of Canada's mainland, the British decided to send a few expeditions overland to map the Arctic Ocean's coastline to the west of that already reached by ships.

To this end, Captain John Franklin was commissioned to undertake a fact-finding journey across the Barren Lands of northern Canada and explore the Arctic coast to the east of the Coppermine River. This mission proved to be entirely different from anything Franklin, a professional naval officer and navigator, had previously attempted.

Because his first expedition in 1819-22 almost ended in disaster when they ran out of food, Franklin chose the western end of Sahtu where there was a reliable year-round supply of fish for his second expedition headquarters in September of 1825. The Hudson's Bay Company built a new, sturdy fort for Franklin, which was to be the home of some fifty persons for the next two winters. It was situated among the pines on a low hill near the Little Lake off Keith Arm. Franklin had intended naming it Fort Reliance but his men had already named it after him. Franklin spent the short summer months of 1826 exploring the Arctic coast, then returned to winter at Fort Franklin, departing for England in February 1827.[2]

For the next twenty years the Sahtuot'ine of western Sahtu were left alone. However, when Franklin and his two ships, *Erebus* and *Terror*, disappeared in the Arctic waters in 1845, several European would-be rescuers arrived to winter at both Fort Confidence at the eastern end of Sahtu and at the fishery near old Fort Franklin/Déline. Demands on the Dene to provide the explorers with food and furs continued until these sporadic visits came to an end in 1851.

The traders and explorers at Sahtu did more than establish a new economy. It was not simply a question of less hunting and more trapping, of famine and disease, of guns instead of bows and arrows, of European clothing instead of caribou hides. An entire way of life, one that had served the Dene so well for thousands of years was in jeopardy. The Sahtuot'ine's standards of right and wrong, as well as their beliefs—all the things that had given meaning and significance to their lives—were being threatened by traders and explorers alike. Taboos and superstitions of various kinds that had in the past formed the buttress of their religious beliefs now aroused only incredulity and denigration. Even the powers of the medicine men no longer had any effect against the new forces engulfing them. Economically and socially they were being cut adrift from their old moorings at the very time when their ranks were being decimated by disease and famine.

It was during this time that the first missionaries arrived at Sahtu. Catholic and Protestant missionaries, in their movement northwards in search of Indian souls, had been active in the Tucho region since the late 1850s. News of their teachings was carried further north by the nomadic Dene, and in 1859 Father Grollier erected small missions at both Fort Norman and Fort Good Hope on the Dehcho. Then, in the fall of 1864, Father Emile Petitot built a small hut that served as a home and chapel during his visits to the Fort Franklin/Déline site on Keith Arm.

Petitot, like most Catholic missionaries in the North, became fluent in the Dene language. During the next fourteen years, this energetic French missionary spent eight winters, travelling hundreds of kilometres on snowshoe or by canoe, to visit the scattered Sahtuot'ine camps. Besides all his travelling and missionary activities, Petitot also mapped the area with considerable accuracy and wrote several books describing in detail the life of the people.

In 1869 the Hudson's Bay Company trading post and, three years later, the mission were again moved from Keith Arm to Fort Norman where Father Ducot arrived in 1876 and remained for forty years. He, too, periodically visited the Dene in their far-flung camps within the immense Sahtu district. During one such visit, Fr. Ducot told the Dene "that for the first time he would be keeping Christmas that year at Fort Norman, and there would be Midnight Mass."[3] It then became customary for the Sahtuot'ine to make two annual expeditions to Fort Norman.

The Dene in this region appear to have accepted many of the new religion's ways and the nomadic priests soon baptized the majority of them into the Catholic Church. It is difficult to evaluate their degree of conviction for, and understanding of, the new religion, but it appears that practices of the Church were easily superimposed on to the aboriginal religion, with beliefs in the potency of good and bad spirits existing simultaneously with Catholic beliefs. The shaman's power was diminished but not entirely broken.

The missionaries visited the Dene in their camps and encouraged them to continue hunting in the bush. At the same time, they also provided the Sahtuot'ine with small calendars, a cross marking every seventh day, at which time the people in the camps banded together for prayers and refused to work on the Sabbath, considering it wrong to even fire a shot on the "Lord's Day, unless in the greatest necessity."[4]

Even though their actions were clearly performed with the best of intentions, the missionaries' activities continued to consolidate the earlier effects of the traders and explorers by further ridiculing and undermining Sahtuot'ine traditional religious beliefs and customs. They neither understood nor valued the Dene's deep spiritual beliefs and their intensely personal relationship to the land and all it provided. Nor did they understand the relationship between men and women and the demands of a hunting existence, and much of their efforts were directed towards "improving" the position of women in Sahtuot'ine society. They also strongly criticized the Dene for their practices of abandonment, infanticide and abortion, practices that were, to a large extent, the result of decades of debilitating famine, sickness, and despair. Similarly, the missionaries attacked the aboriginal marriage practices, many of which they considered to be incestuous. Only marriages approved of by the missionaries were to be sanctified by the Church.

The incompatibility that existed between the Dene's traditional norms and values and those implicit in the new trading economy and the new Christian religion resulted in considerable confusion and stress for the people. Petitot described several prophet, or nativistic, movements around Sahtu. Such movements are considered symptomatic of extreme cultural conflict such as that experienced by the Sahtuot'ine in the nineteenth century.

It seems ironic that, in the name of a new religion, many of the Christian values that the Church attempted to teach these "heathens" had long since been an integral part of their character and culture as expressed in their Dene laws: their sharing of resources with each other in times of scarcity; their hard-working way of life; their honesty; their sincere caring for their children and family members; and the strength of the family unit, both nuclear and extended. But the missionaries were too intent on saving Dene souls and obtaining converts for their own religion to see these characteristics, as they tried to mould the Sahtuot'ine to their own image.

On the one hand, the priests rejected and denounced what remained of the Sahtuot'ine's past customs and beliefs, yet they also provided, at a critical time after many decades of social turmoil, a necessary channel for renewed and orderly social relations. With the gradual acceptance of the new religion, a certain measure of meaning and security was restored again to the Sahtuot'ine's lives. They adopted many of these Christian traditions, replacing some of their own, but more often just grafting them on to their traditional ways.

By the end of the nineteenth century, the lives of the Sahtuot'ine had changed dramatically. There had been a considerable reduction in their numbers as well as in their health and strength due to the many waves of debilitating sickness. Trapping furs in larger numbers to meet the demands of the traders had become an accepted addition to their livelihood, as had the introduction of dogs for pulling sleds. As supplies tied them to trading posts the Sahtuot'ine often found themselves hundreds of miles away from the best hunting grounds at the very time when the caribou were in prime condition. This decline in mobility often led to a loss of adequate and appropriate food and clothing supplies. Traditional beliefs and accompanying rituals that had given meaning and strength to their lives for so long had also been weakened and the *ik'o* of the shaman seemed less effective.

The old fabric had been torn apart. No longer was there a balance between the people and nature. Some fared better than others, usually those who had as little as possible to do with the white man, but others, who were forced to accept assistance from the newcomers because of their weakened state, had difficulty surviving once the traders and explorers left.

Over time, however, the long-proven ability of the Sahtuot'ine to adapt to the land, with its constantly fluctuating resources, eventually enabled them to find ways of adjusting to the changes brought about by the successive waves of newcomers. As the people were left alone and as they again drew strength from the land, their spiritual beliefs and their drums, they regained pride in themselves. A new and strong fabric was woven, one that blended many of the newer elements with the old traditional ways. It was this hard-won balance of the old and new that I came to witness as I lived with the people of Fort Franklin in the late 1960s.

CHAPTER EIGHT

SECOND YEAR: 1966–1967

The start of the school year saw me moving into my new home. Joe had mentioned in the spring that the numbers of school children now warranted an additional teacher. When he said that the new teacher could either have the rooms above the school or the "512" across the road from Claire and me, I quickly investigated the small cabin. The rectangular building had a square footage of 512 (32' by 16'), hence its name. It comprised a large living room-cum-kitchen, with a small bedroom and ration room partitioned off at one end, and the bathroom and entrance porch at the other. The water supply was stored in an old galvanized cattle trough—heaven knows where it had come from—and I would have to make do with a honey bucket for a toilet. An old oil stove provided heat and the means of cooking. Although it lacked many of the amenities of the duplex, I fancied having my own place and felt sure I could fix it up. Joe agreed to my moving into the cabin in September and the new teacher had my half of the duplex.

One of my first tasks into making it habitable was to brighten the outside.

"Why you want to paint this place?" asked Peter, as I proceeded to splash red paint all over the doorjambs, window frames and myself.

"Why you leave other place and go live here? Other place much nicer." That was Raymond and he was right. The cabin didn't look very livable yet.

Painting the outside trim in red provided a nice contrast to the whitewashed walls. Of course it wasn't long before one of the kids wanted to know if I now worked for the Hudson's Bay Company! Once the inside had been cleaned, the sparse furniture rearranged, my red-and-blue check gingham curtains, purchased during the summer, hanging on the windows, it soon looked cozy and bright.

Eventually, the cattle trough was replaced with a standard 250-gallon (950-litre) water tank. (During the summer a large water truck, purchased by the government, had arrived by barge. This was now used to deliver lake water to all the government employees. Previously the lake water had been pumped directly through long hoses into the government dwellings, including the school, a time-consuming job that our custodian, William, had to perform.)

It was also decided that I, as a teacher, must have a flush toilet, although I kept insisting that the honey bucket was fine. The workmen then discovered that it wasn't possible to bury the septic tank below ground because of the permafrost. In order to provide an adequate flow for the run-off, my toilet would have to be raised. A two-tiered, two-foot-high dais was constructed, upon which sat my toilet, a veritable royal porcelain throne. Just as my flush toilet had provided the kids

Teachers Claire Barnabe, Judy Zehr and Lorraine Griffin at the ski hill in the fall of 1966.

with a source of amusement at the duplex, my unique throne toilet became the butt (pardon the pun) of many rude jokes from the various people who visited me on their way through Franklin. One day, one of the pilots arrived brandishing an old DC-3 seat belt. He attached it to the bathroom wall and announced that he would feel much better knowing that I could now sit safely on my lofty perch, when secured by this seat belt!

With a few more plumbing repairs, my 512 was in great shape. I loved my cozy cabin. The kids must have, too, as their evening visits became more frequent.

Several other changes had occurred among the non-Dene community while I was on holiday. Helen had been transferred to a post in northern Saskatchewan and Mary Douhaniuk was now the nurse-in-charge. The new teacher, Lorraine Griffin, now joined Judy Zehr who had replaced Liz Robinson in April when Liz went on maternity leave. Bruce Miners joined Harley at the power plant. Pete, Liz and baby Karen had returned to British Columbia and Ian McDonald was now the new Bay manager.

Two brand new snowmobiles had arrived on the summer barge, one for Claire and the other for Bruce. What with a couple of new trucks, a Nodwell[1] and the new Ski-doos, signs of change were well on their way in Franklin—but the Sahtuot'ine still preferred their dog teams.

My summer visit marked the first time I had been back to Wales and England since arriving in Canada in 1963. Relatives and friends were most intrigued with my new life, especially my life up North. I soon realized, however, that in talking a great deal about Fort Franklin and very little about my previous two years in British Columbia, I was merely confirming many of their misconceptions about Canada. After all, didn't all Canadians live in log houses and drive to work by dog team?

I was frequently asked, "Don't you get lonely living in such an isolated place?"

My answer was always an unhesitating, "No. There is so much that is new and interesting to do and learn in Franklin that there is no time to feel lonely or bored."

In spite of my assurances to the folks back home, as the fall of my second year progressed and all the newness of last year's discoveries became commonplace, I did find some loneliness creeping in. Mary, the new nurse, was a pleasant person but I missed Helen's sense of fun and the long discussions we used to have. Claire, too, seemed to have withdrawn more into herself and spent much of her spare time either on her Ski-doo or back in her duplex, cooking, reading and sleeping. Little by little we noticed Lorraine and Joe becoming good friends, as did Judy and Bruce. Although we periodically got together for dinner or a party, I found myself turning increasingly towards the kids and events in the village.

I continued to enjoy my days at school, encouraging my students to learn and I looked forward to their company in the evenings when they often taught me much. I also enjoyed going to the occasional movie, running Bingo, participating in drum dances, going for long walks either by myself or with others along the lakeshore or into the bush, going fishing and, as the days grew colder and darker, more reading and letter writing. I often wished that I had come to know some of the women in the village better, but since few spoke any English and I had learned no Slavey, communication between us was virtually nonexistent.

It is difficult for me to understand all these years later why I made so little effort to learn Slavey. I certainly had both the time and opportunity to do so, even if only enough to carry on a basic conversation. Critical though I was of an education system that insisted on forcing an inappropriate southern curriculum on these children, and although I recognized the need for them to maintain their culture and language, still I made no effort to learn their language beyond a few very simple phrases. Perhaps it was because I never expected to stay at Franklin for long. Whatever the reasons, it demonstrated a serious and foolish omission in my understanding of the importance of a person's language to their identity, as well as in my ability to get to know some of the women.

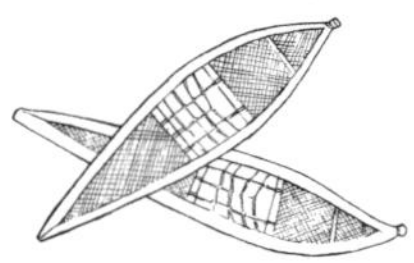

Halloween was upon us and this time, at the kids' request and for our amusement, the school went all out. We decorated our windows with pumpkins and ghosts and witches and black cats. I shared some of the history of Halloween with my students but they really weren't that interested. They were, instead, very keen to dress up for the parade involving the whole school, followed by several class parties. My grade five and six kids loved all the games, such as balloon bursting, biting a quarter off a plate filled with flour—there were no apples available for bobbing—followed by the class dance. A fun time was had by all but I couldn't help wondering what the parents thought of all this.

The last words uttered from my brother, John, as I left Britain in the summer, had been, "Sue and I are getting married on December twenty-seventh. It would mean a lot to me if you could come to our wedding, Miggs. It's going to be very small." I told him that I would love to be there but that, realistically, I couldn't possibly see myself flying back to Wales again at Christmas. However, as the months went by I thought about my brother more and more and wished I could be there with him. One day, early in December, while playing some of my records, the sound of Bing Crosby crooning "I'll be home for Christmas" proved too much for me. I had to go, regardless of the cost and the obstacles.

I made my arrangements. One of the construction men was chartering a plane to take him out on the twentieth of December and he said I could go to Norman Wells with him. There I would catch a PWA flight to Edmonton and then an Air Canada flight to London, England, and be home in North Wales on December 22. Knowing how unpredictable things could be up North I decided not to tell my family, just in case I wasn't able to make it.

The morning of the twentieth arrived. My bag packed, I went to school. The plane wasn't due until close to noon when there would be some light. Joe had already arranged to have some of his older students cover my class for the last three days of the term and I had made up a quantity of work for them. Daylight finally appeared, but not the lake. It was totally invisible. Thick fog blanketed the village and lakeshore. Such fog was usual where the open waters of Bear River exited from the lake but it rarely spread to the village. There was no plane that day.

Disappointed as I was, I wasn't too worried as I had allowed for the possibility of a day's delay in my flight from Edmonton. But when the twenty-first arrived with no change in the thick fog over Keith Arm, I began to panic. Father Fumoleau, who knew I was trying to get to Britain, began calling around on his short wave radio to see if anyone could fly in to Franklin, but without any luck. Needless to say, by that evening I was very despondent. Even if a plane arrived tomorrow, it would now be too late for me to make my connections.

I could not bring myself to unpack my suitcase and, for the third day, I went to school dressed in my travelling clothes: jeans, shirt, sweater and mukluks. Somehow it didn't help at all to see that most of the fog had now lifted. About 11 AM Father Fumoleau burst into my class yelling breathlessly, "Miggs, quick! I managed to contact a plane on my radio! It will be here in a few minutes and will take you to Norman Wells!" I started to protest and tell him that it was now too late, then changed my mind. What the heck. At least I could stay with friends in British Columbia for Christmas even if I couldn't get to Wales. I said goodbye to the kids, picked up my small suitcase and jumped on the back of Father Fumoleau's vintage Ski-doo. Into the plane I leapt, accompanied by the construction man who had been waiting for his still nonexistent charter.

When I arrived at Norman Wells airport, I was approached by a man who asked, "Are you the school teacher trying to get to your brother's wedding in Wales?" I guess Father Fumoleau had done a lot of calling around for me.

"Yes," I replied, "I was, but now I've missed my connection in Edmonton as the PWA flight has gone for today, hasn't it?"

"Yes, but I tell you what. There's an Imperial Oil plane coming through here in about an hour's time taking all their employees home for Christmas." He handed me a name scrawled on a piece of paper and said, "Give this guy a call and explain your situation to him. I bet he'll give you a ride to Edmonton." And he did.

Thirty-six hours later, the skies over London, England, were grey and overcast and I saw very little of the sights as we came in to land, but I couldn't care less. I was here, thanks to a last minute stand-by seat from Edmonton to Toronto and a last minute seat cancellation from Toronto to London. I took the bus to Euston Station on the morning of December the twenty-fourth, purchased my train ticket to North Wales and phoned my mother.

"Hi mum. I shall be home in eight hours."

"What? What do you mean?"

"I've just arrived at Euston Station and will be catching a train home in a few minutes."

"Oh, that's wond—" and the phone went dead.

"Hello! Who's there?" It was my brother.

"Hi John! It's me. What happened to mum?"

"She just fainted. But you know mum, she'll be OK in a few minutes. Where are you, Sis?" and so I told him and gave him my arrival time in Colwyn Bay. He said he'd be there to meet the train.

Now I could relax. I didn't have long to wait for my train. It was only then that I began to notice how people were staring at me. I was still wearing my northern parka with its wolverine fur trim, my big moose hide mittens strung around my neck and the beaded mukluks on my feet, dressed just the way I had been when I had left Franklin. I suppose I did look somewhat incongruous, dressed like this in the heart of London.

A little while later, while standing on the train platform, I became very aware of a long line of big, wet footprints leading up to me. Moose hide mukluks might be great in the frozen North but they were quite useless on the wet streets of London where the hide became saturated. I tried stepping away from the wet prints but they kept following me! Once on the train, I rested my cold, soggy feet against the heater under the opposite seat and before long they were dry but the moose hide was as stiff as a board. My mother and brother greeted me at the station with big hugs. "This is great, Miggs! I knew you'd be here," said my brother. I then explained how close I had come to not making it. But for a number of lucky breaks I wouldn't have.

The wedding day dawned cold, damp and blustery, so although I had borrowed a pink suit, a blouse and a pair of shoes from my mother, I needed to wear my parka over top. Several newspaper journalists who often stayed at the small hotel owned by Sue's father had been invited to attend the wedding reception. Some had taken him up on the invitation—"for the free booze," I had heard one explain. Their curiosity piqued by my parka, details of where I lived and my adventurous journey soon found their way into their journalists' notebooks. Several photographs of me on my own, as well as with John and Sue, were also taken.

The newlyweds left by car to spend the night at a small hotel before heading on to London the following day. That next morning a shriek from my mother had me up in a hurry. There she stood in the hallway, a big smile on her face, waving the *Daily Express*. "Look at this!" She pointed to a large photo on the front page of Sue and John in their wedding attire, and me, standing in the middle, wearing my parka with its hood of wolverine, under the headlines "Sister Flies 8000 Miles to Brother's Wedding!"

Later on we discovered that several newspapers had carried the story, with similar photos and accompanying headlines such as "Guest Drops in From the Arctic," "Wedding Guest Flies to Wales from Canada's Arctic." When I met up with John and Sue in London a couple of days later on my return to Canada, we all had a good laugh about all this publicity. My brother's final comment was, "Good, now I won't have to write to all my friends and tell them I'm married." And he didn't, but he did receive letters of congratulations from friends in Ireland, Scotland, England and Wales.

My flight all the way back to Norman Wells was quite relaxing and uneventful, but then I got weathered in there for a couple of days and arrived late for school. Joe had again covered for me but I insisted on making up most of the time by holding school on Saturday mornings during January. I wasn't sure how many kids would come but I felt better doing it. Much to my delight, all the kids came and it became a kind of special time for us, being the only people in the school. When I eventually told the kids that they didn't need to come any more, they were so disappointed that I continued running our Saturday school well into February. Then I had to stop as I inherited another part-time job.

In mid-February, Father Fumoleau left for a three-month holiday to be with his family in France, his first holiday in seven years, leaving me in charge of the Post Office. He had explained all the procedures and paperwork necessary, so each Saturday I delivered the mail to the scheduled flight, "the sched," and then sorted the incoming mail. Best of all was when the villagers came to pick up their mail: letters, and packages of clothing for children and babies, or toys, or small household items. These items, not available in the local Bay store, arrived from Eaton's or Sears or from friends and relatives in other northern communities or Edmonton. They opened them right there in the Post Office and took delight in sharing their contents with me.

Pleased though I was to see Father return in May, I missed my Saturday morning contact with the village people. It had been one of those rare times when we were able to communicate with each other, despite the barriers of language. We both recognized the tangible subject of our conversations and so were able to share the enjoyment together.

The time had come to expand my curriculum and teach my students some skills other than just "book learnin'." My first tentative ventures were in the area of cooking and sewing for the girls, and Joe took my boys, though I can't now recall what he did with them. During their visits, the girls had indicated a real interest in learning to cook foods available at the Bay store, so I decided to give it a try and held the classes in my cabin. There was nothing fancy to our cooking. We baked cakes and cookies from mixes, baked several kinds of breads and buns, and cooked canned and frozen vegetables, and they took great delight in making, eating and also sharing their efforts with their families. In exchange, the girls taught me how to make bannock, the flat Indian bread that I had eaten many times by then. They also tried their hand at sewing aprons and curtains. We didn't have any sewing machines so everything had to be sewn by hand, a tedious process, but they didn't seem to mind.

Useful and enjoyable though these activities were for the students, it never entered my head that it would have been equally, and in some respects, more beneficial, if I had asked some of the women in the village if they would like to be involved in teaching these classes too. They could have taught their daughters how to sew and bead slippers and mukluks and mittens, or how to tan a moose or caribou hide. These were tasks that in past years the girls would have acquired just by working alongside their mothers. Now, with so much of the day spent in school, these skills were not being learned. The girls might not have enjoyed these sessions as much simply because they often placed little value on things "Indian" and a great deal on things "white," a message that we continually reinforced, as did I with my cooking classes. However, a balance of both traditional and "white" skills would have left open their options for the future and would have given the message that traditional Dene ways were to be valued too.

Our next venture was a class bank. One evening when several of the children came to visit me they noticed my big, fat, red piggy-bank sitting on my dresser. "Why he have hole in his back?" they inquired. I explained why, whereupon they dropped several coins into the pig. I reiterated that this was money that I was saving for my next summer holidays but they just laughed and fed my pig more coins the next time they visited. I then broached the subject of us having our own class bank where they could save and withdraw their own money as needed. They liked the idea and so our classroom bank was born, a bank that was run by students, under my guidance, for students in grades five to eight.

The money they deposited came from a parent's occasional win at a card game or from money earned by those students who helped run the movies, selling pop and candies, running the projector, or selling tickets at the door. Withdrawals were used to pay for CODs from mail order catalogues, such as the student who saved for a bicycle, or for the weekly movie shows and edibles available there. At the end of the year when all the interest paid out and loan money collected was calculated we didn't make a profit, unlike most banks. But the loss of ten cents was certainly cheap for what proved to be a worthwhile venture.

In early March, the band council decided to hold a winter carnival for the first time in several years. My students were excited and could talk of little else for days before the event. It would take place on the lake and there would be dog sled and snowshoe races and various shooting competitions. It sounded like fun and was certainly just the right medicine to cure the winter blahs that had settled in, as spring still seemed a long way off.

I'll enter the snowshoe races, I thought. Johnny Neyelle had already made me three pairs of beautifully crafted snowshoes. He had even helped me hang one pair on my cabin wall where they looked most attractive. The other pairs were gifts for friends in British Columbia, I explained to Johnny. Now I asked him to make me another pair. He brought them around a few days later and I paid him. What a beautiful job he always did of the narrow, pointed design with its wooden frame and criss-crossed babiche webbing, along with oil lamp wick for the foot ties.

The day of the carnival arrived and almost everyone in the village had gathered to cheer on the competitors. The snowshoe race was one of the first events. I was to race against about a dozen other women but I felt confident of doing quite well, since I had used my snowshoes a great deal when we had been camping or when I had gone for walks in the deep snow of the bush.

We lined up. At a given signal, off we shot with a fast semi-shuffling step, our eyes glued on the two oil drums standing on the ice about fifty metres ahead of us. All of a sudden, having taken only a dozen or so steps, I heard a loud crack. Then I stumbled and, with my arms flailing in the air, I fell headlong onto the ice, almost knocking over one of the other women. My beautiful new snowshoes had snapped and were now quite useless. I undid the foot ties and carried the snowshoes and my hurt pride over to the sidelines to watch the rest of the race. Then I spied Johnny and marched over to him. Angrily, I held out the remains of my snowshoes and exclaimed loudly, "Johnny! These snowshoes are no good. I only ran a few steps and they broke."

For several moments Johnny just looked at me and then calmly replied, "Teacher, you not tell me you want to race in them. Before, you only buy snowshoes to put on wall. I use different wood for those. They don't need to be strong." And he turned and walked away. I, of course, hadn't realized this practical difference.

When next year's winter carnival rolled around, I asked Johnny to make me another pair of snowshoes "for racing," I said cheerfully. A few days before the carnival he arrived at my cabin and handed them over to me. His face lit by a big smile, he gave me a detailed explanation of their special strength features and how they differed from those made "for the wall." But despite having my own custom-made, strong snowshoes I still didn't do very well. I was easily outclassed and out-paced by most of the women.

The next day I was once again reminded by my students, their faces beaming with delight, that their older Dene mothers were indeed better at some things than was this young school teacher from the South.

CHAPTER NINE

COMINGS AND GOINGS

Much of the village discussion that spring revolved around construction in the fall of a new community hall. I attended a couple of public meetings where Victor Beyonnie, the village chief, explained the need for a large hall and outlined the activities that it could be used for. Then, as was customary, he asked for input from the villagers. I enjoyed listening to Victor's powerful delivery; he was a fine orator, and, although I understood very little of what he actually said, I could often glean a sense of his message from his expressive face and body language, when supplemented by the comments of a nearby student. The project was clearly an exciting new venture and a community hall committee was formed. I willingly agreed to serve as the secretary-treasurer.

Since movies would be held in the new community hall, I broached the idea of allowing some of the older students to look after ordering and running the movies, as well as providing a concession stand. Several students were already performing these tasks on a small scale at the school movies and this was a chance to provide them with additional skill development. Permission was granted.

I took aside my grade six students, explained what I had in mind, and requested volunteers who were willing to accept this increased responsibility. They would not be paid but would receive a small percentage on the profits earned. Everything would be ordered in advance from a wholesale supplier in Edmonton to be brought in by barge during the summer. Up until then we had been buying our supplies from the local Bay store which left little room for any mark up. When the kids discovered how much cheaper the Edmonton supplies were, they soon calculated that the money made on these sales, even if they charged slightly less than the Bay, would enable them to rent more new, full-colour movies. I seem to recall that we ordered every one of Elvis' movies that first year. With the ordering completed, all we had to do now was wait until the summer barge arrived and the community hall was built.

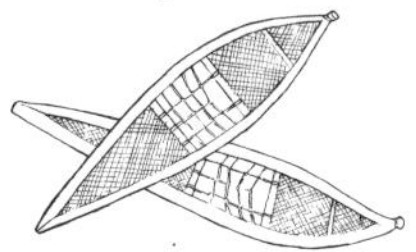

Spring also brought the wedding season, with a double wedding announced for April. Apparently, double and even multiple weddings were quite common at Franklin. When I asked the kids about this, they said it was because people didn't get as nervous about getting married if there was more than one couple. It was also more fun that way. Another fiscal and practical consideration was that only

Raymond Tutcho, John Mantla (Bekale), Jimmy Tutcho and (*in front*) George Cleary of Fort Franklin enjoy an ice cream between rides at the Calgary Stampede, July 1967.

one community feast and drum dance was necessary. The wedding was a delightful experience. Although similar to southern weddings in many ways, it had a unique northern charm of its own.

Father Denis, who was filling in for Father Fumoleau, was to officiate. He asked me to be the "official" photographer since I usually had my Pentax camera with me. He also asked if I could play the organ? I couldn't, nor could I play the piano. But since no one else could either, I agreed to give it a try. I could hum both the "Wedding March" and the ending "Recessional," and so, after much trial and error during my practices at the church, I managed to figure out the notes and a few chords on the small electric organ.

The big day arrived. Although the skies were overcast, the temperature was quite mild for April. The grooms had only been waiting at the altar for a few minutes when, at a signal from Father Denis, I began the "Wedding March." Rosie and Cecile walked down the aisle, escorted by their fathers, to meet Hughie and John, respectively. The grooms and the best man looked smart in their dark suits, crisp white shirts and ties; the lone bridal attendant wore an attractive blue dress. The brides were formally attired in calf-length dresses with matching net veils, Cecile in pink and Rosie in white. All three women carried realistic bouquets of artificial flowers. Everything went off smoothly.

Mary had invited the wedding parties over to the nursing station for their special, three-layered, pink and white wedding cake, and more photos were taken. Then everyone participated in a drum dance held in Joe's room at the school. The only thing missing was the honeymoon send-off since there was nowhere for them to go but, presumably, other special arrangements had been made.

"Miggs. We're going to have some very special visitors come to Franklin tomorrow," announced Joe one day as I was leaving school, "and I wondered if you, Claire and Lorraine would look after making lunch at my place?"

I was intrigued. Joe often had visitors but he had never asked us to cook for them before. "Sure, Joe. Who's coming and how many do we cook for?"

"Stuart Hodgson, the new commissioner of the NWT, and about half-a-dozen other people."

This was, indeed, exciting news. Even in our isolated little corner of the North we knew that Yellowknife had become the official capital of the new Northwest Territories on January 1967 and that governmental power for running the NWT had been transferred from the federal government in Ottawa to Yellowknife. In order to break the bureaucratic hold of Ottawa on this new government, Arthur Laing, the federal minister for Northern Affairs, appointed his new commissioner from outside the Ottawa circle. Stuart Hodgson, a union leader in Vancouver and a man used to representing the rights of employees, became the new commissioner, and John Parker, the mayor of Yellowknife was appointed deputy commissioner.[1]

This move, with decisions being made closer to the action seemed sensible to us. How could politicians and bureaucrats living in far-off Ottawa possibly know what was going on in the North? Later on I was to discover that things were not quite as simple as I had then perceived them to be. Although the seat of government had been transferred, it would be many years before real decision making power emerged in Yellowknife.

In the meantime, the commissioner and his entourage were coming to Fort Franklin for lunch. None of us had any caribou or moose nor were we able to acquire any locally, so they would have to make do with the canned beef that we only had left because it was our least favourite canned meat. "We'll doctor it up with mushroom gravy," said Claire. "I'll look after making some soup, too."

"I can throw in fresh-frozen vegetables," I volunteered. "How about carrots and peas?"

"I'll look after dessert," said Lorraine, and, although I can't now recall what it was, I do remember that it was quite scrumptious.

Our students were sent home early that day so that we could concentrate on preparing the feast and then enjoy the company of these special guests. After all, to us the commissioner was on a par with a provincial premier and it wasn't every day such a person came to lunch. Shortly after noon the Twin Otter circled over the village. Our guests had arrived. Joe walked down to the lake to greet them as we three finished our preparations, even down to a bouquet of artificial flowers placed on my best, and seldom used, white linen tablecloth.

Stuart Hodgson's imposing tall frame was clad in a brightly striped coat made from a Hudson's Bay Company blanket. The toque on his head was similar to the kind formerly worn by the voyageurs. In time his imposing presence, deep voice, bristling mustache and his genuine interest in the people whom he met in every village across the Northwest Territories, became familiar to many. He came to be known as *Umingmuk*, the Inuit word for a muskox. On this trip John Parker, the deputy commissioner, and five other people who were all new to Yellowknife and the North accompanied him.

Lunch proceeded smoothly as our guests plied us with dozens of questions. Even the beef, thanks to Claire's special gravy, tasted quite palatable. Certainly, many compliments were showered our way as they kindly assured us that this was one of the best meals they had received on their travels. We promised them real caribou or moose the next time they visited (I was able to keep my promise the following year). We cleared up while Joe took them on a tour of the village and introduced them to Chief Victor and other important elders before they left for Colville Lake, where they would stay the night.

Increasingly, over time, the communities were to feel the impact of the territorial government on their lives, with mixed blessings. During the first few years after the transfer, Yellowknife continued to be run by transplanted federal bureaucrats accustomed to taking orders from the deputy minister in Ottawa, who was still their boss. Stuart Hodgson's duties and functions were still ill-defined and, during this initial period, the bureaucrats perceived him as an outsider to whom they felt little loyalty. Many years were to pass before Hodgson and Parker were able to convince Ottawa to bring about the kinds of changes that would really put power in the hands of the territorial government and, eventually, into the hands of the northerners themselves.

"Why do you go camping when you got such a nice place here?" asked Judy one day when she and Jane were over. They and several other children thought that we teachers were quite crazy to leave all our comfort and warmth to spend a night or two under the stars at -40°C, lying on the snow in our sleeping bags, and doing all our cooking and boiling snow water over a camp fire. But once the days got a little longer and warmer, we loved getting away on occasional weekends.

Now that both Bruce and Claire had snowmobiles it made it easier for a bunch of us to escape a few miles into the bush. Setting up camp and performing the necessary chores took up some of the time. I also loved lying in or on my sleeping bag close to the blazing fire, just reading or daydreaming while taking in the surrounding bush through my senses. At other times we played cards or sat around in the evenings swapping stories. Sometimes some of the teenagers from the village came with us. This time, Francis, one of my grade six students, accompanied us. Mature for his age, he loved any excuse to drive a Ski-doo.

Francis had become a frequent evening visitor, sometimes coming with friends but often on his own. Most times he was cheerful and gregarious. It was during these visits that he told me about the legendary Bushman who had been known in the past to abduct women and young girls while they were picking berries. I was never quite sure how to react to these stories. Occasionally, he would spend a whole evening just looking through my magazines and saying little as I carried on with whatever I had been doing beforehand, comfortable with the silence, and letting him engage me in conversation if and when he felt like it. Sometimes he would arrive upset, but he never shared his concerns with me nor did I prod him to and I think he was grateful for that. One time, when I was visiting Mary at the nursing station, I returned to my cabin to pick up something only to discover Francis, fully dressed, boots and all, lying fast asleep on my bed. He didn't stir and I left him there. When I returned a couple of hours later he had gone and neither of us ever alluded to his brief stay.

Often, when I left to go on our weekend camping trips, Judy and Jane, who spent more time visiting me than anyone else, stayed behind at the "512." It was such a joy to return home to a clean house, with my clothes washed and ironed, for which they would never accept any financial payment. I recall a time when I was really sick with the flu. Without a word from me, they moved in for the few days. They still attended school and went home to sleep at nights but otherwise they stayed and looked after me, making me soup and bringing me lots of cold drinks.

Of all the kids who continued to visit me in the evenings, I enjoyed visits from Jane and Judy the most, perhaps because there was a maturity about them that belied their years, perhaps just because they were such neat kids. They both spoke good English, especially Judy. Jane was quieter. They were both intelligent and had soaked up a considerable amount of general knowledge. Judy, in particular, also showed a great deal of curiosity about the world beyond Franklin and never ceased to ask questions—which is probably why they could never quite understand why I did not choose them to go south with me that summer of '67.

News of the centennial celebrations for Canada's hundredth birthday had reached us. We had already heard that Georgina Blondin, originally from Fort Franklin, had been selected as princess of the Northwest Territories and would be travelling by barge from settlement to settlement during the summer. I, too, wanted to do something special, as a token of my appreciation for my almost four years of living in Canada. An idea had been brewing in my mind for several weeks. What about taking a couple of my students south for a while in the summer, perhaps to Alberta and then on to British Columbia? Judy and Jane were, in many ways, my immediate and obvious choices, however after giving it more thought, I decided that such a trip, in the long run, might be more beneficial for boys. I thought they would be more likely to explore other avenues of future employment than would the girls, who, it seemed to me then, in the context of those times, would be more likely to get married and stay home. (Pretty feeble reasoning when I look back and I was wrong, at least about Judy and Jane.)

My plans began to take shape. We would begin in Edmonton, so I wrote to Jim Casey, whose work with the northern Co-op movement had brought him to Franklin on a couple of occasions, and asked for his help in acquiring a rental car. From Edmonton we would continue on to Calgary for the Stampede, then camp through the Rockies, eventually ending up in Abbotsford, BC, which would be our base for travelling through the Lower Mainland. I then wrote to my good friends, the Hardys in Abbotsford and the Lesters in Langley, and soon heard back that we would be most welcome.

With that done I then wrote to Pacific Western Airlines, also known locally as "Pray While Aloft" or "Please Wait Awhile," to buy tickets for the three of us. I must have told them of my plans because PWA very kindly sent me two free student airfares. This was so unexpected that I decided to invite two more boys to come along, buying two student fares to add to the free ones, after all, I had already earmarked a certain amount of money for this trip. I also felt that four boys would probably feel more comfortable than two. It was now time to decide which boys to take. I certainly had several worthy students to choose from and I knew my decision would not come easily.

I was very keen to take Jimmy who had been struck by polio at an early age. It seemed obvious that he would never be able to earn a living from trapping and hunting, so the exposure to other forms of employment might be useful for him. But the choice probably had as much to do with how impressed I was by Jimmy's determination and cheerfulness. He invariably joined any activity the other kids were involved in, finding a niche for himself, such as his one-armed swings at bat in softball games. The other kids willingly assisted him if needed, but most times Jimmy just tried his best and did things in his own way, and invariably with a smile on his face, whether he succeeded or failed.

Although only in grade five, Georgie was one of my best academic achievers. Studious and quiet, as well as mature for his age, he also enjoyed the occasional prank. John, an extrovert in the class, had a considerate and sunny disposition, with a natural ability to get along with anyone. He also demonstrated considerable initiative. My fourth choice was Raymond, Jimmy's younger brother. Raymond was a quiet boy who seldom spoke, or to be more accurate, seldom spoke English. He often had a nice twinkle in his eyes but I didn't know him very well, and he was not an immediate choice. I also wasn't sure if it was fair for me to take two boys from one family. On the other hand, I felt sure Jimmy's parents wouldn't let him go on his own and that there would be a better chance if Raymond came along, too. However, soon after our trip began an incident occurred that made me very glad that Raymond was with us.

Although I had enjoyed planning the trip, I had still to find out how the parents would react to my taking their boys south. I talked to Paul, an older adolescent who helped William at the school and who was reasonably fluent in English. I explained my plans in general terms and then asked if he would translate for me as I visited the three sets of parents. We began with Mr. and Mrs. Tutcho, parents of Jimmy and Raymond. With Paul translating, I outlined my plans. They asked only a couple of questions, then smiled, shook my hand, and with a "*Mahsi cho*," agreed to the boys going. I was amazed that they had agreed without asking for more details. However, the same thing happened when I visited the Mantla and Cleary families. Whatever their real thoughts were, they all seemed pleased, and despite my prompting of Paul to ask them if they had more questions, they didn't. We agreed that they should be the first to mention it to their sons who were clearly curious about these visits. I had visited many families at home before but never with an interpreter, so they knew something was up.

That evening the boys came to see me and I shared my plans in more detail with them. Even though their responses were subdued, they seemed excited. However, they didn't ask many questions either. In retrospect, what was I expecting them to ask? They were familiar with airplanes, camping, staying with friends, and with me. They knew something of Edmonton and even if most wasn't very flattering, they would only be staying there for a couple of days, and then with Jim Casey, someone who had been to Franklin. Instead, during the next couple of months they asked few questions and appeared content to wait and find things out for themselves.

The next day I talked to all the class about our plans and announced whom I was taking. I couldn't tell if the others were disappointed or not. They didn't say very much and their faces were difficult to read. Only Judy and Jane appeared disappointed, but then I might have been reading that into their expressions because I felt guilty at not sharing this experience with them. In many ways no two individuals had deserved it more. But they never expressed their feelings overtly to me nor questioned my choices when I took them aside to explain my reasons.

At the end of the school year, while I was in the midst of planning our trip, I was sorry to learn that both Joe and Claire had decided to leave the North. For all of her tough and blustery manner, Claire had a kind heart and had been a good friend. She had also taught me a great deal about the North. Joe, too, in his quiet, unpretentious manner, had been an excellent principal to work with and I had appreciated his support and friendship. I also respected his understanding and sensitivity in his dealings as an administrator with the Sahtuot'ine.

At last it was time for my four young men and me to head south. Our flights from Franklin via Norman Wells to Edmonton were uneventful. The boys chatted amongst themselves most of the time but their observant eyes missed nothing. Jim Casey met us at the airport with some great news: a local businessperson had donated a station wagon for a month. After dumping our luggage—one bag each—with Mrs. Casey and receiving long cold drinks, Jim drove us to a local food store to purchase our supplies for the first part of the trip. The store was at least twenty times bigger than the Bay store in Franklin and, judging by their expressions, the boys clearly wanted to empty everything off the shelves into our two shopping carts. However, they restrained themselves admirably and just reached for the items requested by me. I also included a few treats.

I was in for another pleasant surprise when I came to pay. The manager, Mr. Newhouse, insisted that it was his pleasure to donate the food. We thanked him profusely and loaded all the bags into the back of the station wagon whereupon John sidled up to me and whispered, "If we know he going to do that we could have got more food, then that save you money in the future!"

We spent the first afternoon at the drag races, then, with many "thank-you's" to the Caseys for all their generosity, we headed for Calgary the next morning.

I explained to the boys that I would pay for motels and campsites, for meals, and for main admissions to places. Every week they would each receive a sum of pocket money that they could spend as they liked, but once it was gone they would then have to wait until the next week for more. I also told them that in exchange for the money I expected them to assist with all the chores along the way, especially when we were camping. I didn't think for a minute any of them would have hesitated to do this anyway, but I knew it would make them feel better about accepting my money. They seemed to like our system and it worked well.

I often smile when I remember that month we spent together. I know I enjoyed myself immensely and the boys were the easiest bunch of kids I have ever taken on a "field trip." They were helpful, polite with others, considerate of my needs, and appreciative of everything we did. Never once did they give me cause to worry about them—either worries about their behaviour or of losing any of them. At first I kept close tabs on where they were, especially when we were in large crowds. I even made them carry little cards with them on which was written my name and the Hardys' phone number. But losing them soon ceased to be a concern. As I later explained to a friend who thought I was being very casual letting the boys wander off on their own, "I may not know where they are, but they ALWAYS know where I am. Hey, I'm their ticket home." By then I had also discovered that they were far less likely to get lost in unfamiliar places than was I. Their sense of direction and awareness of where they were never ceased to amaze me. It was one thing to have these skills in the bush up North close to a village of some two hundred and fifty people, but to be able to transfer them to large cities such as Calgary and Edmonton was difficult for me to comprehend.

I remember the day when we parked our car several blocks away from the entrance to the Calgary Stampede, the day I was very glad that Raymond was with us. As we were getting out of the car, a hot-air balloon flew overhead. The boys couldn't take their eyes off it, so it was left to me to notice the name of the street where we had parked, the number of streets away from the stadium, and the direction in which we walked.

Several hours later, having enjoyed all kinds of rides, played a variety of games, stuffed ourselves on junk food, and watched the evening show at the main stage, we headed back to the car. I counted the streets, found ours, turned left and walked the short distance to where the car was parked. But there was no red station wagon parked there. My heart sank. I couldn't believe it. Our vehicle had been stolen. Now what was I going to do with the boys? For several moments I just stood there, close to tears and my stomach in knots, staring in disbelief at the emptiness.

Raymond, who had said little until then, came up to me and said, "Car over there," and he pointed in the opposite direction from which we had just come.

"No, Raymond. It can't be. We had to turn left not right at this street," I replied, tense from feeling frustrated and worried.

"Miss Morris. Car over there," he repeated, still pointing to the right. This was so ridiculous. It couldn't be "over there." The directions were all wrong. Anyway, how would he know—he hadn't been paying any attention to the car when we left. He and the others had been watching the helium balloon overhead. However, since I didn't know what else to do, and since the other boys seemed to agree with him, I let them lead me to where Raymond had pointed.

Four blocks later, on the same street, there stood the red station wagon, just where I had parked it. Although I felt a tremendous sense of relief at its sight, I still couldn't understand what had happened. After all, I prided myself on my sense of direction and I knew I had traced the reverse steps exactly. So how could this be?

Reading my confusion, Raymond explained quietly, "We go into Stampede one way. We come out different place."

Despite all the rides the boys had been on, despite all the many exciting displays and games they had watched and participated in so eagerly, despite the lapse of some ten hours, despite the fact that it was dark, despite having just met Paul Anka back stage after the evening show, which they were still very excited about, despite all the milling crowds in this totally unfamiliar environment, and despite the fact that Raymond had never been anywhere else before except for his own small village, this young man, from virtually another world, had noticed that we had entered and exited from different gateways. I was absolutely astounded, and I was very grateful for his excellent powers of observation.

It was love at first site when we rented horses from Happy Valley just outside Calgary. Somewhat tentative at first about touching them, the boys soon looked like they had been born in the saddle. I asked the horse owner to select two very docile ponies, one for Jimmy and one for me since I am no rider. In fact I was just as nervous at the thought of Jimmy perched on a horse as I was about myself. But Jimmy was only anxious to get going. John led the way along the narrow trail at a nice walking pace. This is going to be just fine, I thought, as I relaxed a little.

Then, as if on some given signal, the horses began to trot. I tensed again. Sitting two horses behind Jimmy, I watched him bounce all over the saddle, not having the strength in his legs or arms to hold on tightly. This hadn't been a very smart idea, after all. And so much for my request for a docile horse for Jimmy. Jimmy, however, while still bouncing, turned around, flashed me a big smile and yelled back, "I real cowboy now!" I gave up worrying. It was a beautiful half-day's ride as we meandered upwards through the forests of pines growing on the lower slopes of the Rockies.

"Did I understand you to say that these boys have never ridden before?" said the manager upon our return.

"Not only have they never ridden before, they've never seen real live horses before. We're from the Northwest Territories."

"That's amazing," he said. "They're naturals, especially that kid in a red jacket." That was John. "Never seen anyone get on a horse for the first time and ride like that. And even the kid you were worried about did fine. Would they like to come over to the paddock and see our foals?" Would they ever! They stood around for a while, content just to look at the horses grazing in the field. Then they walked quietly towards where the manager was holding one. I can still see Georgie extending his hand tentatively towards the muzzle of one horse, then touching it, not with fear but almost reverently.

I hadn't really intended taking them riding again since horse rentals were expensive. Then we arrived at Lake Louise and passed by some horse corrals. No one said anything, no one asked to ride again, no one begged and whined, and they certainly knew that they didn't have enough of their own pocket money. They even tried to avert their eyes from the horses when they felt I was watching. So, of course, I gave in. This time we booked the horses and a guide for a whole day. High up into the mountains we rode, with the boys feeling confident enough to wear their Calgary Stampede Stetsons, all except for Georgie, who was very attached to his green "Robin Hood" cap. That day was a breathtaking and memorable experience for us.

Camping routines were easily established and everyone pitched in with all the chores. However, they weren't fond of the long car rides sometimes necessary, especially through the heat of the Okanagan. In fact the plus 40°C temperatures made us all rather irritable. So we took several ice-cream and air-conditioned restaurant breaks to assuage the effects of the heat.

One day Georgie checked the restaurant tab and discovered an error. "She charge us ten cents too much," he said. So she had.

"I'll mention it to her when I pay."

Georgie looked at me and said, "It OK. I will tell her," and with that he walked up to the waitress and dealt with the matter calmly and appropriately. From then on I designated him as my official "accountant" and let him handle all the bills and keep track of our finances, which he did with care.

We stopped at Hope in the Fraser Valley to visit Pete and Liz, and the boys thoroughly enjoyed their brief stopover with "Mr. and Mrs. Robinson" and Karen, who was now walking. Even though more than a year had passed since the Robinsons had left Franklin, they still seemed like "family" to the kids.

We eventually arrived at Merle and Norris Hardy's, my good friends in Abbotsford, tired and dusty from the long hot drive. Merle insisted that I sleep in the next morning. She would look after the boys and their breakfast. "They don't eat much," were my last words as I drifted off into a sound sleep in a wonderfully comfy bed.

Next morning Merle poked her head into my bedroom and announced that she was on her way out to do some more grocery shopping. "What was this about the boys not eating much?" she laughed. "They all had four eggs each and a ton of bacon and toast, so I'm off to replenish my larder." I started apologizing, but Merle cut me off. "It's fine, Miggs. They are growing boys with big healthy appetites and I'm only too happy to feed them. Don't get up. Just stay there. They've gone over to the neighbours to pick cherries. I won't be long."

It was just as well that she did buy more groceries. They ate like horses while we stayed in Abbotsford, with Merle continually piling up their plates. Later on, recalling the small meals I had served them, I asked the boys why they were now eating so much when they had eaten so little with me. "You pay for food then," replied Georgie for the group. "We don't want to cost you lots of money. But these people, they rich. They live in a big house, got two big cars, and that Merle she keep telling us to eat lots!" I just smiled, after all, Merle and the boys were enjoying all this feasting.

Although we visited the Vancouver zoo as well as the aquarium, Stanley Park, Simon Fraser University, and many other sights, and although the boys enjoyed learning to ride bikes and cutting the grass with a ride-on mower, without question the biggest hit of all was the swimming pool, whether at Merle's friends' or at the Lesters'. They absolutely loved being in a pool—diving, swimming and playing games. The hours just flew by. Although none of the boys were very good swimmers when they arrived it was amazing how quickly they improved over the few days.

Jimmy was unable to swim as his lack of arm strength prevented him from keeping his head above water. So he amused himself paddling around in the shallower end. But when the boys started throwing small rubber rings into the pool and diving for them, Jimmy decided to give this a try. He swam to the bottom of the pool using only his legs, grabbed the ring in his teeth, and then kicked back up to the surface. After dropping the ring and taking a deep breath of air, he always flashed one of his marvellous smiles. Much as I admired all the boys, Jimmy's willingness and his never-ending struggle to participate in everything never failed to stir within me a very great sense of admiration for him.

All too soon the time for our speedy return trip to Edmonton arrived. I had thoroughly enjoyed my month in the company of these four young men, and felt they had too. As they turned once more at the top of the stairs leading into the aircraft, three in Stetsons and one in his green Robin Hood cap, they waved a rather sombre-looking farewell to me before stepping into the PWA plane bound for Norman Wells and then home. I knew that they had left me with many wonderful and happy memories, but at that moment I could only feel a sense of sadness at seeing them depart.

With gratitude for its free use, I returned our much travelled station wagon, now washed inside and out, to our benefactor then spent the night with the Caseys, overwhelming them with tales of the wonderful adventures the boys and I had shared. The next morning, as I was now broke, but happily so, I set off to hitchhike across the Prairies and Northern Ontario, and eventually to Expo '67 in Montreal where I arrived some five days later.

CHAPTER TEN

THIRD YEAR: 1967–1968

Plywood sheets, two by fours, two by sixes, two by eights, and two by tens of spruce. Pounds of nails of all sorts and sizes. Flashing, windows, doors, bundles of roofing shingles, builders' aprons. Mounds of materials left by the summer barge, all destined to produce a large, new community hall, greeted us when we returned from our summer holidays.

As construction began, an air of anticipation and quiet excitement hung over the village as the sounds of hammers pounding and saws humming carried across the tundra towards the lake. I walked up to the site where about half a dozen men were already busy framing the floor. Another dozen or so younger men were out in the bush cutting down the largest pine trees and hauling them back by dog sled for building the walls.

A few days later Chief Victor visited me, and, blueprints in hand, informed me that the foundation and floor were now complete and what should they do next?

"Hey, Victor. I don't know. What do you think you should do next?" and so he told me. "Sounds good. But, Victor, if you knew what to do why did you come and ask me? Why didn't you just go ahead?" He just shrugged his shoulders, smiled and left. The answer was obvious. I was the only white person on the community hall committee, and so, in deference to me, he had come and asked my opinion. Had I known what to do I would have told him and he would have continued to come and check things out with me. That was the way things went. The Sahtuot'ine had learnt well to always ask the white person's permission and let him, or in this case her, assume the authority role. Fortunately for Victor and for me, I couldn't give him a knowledgeable answer. How easily whites and Dene took on those roles almost unconsciously. Certainly there were times when southerners could provide assistance in areas where we really did have some expertise, but often, even if unintentionally, we deprived the Dene of the opportunity of demonstrating their competence even in areas where they already were knowledgeable, because we assumed that we knew best.

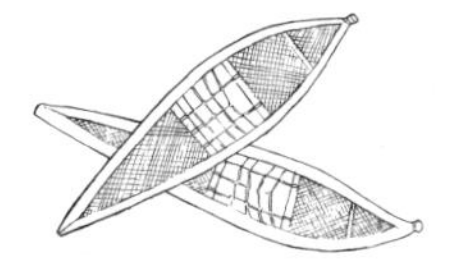

The new term brought several new faces to Franklin. Most significant for me were John and Peggy Talbot, and their two young children. Originally from Edmonton, for the past two years John had been the lone principal-teacher at Fort Liard in the Nahanni Valley. He was now to replace Joe, and, as both prin-

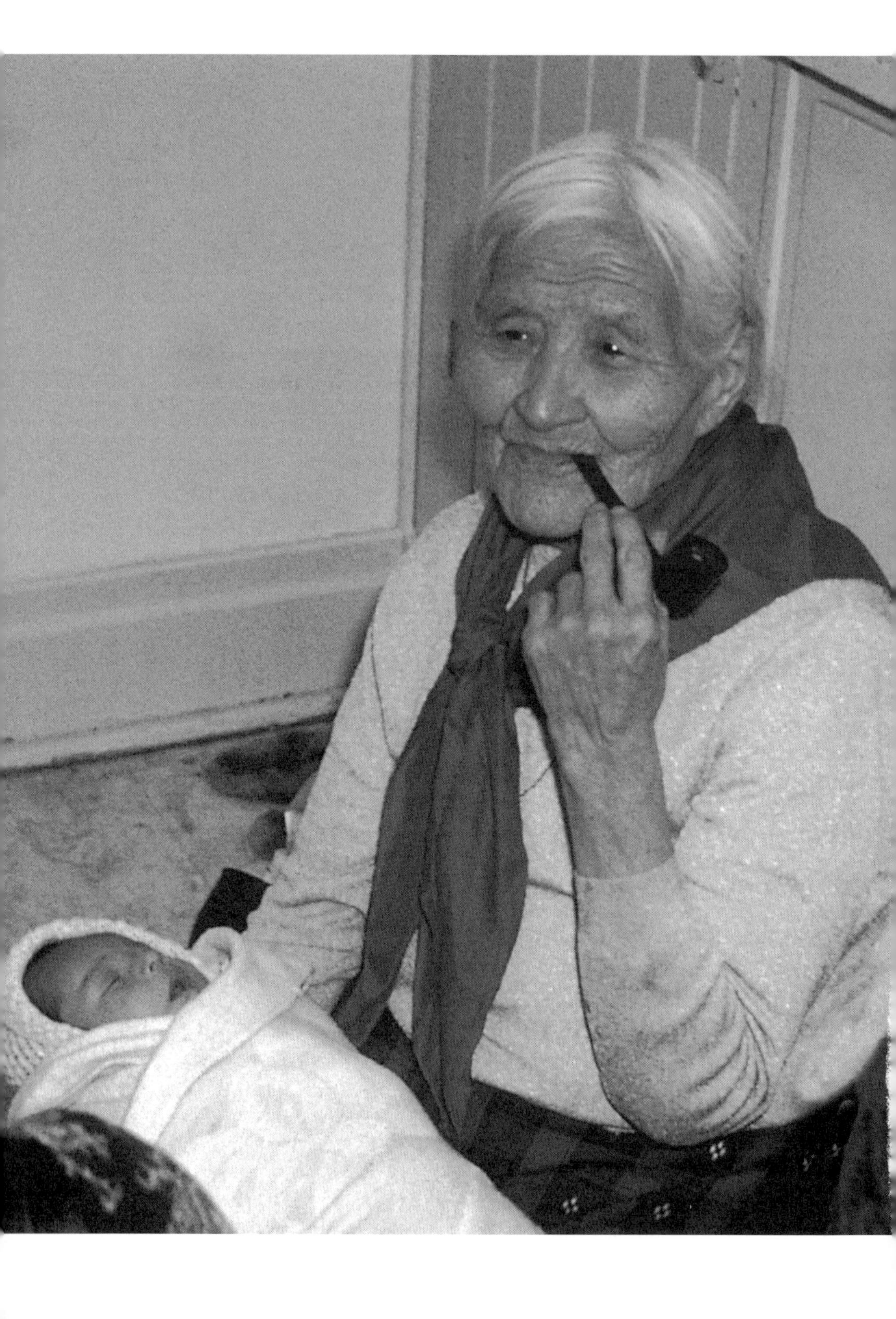

cipal and administrator, John's dynamism and energy were soon evident.

And what about my four cowboys, well, three cowboys and one Robin Hood? They came to visit soon after I had returned and we had fun chatting about the holiday as I showed them my slides. It was great to hear them laughing and teasing each other. They obviously enjoyed reliving the experience. I had several photographs made from the slides for each of them to keep but when I suggested putting on a slide show for their parents, friends and relatives they didn't want that. The photos would be fine, thanks. They also showed a great deal of reluctance to share their experiences with their classmates, which was, in many ways, understandable and considerate of them. However, for a long time afterwards, when we were alone, they would refer to various incidents of the trip with obvious delight.

We watched the community hall construction with growing anticipation. Most of the men had long since departed to trap in the bush, leaving only a small skeleton crew behind, but hopes were high that it would be completed by the time the men returned at Christmas.

Back at the school, we were heavily involved with making Christmas decorations and practising for the annual concert. John, who had a strong artistic bent, had shamed the rest of us into developing more of our own creative talents, and before long my class looked much like Santa's workshop. In fact, the kids and I had to admit that the whole school, including the hallways, really looked very bright, cheerful and Christmassy. John had also begun a school choir in preparation for the annual Christmas concert, and magically, the calibre of music produced under his direction was quite melodious.

John and Peggy invited me to stay over with them for a few days at Christmas. I enjoyed the warmth and friendship of their family as well as all their many visitors of village children and adults. It was especially enjoyable for me to spend a little time with my former students who had moved on to the higher grades with John. Although they still visited me from time to time, it was less than before since my present class of students now monopolised my evenings.

At last, after much feasting and visiting during the Christmas holidays, the community hall was opened early in January, and all the villagers gathered together for a large celebratory feast. Many of the school's Christmas decorations had been transferred onto its bare walls, adding an air of festivity. In preparation for feeding the whole community, three long rows of clear plastic were rolled along the plywood floors. Each of us found a spot beside the plastic and placed our empty plates, cutlery and cups in front of us. Some older folk sat along the walls on chairs, but most of us sat on the clean floor—all two hundred and fifty or so Sahtuot'ine and a handful of whites. Soon the plates were mounded with food as several young men walked around the room sharing everyone's contributions—a full ladle of caribou meat, a handful of cookies, a spoonful of canned fruit, a hunk of bannock,

Granny Zaul, January 1967.

a smaller helping of moose—and cups were filled with steaming, strong tea.

A hush settled on the crowd as Father Fumoleau, sitting at one end of the room with Chief Victor and several of the elders, stood up and blessed the new hall and all the people within with several prayers in Slavey. It was clearly a moment of considerable significance for all the people. Then we tucked into our food and chatted with our neighbours. When we had finished and plates had been temporarily wiped clean and tucked away, the young men rolled up all the plastic and swept the floor and we all moved to sit around the perimeter of the huge room. Another hush settled over the crowd as Chief Victor stepped forward to address us. He thanked all those involved in its construction and told everyone that they should appreciate this new building and take good care of it.

Out came the drums to be warmed on the three wood-burning stoves followed by a drum dance lasting several hours. We all enjoyed ourselves but I felt that the atmosphere in this large hall couldn't compare favourably with that of the many drum dances I had participated in within the confines of a small, crowded, smoky, steaming hot cabin with the beat of the drums reverberating off the walls.

The hall was now ready to be used for a variety of community activities, including movie night. The older students were pleased to set up the concession booth, sell the remainder of their wares barged in from Edmonton, and look after running the movies. They already had plans to purchase much more pop, chips and candy for next year, from their Edmonton suppliers—healthy nutrition was obviously not a consideration for us. As expected, they proved to be very capable at running things and before long I had little to do with the daily operation.

One day Chief Victor came to see me with a new concern. Some of the younger children had vandalized the hall by throwing stones and damaging the fluorescent lights. In addition to being disturbed by the act itself since vandalism was almost nonexistent in the community, Victor stated that only a few spare fluorescent lights had been ordered and once they were depleted new ones would have to be flown in at considerable expense. So he asked me to speak to the children at school.

"I'll gladly do that, but why don't you come to school and tell them yourself?"

"My English is not good," he replied.

"So why do you have to talk to them in English? Why don't you come and talk to them in Slavey?"

"Speak Slavey in school? But school is a place for English."

"Well it shouldn't be. Why don't you come and speak to the kids tomorrow?" He arrived the next day and addressed children from several grades, berating them for about fifteen minutes. They sat in stunned and respectful silence, taking in every word: this was their chief. And that was the end of the community hall vandalism.

It was cold inside the church on that January day. Only a few hours had passed since the wood furnace in the basement had been lit. It always took a long time to warm up when the church had not been used for some time and Father Fumoleau had now been on retreat in Fort Smith for almost three weeks. But no one seemed to notice the cold. We were, perhaps, only aware of the chill in our hearts, aware of the draped coffin in front of the altar, and aware that inside lay a peaceful old lady, now in the company of her Creator.

The evening before she had quietly told her son that she was going to die that night. Her time had come. She knew it with the simple conviction of those who have lived many years and who feel no regret at leaving this preparatory earth. Throughout the evening the people of the village made their way to her bedside to whisper a last farewell and to join in the ongoing chanting of the Hail Mary in her own beloved Slavey tongue. Slowly, in the early hours of the morning, surrounded by friends and relatives, enshrouded in the mystical, musical murmur of prayers, she slipped serenely from one life to another. Old Granny Zaul's body was wrapped in a blanket and then, while the candle-lit prayers continued, gently placed on the wooden floor to lie there until morning.

Johnny Neyelle had already started her coffin. With care and craft of old, he fitted the sawn pieces together. The minutes ticked silently by as he smoothed and curved the rough edges of a six-foot cross. With the world still dark outside and the silence broken only by the occasional howl of a sleepless dog, in the dim light of an oil lamp, his wife patiently sewed dozens of tiny white crosses onto the dark blue stroud material that would cover the coffin. Before they had finished, the sun was already glistening across the golden morning ice.

I was on my way to school when I heard that old Granny Zaul had died during the night. Her son, Joe Blondin, and Chief Victor had already contacted John Talbot. With Father Fumoleau away, would John have a service for her? The coffin would soon be ready. The time was set for one o'clock. By then the church should have lost some of its chill and the simple preparations completed. Later in the morning John went over to the church and prepared the altar and vestments. One of the altar boys made a beautiful wreath of artificial flowers. There was little excitement, little fuss, just an unhurried getting ready.

Shortly before one, I headed for the church. The slow tolling of bells from the mission and church, each echoing the other, rang out solemnly across the drifting snow. I entered the church only to find it empty but for two isolated figures kneeling in the pews, and John, standing and waiting in surplice and cassock, by the altar. We glanced at each other in questioning surprise. Then, as if in answer, we heard the sounds of feet shuffling up the outside wooden stairs. As the door opened the rhythmic tolling of the bells flooded the church and a shaft of sunlight threw the long shadow of the cross onto the altar. Her son Joe carried the cross. Behind him, lifted high on six shoulders, was the coffin with the tiny white crosses clearly visible on the dark blue cloth. Dark silhouetted forms, encased in a cloud of steamy breath, surged forward silently to their seats until the church was filled with muted thoughts and prayers.

John's prayers and readings were simple and appropriate. A hymn was sung. There were few tears. There was no feeling of heavy sadness just a sincere faith born out of deeply spiritual beliefs. As the nasal Slavey chanting of the Hail Mary began, my gaze was on the coffin and my thoughts were with old Granny.

I hadn't known her well, but then you didn't have to know Granny Zaul very well to feel that there was something special about her. I remembered the day she returned from Fort Norman to Fort Franklin two years before. She had been very ill and had decided that she would return to Franklin to die. No one had expected this weak and frail looking eighty-eight-year-old lady to live long. But when the warm summer days came round again there she was sitting outside on the grass under a makeshift tent, sipping strong, sweet tea, smoking her pipe, and swapping stories with other old ladies.

"*Gonezo*, Granny!" I said as I passed by.

"*Heh...eh!*" came the singsong reply followed by some amusing comment to which she and all the other women would laugh cheerfully.

Granny Zaul loved to have her picture taken. As soon as she saw the camera she arranged herself ever so slightly, proudly lifted her chin and tilted her head just a little to one side. Her snowy-white hair framed the deep furrows of her wrinkled, weather-beaten face. But it was the ever-present twinkle in her bright brown eyes and the faint trace of a smile on her lips that made her quite irresistible. Even with her pipe in her mouth, she still managed an enchanting little smile.

She went to every special event. Sometimes, hobbling on her stick, she joined in a drum dance and stepped slowly around the room, laughing in delight. But mostly, she sat quietly in a corner puffing away at her pipe while she rocked a little child to sleep, just watching and smiling and nodding her head.

I wonder what passed through her mind at such times, this white-haired old lady who must have seen so many changes in those ninety or so years. Her father was a French trapper, all the way from Bordeaux, France. Her mother, a Dene from around Sahtu. Joe was her only surviving son but she had adopted fifteen other children. It is impossible for me to conceive the hardships she must have endured in bringing up her children in the frozen wastes of the northern bush, and yet her whole being radiated a tranquillity and faith born out of such hardships and happiness. She lived in an era when there was nothing of importance but the moose, caribou and fish; dogs, sleds and snowshoes; long, cold starry nights and days of tanning hides and sewing clothes; of cooking and caring for her children; of mending nets and listening to the wind. Yet, she sent every one of her children to the mission schools to learn French as well as English. And oh! The stories she told. Is it any wonder that her son, Joe, was one of the best storytellers in the North?

She had witnessed the coming of the white man: missionaries, traders, and lonely trappers and miners hungrily seeking their "El Dorado" in this harsh, forbidding land. They had all brought changes to her life that were but small and few at first, creeping in slowly, almost imperceptibly. But as occurs with all such changes, they soon increased. It must have seemed that in no time at all she was surrounded by barges, planes and strange white people; churches, schools, nursing stations, power plants and stores with unfamiliar foods; bigger planes, Ski-doos, record players and government people bringing rules and regulations as well as a few benefits; and then the beginning of a restlessness among her people as they saw their old ways disappearing with the arrival of even more white people and their unfamiliar ways. And yet, this little old lady could sit in her corner and smoke her pipe with just the faint trace of a smile.

When the Hail Mary was over, John said the closing prayers. Chief Victor announced that there would now be a feast at his house. School had already been dismissed for the rest of the afternoon. We took some food over to Victor's and waited as people kept arriving with their bags of food. Soon it seemed that no more could enter and still they came. We squatted close together on the floor behind our plates and cups, as a few men heaped an assortment of food onto our plates. One extra plate was filled.

At last all were served and everyone waited in silence. Bernard Naedzo solemnly picked up the extra plate. The people parted to let him through. The door of the wood-stove was opened and the food emptied into the fire to be consumed by the flames and carried upwards by the curling smoke. Victor then intoned the blessing and we ate. It was not a sad feast. The room was soon filled with jokes and laughter mingling with the thick smoke. As Chief Victor had said earlier on, "She lived a good long life. She's in Heaven now. She wouldn't want us to be sad."

It was decided to bury Granny Zaul on Friday. From Wednesday until Friday she remained in the frozen church, but not alone. During these hours friends stole in from time to time, drew back the cover, removed the lid and shared a few minutes of prayers and memories with her.

Early Friday morning John again lit the church's furnace. The grave had already been dug. Being on higher ground, it had only been necessary to hack through several inches of ice before getting to the easier sand. It was a cold day, the kind of day that seemed to freeze your breath even before you had inhaled. The smoke from the cabins' wood-stoves swirled upwards into the searing blue sky, the blinding sun reflected off the ice and snow and the alcohol thermometer hovered around -50°C (-70°F). Later that afternoon, the church bells were rung again and the people filled the church. More prayers were said, and the coffin, with the lid secured tightly for the last time, was carried in solemn procession to the waiting Nodwell. It was a cold walk to the graveyard some distance away. Children kept disappearing every few minutes to rush into homes for a quick warm and to don some extra clothing before racing back to join the silent procession.

As we walked, I recalled the last time I had seen Granny Zaul. It was at the Christmas feast held in the nursing station by Mary and Dora for the older folk in the village. I had dropped in for a few minutes. We asked Granny to sing an old song and she obliged. When she had finished she added in Slavey, "It is hard for me to sing. It hurts my chest. But I want to sing for you tonight because I am so happy to be here. I will not see another Christmas."

The cold wind numbed my cheeks. I could feel them stiffen. The wind—was it the wind?—brought tears to my eyes, and they stayed on my frozen face.

The Nodwell couldn't make it all the way up the hillside in the thick snow. We stood waiting around the empty grave, while, one last time, the shoulders of the young men easily bore their light burden. They placed her crosswise above the grave while John led the final prayers. Then Joe and Victor placed a rope under the coffin and gently lowered her into the waiting grave, her head facing towards the east. Each of us threw a handful of sandy earth onto the coffin. Men filled the hole. Women knelt in the snow. And the wind continued to blow.

A long way off in the village the church bells were still ringing, slowly and faintly. A long way further off was another world of commotion and commercialism, of elaborate and expensive funerals. But here, an old woman had died, and her people had buried her with simplicity and a silent faith.[1]

John's forceful personality burst with boundless energy and ideas. As the village administrator, he worked closely with Chief Victor and other elder councillors discussing improvements needed in the village to better the lives of the Sahtuot'ine. It was in this manner that plans were drawn up to construct several water faucets at strategic locations throughout the village. Then people could obtain their water from these communal taps rather than having to cut holes in the ice and haul the water in buckets all the way home. Similarly, it was decided to build wooden sidewalks at certain locations in the village to help deal with the annoying springtime muddy conditions when the permafrost melted and turned the soil into ooze. In addition to providing much needed utilities for the people, these projects were a steady source of employment for a number of men, especially during the "off" season, between trapping and summer jobs.

These plans met with everyone's approval. That is, everyone except for the new government. When officials from Inuvik discovered that John was using welfare money to finance these projects, they were furious. I remember the shouting match that ensued at John's house the evening the welfare agent arrived from Inuvik.

"You can't use welfare money for anything but welfare."

"Your government won't give these people any money to build the things that are really needed in the community, so we have no choice," John retorted.

"This way the projects get built and many people are gainfully employed. If they weren't you would have to pay them welfare anyway. So what's the difference?"

"You can only use welfare money for welfare. I'm sorry if you people can't get any money for these projects but that's a different department and I have nothing to do with it. Those are the rules."

"But they're ridiculous rules. They don't make any sense up here. Without these jobs, and with fur prices depressed, many of these people will end up collecting welfare for doing nothing. They would much prefer, for their own sense of pride and for the sake of the community, to earn this money, rather than be given a handout."

The official left with the intent of cutting off any more welfare money to the community, unless the person applying was genuinely unemployed. John was furious and he was right. Such government policies and decisions seemed ridiculous to us, especially when applied to northern people. But the Sahtuot'ine merely shrugged their shoulders. They had a long history of living with government decisions that rarely made sense to them, and that were frequently made against their best interests. This was business as usual for them. So only a few walkways were built, and the central faucets and other projects were all put on hold until some future unknown date.

Several weeks later a young man entered my cabin in a somewhat intoxicated state. I was about to send him packing but decided instead to offer him some coffee. He began talking. He went on about the stupid government this and the useless government that. As he explained, it was too late to go trapping for beaver, so with no employment available in the village, he now collected welfare for doing nothing, and he complained about having too much time on his hands.

"What I do now? I go to bush and cut wood, but mostly I just stay at home, play cards, get drunk and fuck my wife. What else I do?" None of this made sense to me either.

One bright sunny day in March I noticed that all my students appeared restless. They kept glancing out of the windows, but they wouldn't tell me why. Such a beautiful spring-like day is enough to make anyone want to be outside, I mused, and went on with the class. Later that day something on the distant eastern horizon of the lake caught my eye. Just dark specks at first. Gradually, as they approached Franklin, they took the shape of dog teams and sleds. The level of excitement in the class grew as the kids became aware of the visitors. I looked inquiringly at them.

"They Dogribs," Maurice volunteered. "They from Fort Rae."

Soon we could see a string of dog teams approaching on the distant horizon.

This influx of visitors was obviously far more important to the kids than anything I could teach them at this time so we all went outside and joined John's class, already standing on the snow banks beside the lake. It was a most stirring sight as fifteen to eighteen teams of six to eight dogs, each pulling a sled carrying two or three people, drove past us towards the centre of the village.

"They've come all the way from Fort Rae?" I inquired. "That's hundreds of miles away. How long did it take them to come?"

"Oh a few days, maybe a week, maybe two," was all the answer I received. So I stood back and watched and waited until the children were ready to share what they chose to with me. But I did catch the word "prophet" from their chatting in Slavey and was told that they had come to visit Old Man Naedzo, who was considered to be a holy man. For several days I learned little more, other than that some forty adults were being hosted by the Sahtuot'ine.

My curiosity about these visitors was aroused. Why had they come all this way? I knew such a visit was rare. How long were they staying? How could there be room for all these people in the small cabins? And how would so many people and their dogs be fed? I was, however, even more curious about my students' unusual reticence. Normally, whenever anything happened in the village they couldn't tell me quickly enough and almost vied with each other to be the first to share their news. But not this time. It was almost as if they had withdrawn from me as they made little eye contact and rushed out of the class as soon as the bell rang, instead of their customary hanging around to talk and to help with some classroom odd jobs. So, I continued with things as usual in class, asked them no more questions, and just bided my time.

A few days later a couple of the girls addressed me angrily. "The prophet say we not wear jeans any more. We only wear dresses. Mary not wear jeans, so we not."

"And we not use knife and fork and spoon like white man," said the other.

One of the boys had now joined us and added, "The prophet tell our parents they not go to Father's church. They just pray to Jesus and Mary in their homes, the old way."

I ventured a question. "Who is this prophet?"

They told me his name but mostly they referred to him as the Rae prophet. "He say Jesus visit him and tell him he is now a prophet. Jesus also tell him all Dene must go back to old ways. White man's ways no good for us."

A week went by and there appeared to be a shift in the children's attitude.

"Our parents think he a good man and listen to everything he say. They have drum dances and pray all day. Us kids we not like all this. But when we tell our parents this they get mad at us."

"We not get to wear jeans and we not listen to our records," and almost every house boasted a record player and some country and western records, with Hank Williams and George Jones being great favourites.

I said very little to the kids, just allowing them to let off steam. They were obviously disappointed, for they had looked forwards to the arrival of the Dogribs, but this visit was not turning out as they had expected.

After hearing their comments I wondered if I was witnessing a "millenarian movement," which I had read about in the past. Although my memory of such events was hazy, I seemed to recall that these phenomena occurred when a people underwent cultural changes of dramatic proportions over a relatively short period of time. Often, one of the people would emerge as a prophet, claiming to have been visited by Jesus or Mary and stating that he had been chosen to lead his people back to their traditional ways, rejecting anything to do with the imposed white man's culture.

What the kids shared with me sounded very much like this phenomenon. The Sahtuot'ine had been forced to adjust to huge changes in only a few decades, changes that had taken Europeans hundreds of years to move through. Although I believed that the Sahtuot'ine had adjusted remarkably well and had established a balance between the old and new ways, a yearning for the traditional life prior to the arrival of the traders, explorers, missionaries and, more recently, government bureaucrats, all of which had drastically changed their world, must still hold a strong fascination and appeal to them. I also recalled reading that Father Petitot claimed to have witnessed prophetic movements in this area a hundred years ago. Was this one too?

Unfortunately, I learned very little more. After that one vocal outburst the kids clammed up again, and although my "anthropologist's" curiosity to learn more was strong, I had to respect their wishes, as they appeared to withdraw from us whites. Because the kids had mentioned that Father Fumoleau wouldn't let the people attend church while they followed the Rae prophet, I did approach Father Fumoleau, but he, too, seemed reluctant to talk about events.

A couple more weeks went by. Then one day the children announced, with what sounded to me like considerable relief, that the Dogribs were leaving. Their parents had decided that they could no longer feed them and their dogs. Later I heard that it had much to do with the fact that the Rae prophet had started naming the people who would not go along with him and was, as it were, "casting them out." This practice was said to have annoyed the closely knit Sahtuot'ine.

Whatever the reason, the Dogribs were on their way back to Fort Rae. The Sahtuot'ine, according to the kids, had for the most part enjoyed the visit from the Dogribs. In many ways it was just like the old days for them, when people from several areas had gathered together in large groups to relax and enjoy each other's company. Before long, life in the village seemed to return to where it had been before the visit. The girls were again allowed to wear jeans; country and western music blared from the occasional home; Sunday Mass was again well attended and life continued with, apparently, very little lasting effects from the visit.

One of my students surveys the land while standing on a pressure ridge at Keith Arm on Great Bear Lake, 1968.

CHAPTER ELEVEN

SPRING AND SUMMER 1968

"Today is Treaty Day," one of my students informed me.

"And what does that mean?" I enquired.

"Oh, this is when the Indian agent visits Franklin and gives everyone five dollars and some other things for our parents."

The Otter arrived bringing in the Indian agent, an RCMP attired in his famous red serge, and a couple of government people. A table was set up in the Community Hall. Chief Victor sat at the front with the government dignitaries while people from the village passed through and received their money. The whole thing was very puzzling to me so I asked Father Fumoleau about it.

"Well the short answer to your question, Miggs, is that because the band chiefs signed Treaty 11 in 1921 every man, woman and child in the community receives five dollars annually from the Indian agent."

"That's it?"

"The people also ask the Indian agent for things like gas for their canoes and lamps, plywood sheets and other supplies for repairing their houses, then the agent gives them some of these things. They view him rather like Santa Claus."

"Why do they receive this money? There must be more to all of this. So what's the long answer?"

"Come round and visit me one evening when we both have lots of time and I will gladly tell you."

A few evenings later I took him up on the invitation.[1] As Father Fumoleau related events of the past I found myself becoming increasingly angry and agitated as the evening progressed. It was hard to believe that successive Canadian governments could have treated a group of their own people this way. But as I listened, it was clear that the circumstances surrounding the signing of treaties, as well as the unkept promises of the governments that followed, proved devastating for the Dene.

Father Fumoleau began with a summary of the historical events necessary to my understanding of how and why this situation had come about:

Even before Confederation in 1867 the Canadian government had been involved in signing over a hundred treaties with the aboriginal people in eastern Canada in order, in the words of each treaty, to "extinguish Indian title to this land." Then, in 1870, the Hudson's Bay Company surrendered to the young Canadian government its rights to the vast Northwest lands it owned, in return for a sum of money. This huge tract of land comprised all of Alberta and Saskatchewan, most of Manitoba, two thirds of the present-day Ontario and

Quebec including Labrador, and all of the area known today as the Northwest Territories.

Over the next seven years, treaties known as "numbered treaties" were signed between Canada and the Indian people living south of the Northwest Territories. These treaties covered the fertile prairie lands and opened up western Canada for settlement. New transportation routes were extended to transport freight to the new settlers and, eventually, even further, to the northern fur trading posts.

The arrival of many Euro-Canadians, following the opening of these routes, had a huge impact on the Indians who were still struggling to recover from waves of epidemics and diseases brought in by the earlier traders, while also trying to cope with the social and economic changes affecting their lives.

In the past the Hudson's Bay Company had helped feed those Indians who arrived in various stages of sickness and starvation at their trading posts. But having transferred all this land to the government, the Hudson's Bay Company's position was that the government should assist the Indians. The Canadian government, however, stated that they would only accept responsibility for those Indians who signed treaties with them, hence the signing of treaties one to seven. The Indians of the Mackenzie River Basin—the Dene—were in a different position. These northern lands, unlike the prairies, offered no economic gain for the government at that time. So, while stating they would provide no assistance to the Indians until they signed a treaty, the government had no interest in signing a treaty with these people.

In 1897 the Klondike gold rush erupted, and trainloads of gold seekers poured into Edmonton and then to the Athabasca and Mackenzie valleys on their way to the Yukon. Soon afterwards, gold was discovered at Great Slave Lake and prospecting flourished in the Barren Lands surrounding the lake. When the Canadian government finally recognized the possible future wealth of the natural resources available in this northern area, it sent a treaty commission to meet with the Indians at nine sites south of Great Slave Lake, and Treaty 8 was signed.

Those Dene who signed the treaty soon became disillusioned when they realized that all they could expect from the government's promises were a few rations and minuscule amounts of money, such as the annual payments of five dollars cash per head, twenty-two dollars for each headman, and thirty-two dollars for each chief, along with a new suit of clothes every three years. Similarly, the promise of improved medical conditions merely amounted to bringing a doctor to the annual treaty parties to attend to those few present.

Further influxes of southern prospectors arrived in the North. When their mining claims failed to materialize, many turned to hunting and trapping in the areas where the Dene lived and hunted. Often Dene dogs were shot and traps interfered with and destroyed. Furthermore, in their hurry to obtain furs quickly, some prospectors used poison as a bait for the traps. When these newcomers over-hunted and trapped the animals almost to extinction, the government brought in new game laws that restricted and limited the game season to narrow periods of time during the year. Despite the fact that the Dene had always practiced animal conservation and had never endangered the game (except for some temporary over-hunting around the forts when the traders first introduced them to guns), and despite the fact that most were still starving, these new game laws were enforced on them as well as on the whites.

Despite repeated requests by the northern Dene who were not included in Treaty 8, by Indian agents, and by the missionaries to provide assistance to these destitute people, the Canadian government continued to refuse to make treaty, as it clung to its policy of "No treaty, no help."[2] The government's view was that "The Mackenzie, being a missionary field ... the Indians are ... the Church's responsibility"[3] for education, welfare and health. The missionaries did what they could but their resources were far too limited to make an adequate impact on the needs of these people.

Then in 1914, what was claimed to be the biggest oil field in the world was discovered on the Mackenzie River, forty-five miles north of Fort Norman. When the first gusher at Norman Wells came in on August 25, 1920, it caused considerable excitement across the length and breadth of Canada and, before long, a transportation boom and an increase in white prospectors and speculators began to hit the Mackenzie River District. Obviously the Canadian government could no longer remain indifferent to the North—the stakes were too high—and a Territorial government began to take shape in Ottawa to deal with all the issues pertaining to this new-found oil and gas, as well as for those matters concerning the well-being of several hundred white residents of the NWT. Not one word referred to the plight of the thirty-five hundred Indians and Métis living in this district, although all of these regulations, plans and administrative details affected an area that was still Indian Territory. "It was as though the Indians had ceased to exist in the Mackenzie District, with no rights in the past, and no claims to the future."[4]

The government's first step was to secure ownership of the "vast domain of country, rich in natural resources and favourable to development."[5] For these reasons, and "to avoid conflict between Indians and whites, the Government decided to negotiate by Treaty with the Indians, the surrender of their aboriginal rights."[6] In 1921 H. A. Conroy of the Department of Indian Affairs was selected as the treaty commissioner and given instructions to adhere strictly to the terms of the treaty made in Ottawa.

Despite being aware that the Indians who had signed Treaty 8 had been far from satisfied with the implementation of this treaty, the Dene of the lower Mackenzie Valley and around Great Bear Lake had reluctantly come to realize that if they were to receive any assistance from the government, however small, they had little choice but to accept Treaty 11. But they did not rush to sign. As one of the Indians present at Fort Providence in 1921 said later, "But the chief said not to take money right away, for the white man might lie to us...."[7]

There was no doubt that for the government Treaty 11 was about extinguishing the Indians' title to their lands, yet documents and eyewitness accounts all indicate that this was never made clear to the Dene. Treaty negotiations were brief, and initial opposition was overcome by promising to agree to the specific demands made by the Indians, promises that were forgotten once the treaty team returned to Ottawa.

The Indians' main concern was for the protection of their freedom to hunt, fish, and trap on their land as they had before. Over and over again, at each signing location, this same request was made by the Dene. And each time an issue even closely related to "land" came up, Conroy repeatedly assured them that their rights to hunting, fishing, and trapping on their own lands would last forever and that the payment they received was to ensure continued friendship between the Indians and whites. When one of the Indian chiefs was most reluctant to sign, Conroy said that "as long as the Mackenzie River flows, and as long as the sun always comes around the same direction every day, we will never break our promise."[8] Many other similar instances were later reported by those present at these treaty signings.

Had the notion of ceding the land been explained to the Dene, and had they understood it, they would never have agreed to signing. Their view of "land ownership" was, and still is, very different from that of the European concept, which sees land as real estate to be bought and sold. To the Indian, land and all life upon it, including the animals, is as important as life itself. The land holds a very spiritual significance to them and they see themselves as the protectors of the earth. It would have been beyond their comprehension to understand how land could be "owned" or "sold" by one person to another. But they were very willing to share the land, as was their custom and as a gesture of friendship towards the white newcomers, provided the government assured them protection for their basic needs. Chief Jimmy Bruneau of Fort Rae stated later, "We made an agreement, but land was never mentioned ... a person must be crazy to accept five dollars to give up his land...."[9]

Discussion on the treaty lasted but a few hours. The actual treaty was seldom read out in full, and even when it was, how could these people, unable to read and unschooled in legal jargon, possibly comprehend its true meaning? Bishop Breynat, who was also involved with the treaty commission, believed that he was looking out for the well-being of the Dene when he repeatedly assured them that it was in their best interest to sign the treaty, and that the government would keep its many promises to them. He also assured them that nothing would be allowed to interfere with their way of living. Despite their reluctance and suspicion, but with the assurances of the bishop whose role, according to one of the chiefs at Fort Wrigley, "was to keep God's words, so we trusted him,"[10] the Dene finally conceded and Treaty 11 was "signed."[11]

top: My first view of Fort Franklin/Déline taken from the small six-seater Beaver airplane, August 31, 1965. This tiny, isolated village lies on the western arm of Great Bear Lake in the Northwest Territories, 450 kms north of Yellowknife.

In 1965 the village was home to some 250 Dene Indians, nine whites—including me—and four hundred dogs. Hunting and trapping, along with fishing, were the mainstays of the village economy.

top: The tipi-shaped church with its roof of aluminum tiles was a beacon to travellers and a focal point of the village. Near it stood the mission, elementary school and a small Hudson's Bay store, all built during the 1950s, and a large nursing station built in 1965.

Painting the door jambs, window frames and myself in September 1966. Ronald and Peter wondered if I was turning my "512" cabin into a Hudson's Bay store!

A view of my classroom, some of the students and my wall of windows looking out onto the lake.

I'm surrounded by students at the Post Office. I loved my brief stint as postmistress, sorting and handing out the letters and parcels that arrived on the Saturday morning "sched," 1967.

top: Communal activities that go back hundreds of years were still very important in the 1960s. Drummers at this drum dance included Chief Victor Beyonnie, in the foreground.

Moise Beyha makes his decision at the handgame (also known as the "stick-gamble").

Activities such as the drum dance and handgame, shown here in the 1960s, are still very important in present times not only for enjoyment but also for solidifying bonds between the generations.

In honour of Victor and Elizabeth Beyonnie's fiftieth wedding anniversary in July 1995, a more traditional-style feast, reminiscent of the old days, brought back good memories for all.

top: In the 1960s the land provided most of the necessities of life. Men used dog teams to haul logs from the bush, while the women brought home sled-loads of kindling.

Caribou meat from communal hunts was kept in a shed and then distributed periodically among villagers, who carried home large frozen hunks of meat.

Fish, too, was a very important element in the diet of both the people and their dogs. Smoking fish enables it to last longer.

top left: Although winters were long and cold and often harsh, there was much to appreciate and enjoy in Fort Franklin in the 1960s. Here, children are collecting their family's daily water supply from a hole dug through the lake ice.

bottom left: Although dog teams were the most important mode of village transportation, Father René Fumoleau's vintage Ski-doo occasionally provided taxi service to and from our infrequent airplanes.

The whole community enjoyed the school Christmas concert, where students sang and performed short plays.

top: The years from 1965 to 1995 have brought many changes to the lives of children. Modern houses with several rooms have replaced small and draughty cabins.

Traditional clothing, such as these mukluks, has largely been replaced by modern brand-name clothing.

Bicycles, playground equipment, satellite TV and computers are now commonplace for all children in the Déline of today.

l to r: Jane Kenny, Judy Tutcho *(kneeling)*, along with Helen, Christine, Betty, Jane M. and Merine, proudly show off their accomplishments from our cooking classes.

Granny Zaul enjoys the warmth of the spring sun and a gossip with her friends. Nurse Helen Chan is on the left.

Francis Yukon, one of my students, brings home a load of wood from the bush with his brother's dog-team. I loved riding in a dog sled, listening to the swish of the runners on the packed snow and the jingle of the dogs' harness bells.

Blueberry picking with Atanda and Jannine after the almost calamitous accident during our fishing trip in July 1995.

top: Teacher Claire Barnabe and two young children stand on "Main Street" in Fort Franklin on August 31, 1965, the day we first arrived. The small Hudson's Bay store, the only store in the village, is in the background.

middle: Children play on ice-floes as they break away from the main ice mass each spring (1966). The ice will not totally disappear from Great Bear Lake until mid- to late July.

bottom: Boats and boathouses line the shores of a much-enlarged and modernized Déline in July 1995.

LUND
Johnson

A lone dog keeps watch over the village of Fort Franklin in 1966. By 1995 modern snowmobiles and trucks had virtually replaced traditional dog teams.

Father Fumoleau paused. Overwhelmed by what I had heard, I asked, "And were these promises kept?"

"No, at least not to any meaningful extent. The government believed it had what it wanted—title to all these lands and their resources. It no longer cared about the people living on that land. In the years that followed, the only promise kept was that of the annual visit of the Indian agent with money and rations, which brought the Indians together for a few days during the summer. This did nothing to improve their livelihood. Nor was anything done to improve their health. Diseases and epidemics were not eliminated. In fact, during the influenza epidemic of 1928 that decimated every community along the Mackenzie River, no governmental medical assistance was provided.[12]

"Many years were to pass before any consideration was given to the needs of the Dene and treaties eight and eleven were even partially honoured. In fact, it is not an exaggeration to say that there were times when it seemed that government action was designed to speed up the elimination of the Native peoples out of the North, so that their presence would not interfere with the plans and aspirations of the government and other industrialists in this resource rich country.

"But the decades following the signing of Treaty 11 are another depressing story and we shall have to save that for another time."

I sipped my last drop of coffee and looked at my watch. It was after eleven and Father had to be up early the next morning for the daily Mass.

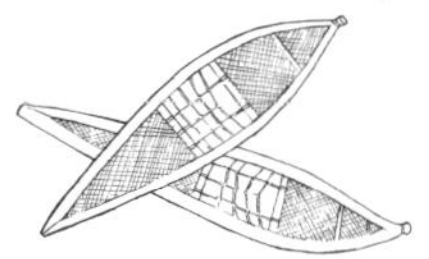

The school year was almost over and this time it held an extra poignancy for me. The time had come for me to leave though I don't recall exactly when I arrived at that decision. After all, I still enjoyed my life in Franklin even if there were occasional pangs of loneliness. The Talbots were very good to me and treated me like a family member, but I seemed to have less in common with most of the other whites now living here. And the language barrier, which I had foolishly done little about, had prohibited my developing close friendships with any of the Sahtuot'ine women.

More significantly, I had grown increasingly aware that our way of educating these children seemed out of step with their lives. Although they obviously enjoyed being at school, and their parents were kindly disposed to us southern teachers, we had imposed an educational structure on them that did not mesh with their way of life and their value system. Surely there had to be a better way, a more culturally sensitive way, of educating their children during this period of immense change.

These children had been brought up in a milieu where interpersonal relations in their homes and communities were informal yet close and strong, where every individual, from a very early age, was treated with respect and, in an atmosphere of non-interference, given the freedom to make his or her own decisions and face the consequences accordingly. Children learned the skills and attitudes they would need as adults by working alongside their parents and listening to the stories of the grandparents and other elders. Egalitarianism was very important, cooperation and sharing was a must, and demonstrating oneself to be better than the next person was discouraged, unless it was to help another. Silence was valued, and someone who talked too much was frowned upon.

Then, at age six, the young Sahtuot'ine entered a school environment that regimented and regulated the students and restricted individual decision-making, where questions were constantly asked and answers expected, and where competition and doing better than their classmates was encouraged.

Stories in the school readers revolved around stereotypical, white, middle-class families that performed activities and visited places totally unfamiliar to these children. (In fact, before long, they ceased to be representative of many southern Canadian families, too.) There were no stories or photos in these books about Dene children and their families engaged in activities that were meaningful for them. None of the skills that were important to their families, and at which their parents and grandparents excelled, had any worth in our schools.

We were taking children who usually had no knowledge of English, since none was spoken at home, and suddenly immersing them, not only in a very strange environment, but expecting them to learn all the new skills we believed necessary, in this new language. Surely their own language should have played a significant role in the schools, especially in the early years? Considering all the differences that existed between life in the village and life in the school, I was often amazed by how well most of these young children performed at school and appeared to enjoy the experience.

Later on, many of the adolescents recognized that much of what they learned in our classes was irrelevant to their lives; they quit school and followed their fathers into the bush and their mothers into marriage. Some left home and went on to continue their education at residential high schools in Yellowknife, Fort Smith or Inuvik. They aspired towards the white man's world rather than emulating their parents' way of life, and they learned to straddle both worlds successfully. Others were unable to cope with life away from home and returned to Franklin.

Certainly the blame could not be attributed solely to the education system. The recent change of establishing day schools in the communities was considerably more enlightened than was the former policy of taking young children away from their families and placing them in residential schools. But many aspects, even of day schools such as that at Franklin, were predicated on the assumption that these children needed to be acculturated and assimilated into the dominant culture, and thus they remained alien to the Sahtuot'ine world and its values.

There had to be a better way. I didn't have the answers but I believed that, somehow, the better way had to involve the Dene themselves. The parents understood that the clock couldn't be turned back, that they couldn't shelter their children from the realities of an encroaching white southern world. They wanted their children educated in schools. But they also knew, in 1968, that there was something radically wrong when years of schooling resulted in so much unhappiness and alienation among too many of their children and themselves.

I was also convinced that we had to develop a partnership where we, as educators, could contribute our teaching skills and our knowledge of the outside world, and where the Dene would share their traditional knowledge, skills and values to create an appropriate and meaningful educational environment. Then, perhaps there would be a chance for these youngsters to end up with an education that allowed them to make realistic and confident choices about their futures.

Despite my few attempts at modifying the curriculum to make it more relevant, I had only been tinkering with the established educational process and I had ignored the contributions their parents could and should have made in their children's schooling. Now at the end of my third year, I knew that it was time to find some answers to these educational issues that bothered me.

Certainly, when I made my plans to leave that summer I had every intention of returning to Franklin, to the Sahtuot'ine who had taught me so much and come to mean a great deal to me these past three years. But other than a brief visit in the summer of 1969, many, many years were to elapse before I did return.

The warm, sunny weather of early summer brought everyone to life. People participated in a whole range of outdoor activities: walks, picnics, and the occasional overnight camping trip in the surrounding bush; midnight fishing trips along the lake shores, travelling warily on the candled ice; groups of women sipping tea in the sun—although Granny Zaul and her pipe were much missed; families fixing their canoes or cleaning fish in the lake waters along the shore before drying the cut strips on the tipi posts; men and women stretching beaver skins on boards; scrawny dogs, now idle for the most part, playing with their pups; ducks and geese honking overhead; and the constant scent of wood fires in the village and lichen on the rocks. It was a wonderful time of the year, when everyone and everything came alive again and life became easier and more enjoyable after the hard struggle of the long winter months.

As had become the custom near the end of the school year, I took my kids for an afternoon picnic to the far end of Keith Arm, and John and his class, my former students, came along too. The chosen June day turned out to be beautifully warm. Some arrived by boat carrying food and drinks; most walked along the shore with John and me. We were even joined by several older teenagers. As everyone claimed to be hungry the decision to eat first was unanimous. So we cooked our hot dogs and fish on the campfires, then toasted our Hudson's Bay-bought marshmallows on the dying embers, accompanied by large containers of Kool-Aid, and the inevitable pot of strong tea.

A game of softball began. Then several of the girls, after the exertion of the game, looked longingly at the lake, and, as if on a given signal, walked straight in. Fully dressed, jackets and all, giggling loudly, the girls frolicked through the shallow waters of the bay. Some even sat down and splashed each other. Yet the water was stunningly cold, made even colder by the fact that there, as a backdrop to this nymph-like display, only some hundred metres away, was the edge of the sheet of ice still covering most of Great Bear Lake. But it mattered not at all to them.

Life in this small northern village could be so good at times and, with this spontaneous burst of enthusiasm, these young girls revelled in the moment, in the warmth of the sun and the coolness of the water, as free from the woes of the world as any children I have ever met.

At length, they ran back shivering to the campfire and dried themselves and their clothes, and still giggling, they savoured their brief adventure. Most of the boys continued to play softball. But one had climbed to the top of a mound of huge blocks of ice, remnants of the pressure ridge formed when the strong easterly winds had blown the vast sheet of decaying ice to abut against the shores. There the ice blocks had come to a temporary rest, close to where the early Sahtuot'ine had come together each summer to raise their tipis, where Bear Lake Castle had been erected by the first white traders, where the stone and wood fortress was built by the men of John Franklin's expedition, and only a short distance away, where Father Petitot had constructed a tiny chapel with his own hands for the glory of his God.

Now, standing on top of the pressure ridge, the young boy, tall and silent, looked across the land, as if glimpsing a view of the shadows of a distant past. How surprised those early Europeans would have been to see these happy, delightful, healthy children and their families, filled with strength of pride and independence. How perplexed they would have been to realize how these Sahtuot'ine people, who seemed so destitute and forlorn in earlier times, had, despite considerable losses of life, survived all the ravages of the terrible and unfamiliar diseases introduced by the white man. How amazed they would have been to witness how well these people had adapted to all the changes wrought on their former way of life by the strangers from far way, and how the Sahtuot'ine continued to overcome obstacles placed before them by a succession of ill-informed and uncaring governments. And there is little doubt they would all have been astonished, perhaps awed, to witness these capable Sahtuot'ine maintaining a way of life, a balance of the traditional and the new, in which their children could laugh and play and learn and experience the joy of living, on such a beautiful warm and sunny day.

The Kenny and Takazo families camp on the land during the summer months of 1969.
Photograph courtesy of R. Fumoleau

PART TWO: CHAPTER TWELVE

THE INTERVENING YEARS

I've done it. I'm going back to Fort Franklin. My flight is booked. I closed the travel agent's door behind me and stepped out into the hustling street. It was an unusually hot day for March, the sky a cloudless blue. Many, attired in shorts and T-shirts as was I, revelled in this unseasonable, but welcoming warmth. With the decision made to return to Franklin, I couldn't stop smiling at everyone I passed and it didn't even bother me that they returned my smiles with looks of indifference, wrapped up as they were in their own thoughts.

I had visited the travel agent that morning only to make some inquiries about how long it would take to fly all the way from London, Ontario, to distant Fort Franklin, NWT, and most especially, to find out what the trip would cost. He soon came up with answers to my questions as he checked on the flights. He then turned to me with, "Shall I confirm your flight now?"

And before I could contain myself I replied, "Yes, do so." And it was done. My plans were indelibly locked into the intricacies of Canadian Airline's computer system. My dates, times, locations, flight numbers and even my seat numbers, were a reality.

The travel agent continued, "Can you give me a contact telephone number in Fort Franklin?"

"I'm not yet sure where I will be staying," I replied, feeling rather foolish.

"Well, the name of a hotel?"

"I don't even know if there is an hotel there. I doubt it very much." His quizzical look prompted me to continue. "This is a very small Indian village about five hundred kilometres north of Yellowknife and I haven't been back for almost thirty years. In fact I've had virtually no contact with the village since then."

"Well, that's all right," he interjected. "I don't need the phone number right away. You can give it to me later. Now I'll get you a print-out of your flight itinerary." He stood up. It was all so commonplace to him—he who was used to making reservations for people flying to Honolulu, or Buenos Aires, or Sydney, or Bangkok. There was no similar magic or excitement for him in my flying to a tiny, insignificant, unheard-of village in Canada's Arctic. Only a moment of frustration when he could not get North-Wright Air in Yellowknife to respond to his computer prompting. "I'll have to call them by phone." How barbaric in this day and age, his tone indicated. But none of that now mattered. The completed itinerary in hand, a huge grin on my face, I floated the rest of the way to my car and sped for home.

I suppose it must be difficult for others to comprehend why I was so ecstatic—and ecstatic is how I felt—at knowing that I was finally, after all these years, returning to Franklin and the North. And it must be equally difficult to comprehend why I had maintained so little contact with a place and a people who had obviously once meant a great deal to me. So let me backtrack and provide some accounting of my years following my departure from Fort Franklin in early July 1968.

A small trunkload of personal effects had been sent for safekeeping to the Casey's in Edmonton until my plans for the future had been settled. I had also given away many items in Franklin. I said my goodbyes to people during my last few days and to those who had come to see me off at the dock. I clambered into the waiting de Havilland Twin Otter float plane, said some "Hellos" to my fellow passengers, found the remaining empty seat, and watched the people on the dock disappear quickly from sight. The seventeen-passenger plane swung around to the right to give me one last look, through my tears, at the village and the expanse of ice still covering most of Great Bear Lake.

There was certainly heaviness in my heart as I left behind the community that had been my home for the past three years and all the people I cared about, and where I had learned so much. But, after all, this was only a temporary departure, I thought. I would be back.

Furthermore, I was embarking on another brief adventure. Stuart Hodgson, the commissioner of the NWT, had invited me to accompany his party for a ten-day trek around the higher Arctic. Twice a year, when members of the Legislative Assembly (MLAs) of the new territorial government were transported in a circuitous plane flight to and from Yellowknife and their respective communities, Hodgson filled the remaining empty airplane seats with other people—an assortment of Canadian dignitaries and press people interested in the North, as well as some of his office staff in Yellowknife. He saw this as an inexpensive way to further the understanding of Canadians on the vastness of the North and the uniqueness of its inhabitants.

When I asked him later why I had been invited to join the group he merely said, "Miggs, when I heard you were leaving, I hoped that taking you on this trip might ensure your return. From my dealings with you and the people of Franklin, I know that you're the kind of person we need to help build a new North." Whether he really meant it or not, in my mind this wasn't necessary since I had every intention of returning soon, but who was I to argue with the commissioner? I was too excited at having this opportunity to see more of the North.

We spent the next ten days flying to the communities of Colville Lake, Paulatuk, Sachs Harbour, Holman Island, Coppermine (where we fished for Arctic char at historic Bloody Falls), Bathurst Inlet, Cambridge Bay, Pelly Bay, and to a most beautifully serene location of only two cabins called Thom Bay situated half way up the Booth Peninsula.

It was a most wonderful experience visiting all these Inuit settlements and meeting, eating and talking with many of the local people. At Pelly Bay, I met an ivory carver of renown whose work had been chosen to give to the Queen and Prince Philip the year before. And then there was the elderly couple at Bathurst Inlet, he in his sealskin two piece "suit" and seal *kamiks*, and she in her "Mother Hubbard."[1] They were such a delightful couple, now in their seventies, but rumour had it that fifty years ago he had killed his wife's former husband in a duel.

Then there was our scary departure from Holman Island where we had stayed overnight in the land of continuous summer daylight. With the coming of "morning," we saw that all the ice floes had blown into the bay leaving us with no clear pathway for our take-off. That's when I discovered one of the many special talents of the Twin Otter. While the rest waited in the village and I sat on a bluff overlooking the harbour, the pilot spent the next two hours repeatedly shuffling the float plane forwards and backwards, edging the floes to each side with his pontoons, until a watery "runway" had been cleared for us.

At his command we hastily climbed aboard. I got to sit up front with the pilot but that only gave me a closer view of how rapidly our clear space was disappearing as the stiff breeze pushed the floes back into our pathway. As the pilot raced, full throttle, down the narrowing span of water, with the ice floes closing in on us, I sat still, gripping my seat, my eyes glued ahead. And I am sure to this day that when the pilot finally pulled back on the throttle and carried us safely towards the next village, we could only have cleared the ice floes by inches. Although the pilot had remained calm throughout, and no doubt had done this many times before, I had been terrified. However, it was our only close call on the entire trip.

In many ways, the small villages reminded me of Franklin and the Inuit were also warm and welcoming. Some day, I decided, I would like to come and live and teach up here too. One day, after I had returned to Franklin. There was so much of this wonderful northern country to experience.

Ten days later, with half of our human cargo left behind in their home settlements, we headed back towards Yellowknife. During the several hours of crossing the Barrens and the Thelon River, I thought about some of those early Europeans who had travelled and lived here: Samuel Hearne and his Indian guide, Matonabbee, on their long journey from Fort Churchill to the Arctic Ocean in the 1770s; John Franklin and his two overland expeditions; Back and Dease and Simpson and many others in the late 1800s who came, primarily, to search for Franklin, lost on his third expedition.

I thought about many other Canadian explorers on personal quests in the early years of the twentieth century, such as George M. Douglas and Jack Hornby, people made legends in their own time. Men, and later a few women, who had all felt the incredible pull of Canada's northern lands, and despite the tremendous hardships all had encountered, had returned again and again. Their tales of endurance and strength of body and spirit, even when ultimately the North defeated them, as was the case with Jack Hornby and his two young companions, are tales worth reading.

Marvelling at the way these Outsiders had endured such hardships led me to recall again the original and permanent inhabitants of these lands—the Indians and, beyond the tree line, the Inuit, people who had lived here continuously for thousands of years, who had to struggle to exist day in and day out, for their entire lives—which they did with a daily sense of gratitude and happiness when sufficient food and shelter was available for them and their families.

I spent a few days in Yellowknife—a Yellowknife which had recently acquired its first traffic light, much to the disgust of the local residents—before heading for Saskatoon. One of Commissioner Hodgson's guests on our trip had been Dr. Lloyd Barber, dean of Economics at the University of Saskatchewan. During one of our many mid-air conversations, I had outlined my plans for pursuing cross-cultural education courses in Phoenix, Arizona. He informed me that the University of Saskatchewan had just begun a similar master's program at Saskatoon, and in his persuasive and erudite manner, he convinced me that I should maintain my loyalty to Canada and enrol in the Saskatoon program!

At that time, in order to obtain a master's degree at the University of Saskatchewan, it was necessary for me to combine my studies in Indian and Northern Education with another recognised post-graduate course, so I also enrolled in the Department of Geography, on the condition that I could pursue a thesis that would enable me to return to the North, and, more specifically, to Fort Franklin. This was agreed to and later on I was awarded a scholarship from the Institute for Northern Studies which paid for much of my travel expenses back North the following summer to obtain background information for my thesis. Under the title of "Great Bear Lake Indians: A Historical Demography and Human Ecology," I detailed the reasons for the decline in the Dene population surrounding Great Bear Lake from precontact days to the end of the nineteenth century.

During that summer of 1969 I first spent a month near Echo Bay, at the eastern end of Great Bear Lake, where I stayed at Arctic Circle Lodge, a sports-fisherman's paradise. I had never been to this eastern end of the lake, where many Sahtuot'ine families had formerly camped while awaiting the caribou, and I wished to explore the area. I made a deal with Arctic Circle Lodge that I would work mornings for them—housekeeping chores—in exchange for my room and board, leaving my afternoons free to search for evidence of Dene habitation in the area.

Then I managed to hitch a ride to Franklin on one of their charters and, with

Chief Victor Beyonnie's permission, pitched my tent along the lake shore not far from the church. It was good to be back although many people were away from the village: several men were working at the fishing lodges or on the barges, and whole families, including many of my students, had returned to the bush or tundra to live off the land for the summer. But I enjoyed my time there: berry picking with the kids, going fishing on the lake or river, talking to some of the older people about their memories of the past, and searching, without success, for signs of John Franklin's expeditionary stone fortress in the vicinity of the Little Lake. A hundred and forty years of ice and snow as well as the growth of moss, shrubs and small trees had hidden all traces of these once sturdy buildings.

None of the children bothered my tent down by the lake, so I was surprised one day to see the flap door open as I approached. Inside, lying on my sleeping bag, was Francis. He awoke as I entered.

"I came to see you but it was so warm in your tent I guess I just fell asleep," he said with a sheepish grin.

"It's OK, Francis. I'm glad to see you. I was hoping I would," and I meant it because I had always been very fond of Francis. I suppose it had a lot to do with all those evenings he would spend at my 512 where we sometimes chatted and sometimes sat reading in silence. He was now seventeen and looked more like a young man than the adolescent kid I remembered. As I made us some soup and Francis made the tea, he asked about my past year and brought me up to date on happenings in his life and in the village. The year's absence disappeared in these mundane tasks and comfortable chat. I saw him several more times during my stay. Tragically, within five years Francis would be dead.

All too soon it came time for me to leave Franklin and head for Fort Smith near the NWT-Alberta border. I needed to study the earliest church birth, marriage and death records pertaining to the Sahtuot'ine for my thesis and the Oblate fathers there had promised to make them available to me. I was also able to spend a very enjoyable afternoon in Fort Smith with Judy and Jane as they now attended Grandin College, a residential high school that had already earned an excellent reputation for educating the most capable students in the North.

Back in Saskatoon I spent the next year working on my thesis, as all my course work in Indian and Northern Education had been completed. Also, for a change of pace, I took classes in Inuktitut—the language of the Inuit, which would eventually prove useful.

In time I wrote to the Department of Education in Yellowknife making them aware of my intention to return to the North and shortly afterwards received a phone call offering me a position in the Keewatin District on the west coast of Hudson Bay. Although my first choice was to return to the Western Arctic, the role of language arts consultant was very tempting and I accepted. For the next two and a half years I was privileged and fortunate to work in the best job possible, and it would take another book to do it justice!

At that time, all NWT government departments for the Keewatin Region were based in Fort Churchill, Manitoba. I was to assist teachers in nine Inuit communities, mainly on the west coast of Hudson Bay in an area that measured some 900 kilometres north to south. My rather vague job description provided me with an excellent opportunity to put my educational beliefs into practice. With the approval of my superintendent Gerard Mulders, the assistance of other educators, especially principal Peter Balt of Whale Cove, and the support of Inuit parents, we worked to create schools where Inuktitut (the Inuit language) would predominate in the early years, while English was being taught as a second language. Local Inuit classroom assistants were trained to become integral in the teaching process, and reading materials that were culturally meaningful to the children were produced in Inuktitut. And it was my job to coordinate and assist in this entire process.

It was a wonderful time in education. There were so many excited, hard-working people involved in the process, both Inuit and Kabloona (white people), and I was indeed fortunate to be in the middle of it all in these early stages. In fact, it took the Department of Education in Yellowknife, whose emphasis was directed primarily towards the Western Arctic, more than a decade before it allowed the Dene to become similarly involved in the education process of their children.

And then I walked away from it all.

All the travelling and living out of a suitcase for some twenty-five days every month began wearing me down. Trips from community to community in drafty DC3s or Piper Comanches or Beechcraft, and long Ski-doo trips between settlements, such as the 120-kilometre journey between Rankin Inlet and Whale Cove, in temperatures that were consistently well below minus 20°C, began to take their toll on my health.

Furthermore, the few days spent back at Churchill played havoc with my social life, and although everyone with whom I stayed in each community was always very kind, I was always a visitor, a guest. More and more, now in my mid-thirties, I began to feel the need to establish roots in Canada. Although I had lived in my adopted country for almost ten years, I still didn't have anywhere to really call home. Fort Franklin had come the closest to that. Should I return there? Should I try to put down roots anywhere else in the North? The doctor finally settled that by telling me that if I were to regain my health fully, especially my chronic chest congestion and increasing back problems, I would have to leave the North.[2]

Despite all these reasons, the decision to leave did not come easily. The North was truly in my blood. My time spent at both Franklin and in the Keewatin had been the most exciting, interesting and productive years of my life. I loved my work and I loved the people I worked with—the Dene of Franklin and the Inuit of the Keewatin. What was it? Their openness, their friendliness, their sense of joy at life despite all its hardships, their sense of appreciation, their willingness to take all persons—Native or non-Native—as they were, their lack of pretence and putting on airs, their sense of optimism and dignity in the face of adversity, their sense of serenity, of fun and enjoyment for even the smallest and simplest of things. Somehow they managed to maintain a core of the wonder of childhood blended into an overall mature sense of perspective and proportion towards life—a sense of wholeness.

But leave I did, in December of 1972, for London, Ontario. Many have described the lure of the North as being akin to a drug, an addiction, and I knew it was true. Only by severing all my connections to the North (going cold turkey!) would I have any chance of putting down roots in southern Canada. Once in London, my involvement in teaching children with special needs soon became my primary school focus and, in time, as I readjusted to the ways of an urban society, I came to enjoy both my life and work, at first in London itself, and later in the nearby countryside.

With my roots now secure in Ontario, I no longer shut out the occasional news of events pertaining to the North and, increasingly, I realized that I still wanted to return for a visit, and most especially to Fort Franklin. I wanted to know what had happened to my former students and others in the village after all these years. Had the people of Franklin managed to maintain their independence and sense of pride with which I had become so familiar, or had events engulfed them, particularly the influence of southern society and inappropriate government actions, as they had with so many other Aboriginal people throughout Canada?

The summer of 1994 brought the World Cup of Soccer to North America, and when I realized that I would see none of it on my TV stations, I rented a satellite dish. Besides providing me with a feast of soccer which I thoroughly enjoyed, having been an avid player and follower in my youth, the satellite dish also brought CBC North into my living room. I was soon glued for hours listening to programs from the North, often in Inuktitut and some in Slavey or other Indian dialects. I absorbed the North back into my being and rekindled memories from the past.

One day, as I watched the Queen and Prince Philip visit Yellowknife, Ethel Blondin-Andrew, formerly of Fort Franklin and now the federal member of Parliament for the Western Arctic, introduced the community chiefs of the Mackenzie District to the Queen. When I heard Ethel introduce "George Cleary of the Sahtuot'ine" to the Queen, I leapt up.

"That's my Georgie! That's my little Georgie who came South with me in the summer of 1967!"

"Does it look like him?" my friend asked.

George must be close to forty, I thought. "It could be. It's hard to visualise an eleven-year-old after all these years. But there is something familiar about him and surely there can't be too many George Cleary's. It has to be him."

Seeing George had made me even more eager to return to Franklin but could I just hop on a plane and visit again after more than twenty-five years? Surely I must have a tangible reason for doing so. What if I arrived and no one remembered or recognized me? Where would I stay? And, in practical terms, could I afford what was bound to be a considerable expense, just on a whim?

I began resurrecting my old slides of Franklin. The memories came rushing back and I began to write about my adventures of those special years in the sixties and, more importantly, to tell the story of these people, these Sahtuot'ine, whom I had loved and admired for so long. Increasingly, I came to realize that this was a story that needed to be told. After six months of looking at my slides and writing about the people, collectively and as individuals, I knew that I had to return, and thank goodness for the encouragement and support of my good friend, Alison, who understood this need.

And that's how I came to book my flight to Fort Franklin, on that beautiful day in March.

In the meantime I wrote to George and told him about seeing him with the Queen in Yellowknife, a little about myself and present life, and that I wanted to return to Déline. I had phoned to enquire about the accommodation rates in the small local hotel and discovered that it was very expensive. So I asked George if he knew of someone who might be willing to rent their place to me while away for the summer.

Some weeks later I received a long, newsy letter from George, accompanied by a photo of himself with his wife, Doreen, and two sons and two daughters. He began by apologizing for the delay in replying. He now lived and worked in Yellowknife and he had not received my letter until he had visited Déline on business. Then he confirmed that he was indeed the George who was my former student. He had become chief of the Déline Band in 1988, but was now president of the larger Sahtu Dene Council, and it was in that role that he had been introduced to the Queen in Yellowknife. He also expressed his great pleasure at hearing from me and to learn that I was planning to return to Déline. Finally, he assured me that I needn't worry about my accommodations—he would look after things. I was extremely happy to hear from him—from "my Georgie," realizing that I would now have to practise calling him "George," as befitted his age and status.

I called George the next day to express my delight at receiving his newsy letter and we chatted for ages. From then on, however, most of our correspondence was carried out by fax as George proved to be a hard man to get a hold of. His business for the Sahtu council had him constantly on the go between Déline, Yellowknife, Edmonton and Ottawa.

My accommodation arrangements were now secured. I would stay with his daughter and family in Yellowknife and with his sister and family in Déline. The relief I felt from knowing this was immense and I was indeed grateful to George for taking charge of things. Now I could finally relax and deal with the relatively minor issues of what to take with me, such as clothes, camera equipment, notebooks, gifts, etc.

Only days before leaving, while I was still scrambling to get everything done, I received a phone call.

"Miggs. It's Judy," said a rather deep and unfamiliar voice, then silence.

Judy. I know several Judys but I immediately realized who this was even though I had not spoken to her since 1969 in Fort Smith.

"Judy Tutcho," more of a statement than a question. "Where are you calling from?"

She was staying in Ottawa for the summer. She had heard that I was returning to Déline and since she could not be there, asked if I could come to Ottawa. In many ways the timing couldn't have been worse since I still had much to do before leaving, but I had to go, even if only for a couple of days.

As my train pulled into the Ottawa station, it suddenly dawned on me that I had not asked Judy for a description of herself, as I recalled a young girl of sixteen with long black hair—would we recognize each other? But I was no sooner off the train when this woman of roughly my height, with short, black, curly hair, dark sunglasses and a huge grin came racing towards with me with arms extended and calling my name. I guess I hadn't changed that much, but her curly hair had certainly thrown me.

Within a very short period of time, after introducing me to her two sons of twelve and six, her brother Earl, and a friend, the talking between us flowed easily. She seemed just as vivacious and gregarious as I remembered and, as we talked, both with so much to say, the intervening years just melted away. Judi, as she now preferred to spell her name, had long since obtained her degree and teaching qualifications, and had been a teacher and principal for many years in several locations in the North and now, much to my surprise, was the principal in Déline.

"In Déline? That's wonderful, but you won't be there when I return." I was very disappointed. However, it seemed that most of my former students, including Jane, would be there.

We talked and talked long into the night about all kinds of things as we tried to cram our lives of twenty-six years into a few short hours. It had been very special meeting again with Judi as well as meeting her sons, Sean and Spencer, but all too soon it was time for me to return to London.

A couple of days later, I was on my way back up North to where I had began my northern teaching career thirty years earlier in the tiny settlement of Fort Franklin on the shores of Great Bear Lake, home of the Sahtuot'ine.

Church organist Louis Taniton and his wife, Rosa, now in their eighties. Taken in Déline in 1995.

CHAPTER THIRTEEN

AND WHAT OF THE SAHTUOT'INE?

And what of the Sahtuot'ine? What had happened to them in the years since I had briefly visited Fort Franklin in the summer of 1969? In order to answer these questions let us pick up the Dene's story after the signing of Treaty 11 in 1921.

Successive governments, unwilling or unable to appreciate the strength and endurance of the people who had survived and lived independently on these lands for thousands of years before the coming of the Europeans, continued policies of assimilation across Canada.

One of the most insidious ways in which the Canadian government practiced assimilation was through the use of residential schools run for the government by the churches.[1] Much has been written about the thousands of Native children throughout Canada who were taken from their parents and their communities and placed in church-run schools and their accompanying residences, sometimes for several years, without any contact with their homes. In fact, many parents weren't even told where their children had gone.

No doubt many of the religious teachers and staff were well intentioned and cared for their charges, yet the methods used were totally alien to the children's upbringing by their parents and extended families. Children were often treated harshly. Many were beaten for speaking their own language, separated from their siblings, and taught to fear God if they did not obey those in charge of their schooling. Much has also come to light in recent years about the extent of sexual abuse perpetrated on these children.

Less has been written about the devastation inflicted on the parents when their children were forcibly taken from them—the silence, the suffering caused by the emptiness in their lives with no sounds of children laughing and playing, and the dreadful lack of self-worth parents felt from being told by the government's actions that they were no longer capable of bringing up and caring for their own children.

When the children eventually returned to their communities many years later, they were scarred by these experiences, unable to speak their native language and therefore unable to communicate with their parents and grandparents, and no longer familiar with the cultural mores and values of their families and communities. Most continued to suffer for years from a sense of disorientation and not belonging.

The toll of this past legacy is still deeply felt in most Native communities, especially across southern Canada. However, as more people speak out, it is coming to light that many children and youth in the North, including those of Sahtuot'ine families, were similarly treated.

In 1946 the federal Department of National Health and Welfare began to address the disgraceful conditions of health for the Northern people where chronic sickness was still pervasive, the infant mortality rate very high, and TB on the increase.[2] Northern Health Services was created and, in the fifties and sixties, small nursing stations were established in most settlements, with flight access to hospitals in the larger towns available for more serious situations.

In 1955 the Department of Indian Affairs began a major restructuring of the northern school program. Under this new policy, the government decided to provide a public school system with elementary facilities for all northern children in their home communities by 1970. Secondary schools, financed jointly by the federal and territorial governments, were to be built in the larger settlements, along with large hostels run by religious affiliations to accommodate the older students.

The Dene of the Western Arctic (Denendeh) had always placed a high priority on their children's education, where they learned their values, skills and attitudes from and through direct daily participation with their parents and grandparents. In time, as changes in the North continued, many Dene came to recognize that there were indeed advantages for young people to receive a good academic and vocational education that would prepare them for the changing future, as long as they could also retain the tradition of learning from their parents in the vocations of trapping, hunting and fishing.[3] But, as usual, the Dene were not consulted about their views on what was best for their children. Southern educational programs and teachers, of which I was one, though well intentioned, taught all academics and some vocational subjects in English, but there were no attempts to involve Native people, nor things that were important to their culture, in the process.

With the construction of many elementary schools in the fifties and sixties and the government actively encouraging the Dene to settle in permanent communities, the enrolment of students gradually increased, and the pattern of family life began to change. The men continued to hunt and trap in the bush while the children and their mothers settled in drafty log cabins close to the school, church, nursing station and trading post. An added incentive was the network of social services such as family allowance payments and old age pensions now available to all Canadians. These increasingly came to provide the basis of the family's food supply for many months of the year. Thus, for the first time, a relationship of dependence on government supports and an economy that revolved around money began to characterize the Dene's lives.

As the rights and interests of the Dene, who formed the majority population in the Western Arctic, were repeatedly disregarded, the gulf between them and the minority non-Natives in the North continued to grow. Feelings of being disenfranchised within their own lands increased among the Natives as they found themselves able to have less say in the utilization and administration of their own land. Every year more mines were discovered and opened, roads built, parks proposed, oil and gas wells drilled—all without the consent of those people on whose land all this was occurring.

After decades of having their language and cultural values denigrated by the church and government, with little incentive to follow the pattern of life practiced for so long, with diminished control over their own lives, as well as the alienation felt by those who had spent years in residential schools, many turned to alcohol in an effort to forget their pain, their boredom, their lack of hope, their guilt and their sense of worthlessness. And with the increased use of alcohol and other drugs came an increase in family violence and the abuse and neglect of children. Community life became a destructive environment. The Dene became increasingly enmeshed in a cycle of dependency and destruction from which there seemed to be no escape. And, worse, they felt powerless to do anything about their plight.

Out of this quagmire of despair and degradation arose a number of Dene who came together to begin the long climb back. A powerful Dene revival was born and it took many forms: a new political awareness, pride in their cultural and traditional values, and the emergence of a spiritual renewal.

In the past, because of their differing dialects and languages, there had been little contact between the various Native groups, and the Dene had usually dealt with the government as separate communities. Increasingly in the late 1960s, as they began having more contact with each other the Dene began to realize that their former patient approach with the government wasn't working. If they were to survive as a people with needs that were clearly different from those of non-Natives, the only answer to this increasing loss of control over their own lives was to organize themselves, politically and economically.

When sixteen Dene chiefs met in Fort Smith in 1969 under the sponsorship of the Department of Indian Affairs and Northern Development (DIAND), the chiefs agreed they needed a more independent organization to represent their concerns and the Indian Brotherhood of the Northwest Territories (IBNWT) was formed, with James Wah-Shee elected as the first president. The hope generated by this new Dene organization was verbalized by an elderly Dogrib woman: "They could ignore some of us, and beat some of us, and steal from some of us, and pat some of us on the head before, but they will never be able to do that to us again, because we have our Indian Brotherhood now."[4]

The Indian Brotherhood turned its attention to the major issue plaguing the Dene since the signing of treaties eight and eleven: the government's total disregard of the fact that the Dene had not given up their land in these treaties. A number of oil companies had already obtained permits for oil and gas exploration from the government, as well as land-use permits to do exploration work on Dene lands. Then in 1971 the federal government, disregarding the aboriginal rights of the Dene, and giving no thought to the severe social and environmental consequences of such an action, announced that it would encourage and support the construction of an overland pipeline to carry northern oil to markets in southern Canada.

Since this pipeline would traverse those lands covered by treaties eight and eleven, the government, in order to avoid any possible political embarrassment, made an offer to the Indian Brotherhood that included promises to establish reserves and provide a financial compensation package to the Dene. The IBNWT rejected the offer, persisting in the traditional Dene interpretation of the treaties and re-stating that they had never extinguished their rights to the land. They also rejected the government's simplistic "cash for land" approach. They knew only too clearly that if their cultures were to survive they would have to secure some degree of ongoing control over their lands. "No pipeline before land claims settlement" became their battle cry.[5]

After spending the summer of 1973 travelling to all the Dene communities to hear evidence from the old people regarding the treaties, Mr. Justice William Morrow, of the Supreme Court of the Northwest Territories, brought down his landmark decision which stated that the "indigenous people" were the owners of the land covered by the caveat and "that they have what is known as aboriginal rights...."[6] He further endorsed the Dene's position by stating that he doubted that aboriginal title to the land had ever been extinguished and that the Dene should be permitted to put forward a claim for title to the land. Judge Morrow also admonished the Canadian government stating that it had an obligation to protect the legal rights of the Native people.[7]

In 1969 Dr. Lloyd Barber, with whom I had travelled in the Twin Otter Arctic trip in July 1968, was appointed Indian claims commissioner for Canada. Five years later in a speech in Yellowknife relating to the treatment of the Indians of the North by the federal government, he said:

> I cannot emphasize too strongly that we are in a new ball game. The old approaches are out. We've been allowed to delude ourselves for a long time because of the basic lack of political power in Native communities. This is no longer the case and there is no way that the newly emerging political and legal power of the Native people is likely to diminish. We must face the situation squarely as a political fact of life but, more importantly, as a fundamental point of honour and fairness. We do, indeed, have a significant piece of unfinished business that lies at the foundation of this country.[8]

Recognizing the importance of the Morrow decision and the sentiments expressed by Barber and others, the minister of Indian Affairs told the Northwest Territories Council in January 1974 that "the time has come to meet and deal with the Native peoples' concerns, including claims."[9]

The sixties and seventies had been heady times for the Dene. Much had happened under the guidance of the Indian Brotherhood that enabled the Dene to believe they were, once again, able to exert some control over their lives. The second annual Joint General Assembly of the Indian Brotherhood and the Métis and Non-Status Association of the Northwest Territories was held in July of 1975 at Fort Simpson on the Mackenzie (Dehcho) River. At this assembly more than three hundred delegates voted unanimously to adopt the historic Dene Declaration. These are its opening words:

> We the Dene of the Northwest Territories insist on the right to be regarded by ourselves and the world as a nation. Our struggle is for the recognition of the Dene Nation by the government and people of Canada and the peoples and governments of the world....

This moving statement of their struggle to be recognized as a distinct people, ended with these words: "What we seek then is independence and self-determination within the country of Canada. This is what we mean when we call for a just settlement for the Dene Nation."[10]

Spoken with eloquence and pride, the Dene Declaration became a milestone in the evolution of Native politics in the North. For the first time, the Dene had declared themselves to be a single nation, a kind of "northern confederacy through which diverse groups drew on cultural similarities to pursue common political goals while still maintaining a sense of connection with local communities and traditions."[11]

But the Dene's troubles were far from over. Of increasing concern was the fact that the oil and gas companies kept applying pressure to build a pipeline and a road through the Mackenzie Valley, the heart of their lands.

In response to an increasing awareness and empathy across Canada for Native concerns, the federal government agreed to sponsor a commission of inquiry into the potential social, environmental, and economic impact of pipeline development and operation in the North. Mr. Justice Thomas Berger from British Columbia was appointed commissioner. In addition to travelling to several cities in southern Canada in 1975, the Berger Commission also visited thirty-five communities in the North where it listened to almost a thousand northerners.

Wherever the Berger Commission's public hearings were held, the Dene felt that, for the first time, their voices were being heard.[12] In each community the people spoke to Justice Berger with passion, eloquence and pride about the life that they once had. And they spoke with pain and despair about the life that had become lost over the decades, lost to diseases left to run rampant throughout families because of the lack of medical assistance, the splitting up of families and the loss of their children to schools and hospitals far away, the loss of their culture and language in schools that were oblivious of what was important to them, the loss of their income and sense of independence with the decline in the fur industry and increasing game restrictions, and the loss of their land to the development of oil, gas and minerals. They talked about the impact of the pipeline and the accompanying development of an infrastructure on the land, on the migratory caribou and other animals, and most of all on the people.[13]

After twenty-one months of debates and presentations up and down the Mackenzie Valley, in English, Slavey, Dogrib, Gwichi'n and Chipewyan, Judge Berger declared at the last session on November 19, 1976:

> There is a kind of conventional wisdom that says that a decision like this should only be made by the people in government and industry. They have the knowledge, they have the facts and they have the experience. Well, the hearings we have held show that the conventional wisdom is wrong....
>
> At this Inquiry we have tried to discover the true North. I say that because we have to understand the condition of the North today if we are going to be able to predict what the impact of the pipeline and the corridor will be....
>
> The future of the North is a matter that is important to us all. What happens here will tell us something about what kind of a country Canada is, what kind of people we are.[14]

When Justice Berger's comprehensive report was submitted to the federal government in 1977, he recommended that the Mackenzie Valley pipeline, or any other major project in the Dehcho Valley, should be postponed for ten years to allow sufficient time for Native land claims to be settled, for new programs and institutions to be established, and for an orderly, not hasty, program of exploitation.

His report angered and frustrated many, particularly those who would experience a loss of potential fortunes. However, for the Dene, it was a vindication of their rights as a people worthy of due consideration. At last, their voices had been heard.

However, despite the recommendations of the Berger Commission, the federal government continued to provide financial support for the development of considerable resource exploitation throughout the North and oil and gas companies continued to plan the Mackenzie pipeline.[15] The Dene and Inuit came to recognize that despite their earlier successes, they could no longer stop the government from exploiting the resources on their lands. Once that became clear, the focus for change for the Dene now turned from exerting political rights to ensuring management rights through the settlement of land claims. This was a major shift in philosophy and direction for the Dene but they believed that settling the land claims would assure them of a large measure of self-government coupled with increased economic self-sufficiency, thus enabling them to deal with the serious and mounting concerns of their communities.

At the initiation of negotiations between the federal government and the

Native people, federal negotiators adamantly insisted that comprehensive claims would only deal with lands and resources. When the Dene and Inuit balked at this, funds were cut off and negotiations went nowhere. Threats to terminate the process were made, so grudgingly, the people agreed to negotiate claims on this basis, but only on the condition that self-government would be addressed in other forums.

The Dene worked within this framework through their comprehensive land claims in the 1980s. This process, begun in 1981, culminated in an agreement-in-principle (AIP) being initialled in 1988. The government made its offer regarding land ownership, subsurface mineral rights, and compensation for land-use lost in the past. In return the Dene would agree to extinguish their aboriginal rights and give up their land claims to remaining lands in the NWT.

That July, a special joint assembly was held at Hay River to study the proposals. Many serious concerns were raised by the Dene, but of greatest concern was that the AIP represented a loss of their aboriginal rights through the loss of title to the lands.[16] Some participants argued that part of the agreement had to be renegotiated and there was talk of pursuing issues again through the courts. But the federal government refused to consider further renegotiations. As a result, the Dene-Métis comprehensive claim negotiations broke down, posing a major challenge to the Dene Nation.

At this point the federal Department of Indian Affairs (DIAND) announced that it would be willing to negotiate separate regional agreements.[17] Those who refused would have their funds cut off.[18] With their backs to the wall two of the Dene groups indicated a willingness to negotiate their own separate agreements with the government. The Gwich'in, located near the northern Yukon border, settled their agreement in September 1991 when it was ratified by a heavy turnout of voters.

The second group were the Sahtu Dene of the Great Bear Lake (Sahtu) region, representing the communities of Fort Franklin (Déline), Fort Norman (Tulit'a), Norman Wells (Le Gohlini), Fort Good Hope (Radeli Ko) and Colville Lake (K'ahbamitue). For several months discussions continued among the people in the five settlements led by their president and chief negotiator, George Cleary of Fort Franklin (Déline). Finally, in September 1993, with Norman Yakaleya of Fort Norman as the new chief negotiator (George remained president of the Sahtu Dene Council and Secretariat), the Sahtu Dene also arrived at a comprehensive land claim agreement for the Dene and Métis of the Sahtu region, similar to that of the Gwich'in and for many of the same reasons.

As stated in the Sahtu Dene claim, "nothing in this agreement or in the settlement legislation shall remove from the Sahtu Dene or Métis their identity as aboriginal people of Canada...."[19] However, they did cede certain rights formerly specified in Treaty 11 in order, in the view of the Sahtu Dene, to receive other more important benefits for their people.

Many Native groups across Canada saw this as a sell-out to the government but such thinking fails to give credit to the Gwich'in and Sahtu Dene who obviously had a clear agenda to pursue, based on what was best for the communities they represented.[20] They believed that, in order to become healthy again, aboriginal societies must have more control over the most fundamental influences that shape and define their culture. Their distinct values and ways of doing things must be reflected in their own institutions. Only by dealing with their concerns together at the local level could the people return to their original values and provide opportunities for people to regain their respect and dignity. It was the local people who best knew the problems each community faced, and they wanted to take an active role in creating solutions for these serious issues.[21]

Although there appears to be a large gulf between both points of view, these differences in priorities and perspectives are no doubt a reflection of each group's unique situation. The very different history and geography of Canada's northern Natives have led to a set of circumstances that appear to require different solutions from those of their brethren in the South.

Many realistic fears about the future persist, for the dislocation and turbulence wrought by such momentous and rapid changes in recent decades has brought its toll on the people. Alongside an increasing wealth of material goods, improved housing and basic amenities, increased opportunities for attainable and often well-paid employment, more relevant educational programs, and easier access to adult learning, all northern communities suffer, in varying degrees, with problems of substance abuse, dysfunctional families, neglect of children, insufficient employment, increased suicide, aimless and confused teenagers, feelings of alienation and a general inability to cope with the rapid changes.

But the people have come a long way since the signing of Treaty 11 in 1921. When at a very low ebb in the late sixties and early seventies, Dene groups, in their hour of need and almost as a last desperate cry for their survival, came together, recalled their pride, talked until a consensus was arrived at, and plans were made for the formation of the Indian Brotherhood and then a Dene Nation. Together they drew on their combined strength and from their renewed spiritual relationship to the land as they continued their daily struggles to survive in a confusing new world of accelerating changes.

Such was my recently gained knowledge of significant events in the Western Arctic (Denendeh), including those occurring between my departure from Fort Franklin in 1968 and my impending, long overdue visit in the summer of 1995, to Déline, as the village was now officially named.

But of Déline itself, and the impact of all these changes on the village, I knew virtually nothing. I had learned that its size and population had increased considerably. Other snippets of information had occasionally come my way from people who worked and travelled in the North. One person had described Déline of the 1970s as "the armpit of the North." Another had said that the people remained proud and strong despite the problems brought by the rapid changes. Yet again, the news of the Sahtu Dene land claim settlement led me to believe that there surely remained much of the fighting spirit of the past in the people of Déline. But my excitement at returning was more than tinged with apprehension at what I was about to discover for myself.

The western end of an enlarged Déline in the summer of 1995. Notice the tipi on the right erected among the newer, attractively built log houses.

CHAPTER FOURTEEN

RETURN TO DÉLINE: JULY 14, 1995

"Miggs. Below you. That's the south shore of the lake." I could barely hear George Cleary's words over the loud vibrations of the small Beechcraft airplane. I peered out of the oval window. There it was, barely visible, a narrow strip of pale yellow sand fringing the waters of Sahtu (Great Bear Lake). A moment later it was gone, shrouded by the dense smoke that had prevented us from seeing anything since leaving Yellowknife a couple of hours earlier.

The forest fires that had plagued much of northern Canada during the early months of the summer of 1995 had brought Tulit'a (Fort Norman) and Norman Wells into national prominence when their entire populations had to be evacuated the previous month to Déline and Yellowknife, respectively. Although the fires were now under sufficient control to enable people to return home, their power to erupt again from the remaining hot spots was still a constant concern and the erratic spewing of smoke continued. This day, a brisk westerly wind had caused the smoke to blanket an area extending for more than two hundred kilometres to the east of the Dehcho (Mackenzie River), reducing visibility above two hundred metres to zero.

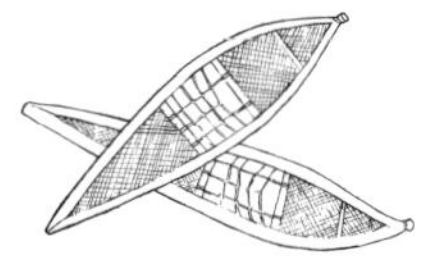

Two days had passed since I had arrived at Yellowknife, landing in bright sunlight at 10:15 PM. I was indeed back in the Land of the Midnight Sun even though Yellowknife lay several hundred kilometres south of the Arctic Circle. The capital of the Northwest Territories, with a current population of more than fifteen thousand, had grown considerably since my last visit in 1969, but, as I peered out of the plane window during our descent, my memories of the former Yellowknife were too vague to make a meaningful comparison of its size.

Struggling across the tarmac with my heavy and bulky hand-luggage, not for the first time did I curse the weight of all my 1960s slides, duplicate photos to be shared with others, and camera equipment. But I would not relinquish them to the mercy of the flight baggage handling system.

None of that mattered for more than a fleeting moment. I was back up North for the first time in more than twenty years, and there to meet me at the terminal were George and Doreen, instantly recognizable from the photo I had received from George in May. The hugs and talking came easily as George carried my precious hand-luggage and one of my other two bags, which was even heavier. I knew I had far too many clothes with me but I had come prepared to face the extremes of temperature that can occur in the summer up North.

George pointed out various landmarks for me to visit during my brief stay, as he drove us to their daughter Cheryl's home where I was to stay, located on the narrow, rocky peninsula in what is known as Yellowknife's Old Town. Here is where modern Yellowknife had its origins when prospectors from across Canada arrived in the early 1930s to lay claim to the rocky areas where gold had been discovered. Gary and Cheryl's newly-built house was representative of many of the spacious and attractive modern houses now replacing the hastily constructed miners' shanties of former days.

Over the next two days, I became reacquainted with George and Doreen and their family. I remembered Doreen in John Talbot's class when the Gaudet family moved to Déline in the fall of 1967 but I hadn't known her very well. She is now a counsellor at a Yellowknife secondary school. In addition to Cheryl, they have two teenage sons and a young daughter.

The next evening they invited Gary, Cheryl, their two young sons, and me over for dinner. Also present was Doreen's mother, Phoebe, whom I well remembered as she had changed surprisingly little. She was accompanied by her present husband, Hugh. Her previous husband, George Gaudet, former power plant operator at Déline, had died in 1992. I was also delighted to meet Doreen's sister, Sarah, who had been in my class that last year. She had arrived from Norman Wells where she had been a teacher and school principal for several years. She was now married with four children.

Later that evening, after we had all feasted on caribou, moose, barbecued lake trout, potatoes, vegetables and sumptuous desserts, John Bekale (formerly Mantla), another of the four boys whom I had taken south in 1967, arrived with his wife. John, as easy going and gregarious as ever, had returned to his original family name when he moved to Behcho Ko (Fort Rae) in the 1970s.

After doing the dishes and tidying up, we all sat outside on George and Doreen's porch, as the three of us—George, John and I—regaled the rest with tales of our southern summer adventures all those years ago. And in the telling of what we best remembered, I found myself fascinated by the different individual memories that each of us had carried over time. But there was no disputing that riding horses and swimming had been John and George's favourite activities.

John went on to share with me events of his past and present life. He is a former Dogrib chief and, like George, continues to be actively involved in local politics as he works to assist his people. The Dogribs are currently in their last stages of negotiating their land claim, similar to that achieved by the Sahtu Dene in which George had been very instrumental. He is also considered to be quite a crack golfer, having won several tournaments in the Yellowknife area.

There was something quite magical about the evening as we drank coffee and discussed events from almost thirty years before in an atmosphere that was comfortable and welcoming, almost as if I had been accepted back into the extended family, a kind of quiet understanding that although events might have kept us apart all these years, a bond still existed between us.

Suddenly George leaned across the aisle again and yelled loudly, "Right below you. That's Déline." Ever since seeing that strip of yellow sand, I had kept peering through the dense smoke for any sign of the village, having long since accepted that there would be no aerial photographs today. And now there it was, a hundred metres below me and to my left. We flew the length of the village before turning and straightening out for a smooth landing on the sizeable airstrip located north west of the village. I had expected Déline to be much larger than the village I had left behind in the late sixties, but I was not prepared for being unable to locate even one of the buildings I used to know: no silvery white church, no yellow school, no pink nursing station, no log community hall, and no white and red Hudson's Bay post.

The small plane came to a halt. I stepped out and glanced all around me, recognizing nothing and no one. But it didn't matter. I was back. Back home. I moved away from the airplane and my fellow travellers and stood on the edge of the runway for several moments, breathing the familiar northern air, gazing around at the shimmering grey-blue waters of the lake in the distance and the short black spruce trees beyond the airport, while half listening to the sounds of Slavey and English all around me. I was filled with an urge to kneel down and kiss the ground. But I did not. Instead I stood silently to one side, feeling an incomprehensible sense of happiness and relief, as another part of me watched an RCMP officer check our bags to ensure that no illegal liquor had been brought in to Déline.

Two young men stepped forward as I followed George towards the truck waiting near the tiny airport terminal building.

"Hello Miss Morris. Remember me?" said one of the men, his hand extended. He did look familiar but no name came to mind. He helped me out with "Albert...."

"Sewi," I added, instantly recognizing signs of a child I had once taught within the face of this grown man, now complete with mustache. "Yes, Albert. I remember you. It's good to see you." And with grins on both our faces we shook hands. "How is William?" Pictures of Albert's father fixing my frozen pipes and showing Claire and me how to check propane tanks came to mind.

"He's good."

"And Rosie?" I wondered how many times I would ask after the older people only to be told that they had long since passed away.

But Albert replied, "She's good too. They are looking forward to seeing you again."

George was calling me so I followed my luggage and climbed aboard a half-ton, extended-cab, pick-up truck, already laden with the luggage of other passengers. I was relieved to find that Albert had been so recognizable once I remembered his name. It had occurred to me during the flight that I might no longer recognize my grown-up students nor would I be able to attach names to them.

My eyes were glued to the view outside the truck as we sped along the dusty red gravel roads, past rows of identical houses and several large buildings. Nothing seemed familiar. After several stops George ushered me out of the truck and again helped with my luggage. We entered the porch of a detached, two-storey log cabin. Kicking off my running shoes, as George had done, I followed him along the shiny clean linoleum floor in my socks. He introduced me to his sister, Cec, who had been sitting at the kitchen table cutting hunks of boiled caribou meat off a large bone while sipping tea and waiting for us.

The greetings complete, Cec led me upstairs, pointing out the bathroom half way up, complete with bath/shower, toilet, sink and closet. She then showed me my bedroom—a good-sized room, complete with a dresser, bookshelves, double bed and round side table, under a slanting roof. How different this house was compared to those one-roomed cabins of thirty years ago. From my small bedroom window I could see the lake and many of the village houses we had just driven past.

I joined George and Cec downstairs where I met Cec's husband, John, and teenage daughter, Atanda. I had been present at John and Cec's wedding in the sixties—one of the multiple ones—and had brought photos of their wedding for them, but I hadn't known them very well. We sat down for an enjoyable dinner of pork chops, rice and canned vegetables washed down by cups of tea.

After a while, George stated that he was going out to meet someone. I also excused myself as I wanted to go for a walk and see more of the village. I arbitrarily chose to head to the right, to the east. But by the time I reached that end of the village some twenty minutes later, I felt quite despondent. I still had not seen anyone or anything familiar. The usual admonitions that "you can't go back" echoed in my mind, as did my own earlier doubts about following my dream of returning after all these years. Had I been foolish and naive to think that I could return and recapture some of the feelings I had once experienced? And what was I going to do here for seventeen days? This wasn't your typical tourist location where there was always much to see and do.

Of course I hadn't expected it to be the Franklin I had known and I was prepared for many changes but not for a place that was so totally unrecognizable. There certainly wasn't anything very dreamlike about this depressing, very uncharming looking village lying below a blanket of overcast smoke. In the space of less than a couple of hours I had swung from feelings of euphoria to a huge sense of disappointment.

The rolling muskeg extended beyond the village and ahead of me, fringed to the south by the grey-blue lake waters gently lapping on the narrow sandy shore and rounded rocks. I left the village and continued in that direction. Here at last was something I well remembered. I walked over the muskeg, spongy and springy beneath my feet, smelling the familiar pungent aroma of the *tripe de roche*, a lichen that had been an important source of nourishment for both the Dene and non-Natives in times of emergency.

I wended my way through shrubs laden with almost ripe berries and a forest of dwarf-sized pine trees feeding off the permafrost never far below, as they forced their way through the muskeg into a world of sun, snow and ice. Here, lying half-buried, I found an old blue and white chipped enamel-ware mug and then a small dish a little further off. Signs of life from bygone days. I knelt to touch and smell a myriad of small flowers—a familiar white potentilla, yellow buttercups, red and purple Indian paintbrush, wild blue daisies and the tall blazing pink fireweed. I felt better.

I turned and walked towards the lake, scanning its shores for as far as I could see. The southern shoreline, though dimly enshrouded in smoke, looked familiar and, for a moment, I was back in my classroom looking over the heads of my busy students, looking out across the lake in all its guises as it echoed the changing seasons. Only "my mountain" was missing, the mountain over which the midday sun of late December climbed and descended during its half-hour voyage of daylight. Now the dense smoke at higher altitudes hid it from view but I knew it was there and that I would see it soon.

A fast-moving boat hummed by in the distance trailing a plume of effervescent spray. Gazing down through the lake's crystal clear waters at the stones below, I extended my hand into the cool, refreshing water, picked up some pebbles, smooth from years of rubbing against each other in the fall storms, and felt their strength in my hands.

I took a deep breath, turned towards the village and started heading back with a new spring to my walk. I had been too impatient. I had not given the village a chance to share its new secrets with me. As for the people with whom I had come to visit and become reacquainted and learn about and, hopefully, share for a brief time in their grown families and adult lives ... well, I needed to be patient here, too. I was a stranger from the past, someone recalled in distant memories, a *mola* (white person) whose ways of thinking and living were very different. It was not my place to put expectations on these people. This was my dream, a dream I had harboured for years and nourished with increasing love and longing, especially during the previous months of recalling their familiar faces and accompanying memories from my slides, and by bringing them to life in the writing of the first chapters of this book. "Give them time," I said aloud. They are still the same people, the same adults and children you once knew, whom you once cared so much for, and who cared for you.

I began retracing my steps, first along the shoreline past a few aluminum boats and outboard motors pulled out of the water and berthed along the shore. Then, with a renewed sense of hope and expectation, I walked back to the dusty roads and headed for the rest of the village.

"Miss Morris. Miss Morris. Is it really you? Do you remember me?"

I did. I paused and from somewhere her name emerged. "Rosie, Rosie Taniton?"

"Yes, but not Taniton now," and she gave me a big hug. "I heard you were coming but it is so good to see you again. And it really is you. You must come and visit me, but I have to rush to the Northern store now before it closes." And with another big hug she was gone.

I didn't fare as well with the names of the many other people who met me on the street and greeted me with handshakes and hugs. "Do you remember me?" became their standard greeting, putting me at a considerable disadvantage. After all, these adults had only been young children when I had last seen them, so most of the time I could not instantly produce a name, as I had done with Rosie. But once they had told me who they were, I could, almost always see the child in the adult, usually in their eyes or in their smiles. Suddenly I had forgotten all about my despondent emotions. I now had a new concern. How was I to remember all the names of the people who kept coming up and introducing themselves to me?

Like many, I am not good at remembering the names of people when I first meet them, even when I am introduced to only one or two people at a time. Already, I had met more than a dozen people. They had chatted with me for a few minutes and left, fully expecting that I would now remember their names, who they were married to, and how many children they had. How was I going to deal with my dilemma? After all, I had, potentially, well over a hundred names of people I used to know to relearn as well as those of their family members.

I escaped down towards the lake where there was no one in sight, and sat on a large boulder. I thought about the people whom I had already met and much to my relief their names and faces returned quite easily. Why not? I reasoned. These were former students with already known personalities to go with the names and faces. These were not new people. No doubt it also helped that I had spent many hours during the past nine months looking at slides of them, as children. Even if I couldn't immediately produce a name in response to the familiar "Remember me?", I was having no difficulty retaining names once my memory had been refreshed. I'll worry about their married names and those of their children later on, I told myself.

It soon became my custom when referring to another person in a conversation to say, for example, "Irene, who used to be Kodakin," then everyone knew who I was talking about. Eventually, I was able to go beyond that and tentatively suggest, "Irene, who used to be Kodakin, now Betsidea?" And then the day finally arrived when she became simply "Irene Betsidea."

Feeling reassured by all of this, I returned to the dusty red roads. Before long I had walked from one end of the village to the other, easily twice as long as it used to be, and certainly extending much further inland. I tried to find the spot on the low hill where Helen Chan, Claire Barnabe and I had stopped and turned back to survey the village on our walk that first evening in August of 1965, but, with many new houses now built on this ridge, I was unsure of its location.

"Miggs!" It was Sarah, George's other sister, whom I had met for a few minutes earlier that afternoon. "Why don't you come in for some tea?" I accepted her invitation, and discovered that Sarah lived in the Cleary's old log house. I had only met her briefly in Déline in the sixties when she was on a visit home from Edmonton where she then lived. But Sarah and her brother Maurice had spent a week at Christmas with my mother and me in Saskatoon in 1969.

Sipping tea in her family's old home, one of the few old cabins still in use, Sarah informed me that her three adolescent children lived with her husband in Edmonton, but she had returned to Déline for a while. She ran the Basic Awareness Program, which acted as a referral centre for alcoholics who had decided to attend treatment facilities elsewhere. The centre also provided ongoing support for those who had returned from treatment centres, as well as preventative programming for adolescents. After receiving an overview of the important programs I promised to visit the centre and learn more about their work.

A couple of young children were already visiting her in her large dining room-cum-kitchen, a room which, as in the sixties, occupied most of the old cabin. While managing to talk to all of them and me, in a mixture of English and Slavey, Sarah also prepared a delicious plateful of hors d'oeuvres for me and cookies for the kids. As the evening wore on, several older people dropped in to visit Sarah. I remembered many of them and we chatted about their families, with Sarah translating as required.

But I required no introduction when Victor Beyonnie, the former chief, entered. He was instantly recognizable. With a grin on my face I walked over to him and extended my hand. He took it and also gave me a big hug. Then, with Sarah translating, we talked for a while. Victor had spoken a fair amount of English before, so the Slavey used now was mostly to include his wife, Elizabeth, whom I had not known well. He informed me that he was soon off to Inuvik to have cataracts removed from his eyes; otherwise, at age seventy-eight, he was in good health. I thought he looked great and was delighted at seeing him again. I was not surprised to discover, from talking to others later in the week, that Victor was still held in high regard and was considered to be one of the best chiefs Déline had ever had.

Much later, after all the other visitors had left, Sarah and I sat and talked about her Déline family—about the death of both her mother and father in the last few years due to cancer, and the death of her sister from Lou Gehrig's disease the previous year. But mostly she talked, with sadness and anger, about her brother

Maurice's death several years ago, when he was still a young man in his twenties, killed in a seemingly unnecessary accident while snowmobiling on the trail along the Dehcho.

Unfortunately, her telling of Maurice's abridged life was but one of many such sad tales I was to hear over the next few days. So many young people, several of whom were former students of mine, had died in boating, hunting or snowmobiling accidents.

Eventually, somewhere around midnight, with the northern sky still light, I sauntered back to my new home, had a brief chat with Cec and Atanda who were watching TV, and slept soundly.

CHAPTER FIFTEEN

TWO WEDDINGS AND A DRUM DANCE

The next morning, after a cup of coffee and some toast, I decided to walk to the Northern store to replenish the shampoo I had left behind in Yellowknife. (These Northern stores had replaced the familiar Hudson's Bay posts in the mid-1980s.) I was rather surprised to find the roads quite deserted until I arrived at the store to read a sign stating that the store would open at 11 AM, almost two hours away. Wondering what to do next, I heard my name called.

"Miss Morris!" I was being hailed by Jonas Kenny, another former student whom I had met briefly the day before. "Why don't you come and have breakfast with me at the hotel's coffee shop?" I took him up on the invitation for another cup of coffee. I was also eager to see Déline's hotel.

Rarely have I seen an uglier building from the outside, a rambling one-storey monstrosity covered in drab grey siding. It looked anything but inviting. But this unwelcome exterior was deceiving, for inside was a pleasant surprise. The rooms were clean and neat, small but cheerful. The beds were covered in brightly-coloured, matching Indian motif blankets, and each room had a TV. All the food I sampled at the cafeteria was tasty and plentiful, especially the homemade French fries, in which I indulged a few too many times. However, I was surprised and disappointed not to find any fresh fish on the menu of a restaurant perched on the shores of such a prolific lake.

We joined Ronald Beyonnie, Victor's son. I was delighted to meet again a former student of Claire's who had spent a considerable amount of time at our duplex that first year. Ronald was still among the shortest of his peers and reminded me, in appearance and demeanour, of the movie actor Charles Bronson. We reminisced and had many good laughs about "the old school days." One of the highlights for Jonas had been the school Christmas play when he was attired as an angel. (Later on when I gave him a photo of this event he went around and showed it to everyone with a mixture of pride and embarrassment.) The conversation flowed easily as they talked about their lives, their jobs and their families and, generally, about people whom I knew in Déline. They also asked me about my life. This pattern of conversation was to be repeated frequently during my stay.

After coffee, I decided to look in on Helena who had arrived as a teacher in Déline in 1972, eventually marrying one of the local young men, John Tutcho, and had lived in either Déline or Tulit'a ever since. Helena, a tall blonde woman in her late forties, was in the middle of icing wedding cakes for the afternoon's wedding feast. It seemed that I had arrived on a weekend of three weddings. The

After the double weddings, a boisterous truck ride around Déline preceded a community feast and drum dance.

first wedding had already taken place the evening prior to my arrival. On this day a double wedding was to be held, followed by a feast and drum dance. (It was still customary to hold several weddings together as there was no longer a permanent priest located at Déline, and the bishop had to be flown in from Yellowknife. In fact, Catholic priests were now in short supply in the North as the Oblates are unable to recruit young men to this calling.)

As she continued to decorate the double cakes, she told me about leaving England to teach in Calgary in the late sixties. She was "from Bath" she announced, pronouncing it in the English manner with the narrow sounding "ah" in the middle, and then adding with a smile, "Doesn't that sound very posh?" Long after the large cake had been attractively decorated we were still sharing tales of our respective experiences in the North. I then returned home and changed into something slightly more elegant than my daily jeans and shirts and headed for the wedding, eager to compare it with those of thirty years ago.

Father René Fumoleau, whom I had seen in Toronto earlier in the spring, had already warned me that the beautiful silvery church had burnt down in the eighties. The priest had gone away on a retreat, leaving a local person in charge of getting the furnace going. However, it overheated when the village generator broke down, leaving the furnace's fan without power. Before long the church was engulfed in flames and all efforts to put it out were in vain. The new church had been built on the same concrete foundation, and, in many ways, the inside was still attractive, but the roof was now sheathed with rust-coloured tiles. It looked rather drab to me, compared to the regal appearance of the old silver and white church, such a welcoming beacon from afar.

On this special wedding day, when two of the Taniton brothers were getting married, garlands of blue and white ribbons and matching balloons festooned the inside. It looked very festive. Each bride was elegantly attired in a white satin wedding dress and long train, and was attended by four bridesmaids in peacock blue and a young flower girl in white. The grooms, best men and four other groomsmen, as well as the little ring-bearers, were all dressed in black tails, rented especially for the occasion.

With the men and bridesmaids waiting at the altar, the brides entered to a tape of Bryan Adams singing "I Do It for You." The church was full, but no longer did the men and women sit on separate sides. Instead, people sat together in families as they had done since the early eighties. Several people in the congregation were involved in the Bible readings, including George whose white shirt I had ironed earlier that afternoon.

The bishop gave a long and interesting sermon, complete with chart paper, on the responsibilities that come with love and marriage. When most of the congregation stepped forth for Communion at the end of Mass, someone broke out into a Slavey hymn and others joined in. It was so good to hear the familiar nasal Slavey singing again. Finally, the newlyweds returned down the aisle to the contrasting taped sounds of "That's What Friends Are For."

Outside, a cool breeze blew off the lake as the wedding party lit cigarettes and posed for several photos. And as occurs in countless weddings across Canada, the new brides tossed their bouquets back over their heads into the hands of the eagerly waiting young girls. I stood to the side for a while, watching the wedding activities and taking photos of my own. It also afforded me the opportunity to meet and chat with many other people. Jimmy Tutcho, of the 1967 trip, came over and it was so good to talk to him again. Despite the passage of thirty years Jimmy had changed little. He is now an accountant at the government offices. "Come and visit me on Monday and I'll show you around," he said, flashing his beautiful smile.

Then Bernice and Morris Neyelle invited me over for tea. Bernice had been a student in my last year. Morris, the son of Johnny Neyelle the snowshoe maker, had been in Joe Matters' class. They owned a very nice log house onto which Morris had recently added on a large room, also made of logs. It was soon clear that people were immensely proud of their modern homes and contents. Morris owned the sewage contract and as such had one of the most lucrative and responsible positions in the community, with several men working for him. He was also a village councillor.

Later on they drove me to the feast being held in the large hall attached to the full-sized skating arena. As in the sixties, more than a hundred people sat on the floor alongside long strips of white paper. Some of the same kinds of foods—caribou, bannock, cookies—sat on plates and in pots before us, along with the newer additions of boiled potatoes, vegetable salads, chicken and turkey. No longer did young men come around and serve us; instead we just helped ourselves.

The large wedding parties sat at a long head table. Prayers and speeches were said before we proceeded to eat. The hall, too, had been cheerfully and tastefully decorated in blue and white, with the names of the three brides and grooms printed on a long computer banner hung behind the head table. Again I was struck by how well the wedding and this feast epitomized the blending of things traditional and modern, very northern and southern. This proved to be the foreshadowing of much of what I witnessed in Déline that summer.

Where would the wedding couples go for their honeymoon, I enquired. Nowhere right now. After spending so much on the purchases and rentals for the wedding itself, real honeymoons would have to wait. However, shortly after the feast, two attractively decorated half-ton pick-up trucks carried the wedding parties all around the village to the accompaniment of blaring horns, rattling tin cans, smiling faces, waving hands and chasing children.

Since a large new culture hall would not be ready until the fall, the drum dance was to be held in the old hall. I arrived around 8:00 PM, thrilled at having this opportunity to participate in a drum dance again. The afternoon breeze off the lake had disappeared as had all the smoke from the forest fires, and, as the evening was sunny and very warm, I was soon glad I had changed into a loose T-shirt before heading for the hall. At first there was little action other than the heating of drums until they were all tuned to the same high pitch. For this task, a double electric hot-plate replaced the old wood stoves. Soon after the wedding party arrived, still dressed in their wedding attire, eight drummers, neatly dressed in white shirts and dark pants, red ribbons dangling from their drums, stood to one side and began a slow chant to their rather subdued drumming, but no one got up to dance. One of the men with whom I had been quite friendly in the past, came and sat next to me. As we chatted about the weddings, Archie asked me why I had never married and made the kinds of flirtatious comments that anyone nearing sixty likes to hear once in a while. Then his light-hearted manner changed as an older man stepped up to the drummers and the beating stopped.

The elder turned to the wedding party as they sat on benches along one side wall and began talking to them in Slavey. Archie summarized his speech for me in whispered tones. He talked about the drum being symbolic of the circle of life, reflecting the stages of birth, marriage, childbirth and death, each with its own time and purpose. He reminded them that during the difficult times that lay ahead, they should take strength from each other and from their families joined together by this union, as well as from their spiritual lives. He also told them to remember that good times would always follow darker days in the circle of life and when they did, they should rejoice and give thanks to the Creator. Then the grooms' father stepped forward and gave thanks to the Creator for bringing the couples together in marriage. He also gave thanks for their health, their families, and for the fellowship of their friends. Then he prayed to the Creator to continue to bless the lives of these young couples.

The sombre mood was instantly changed when the eight drums sprang to life, reverberating loudly around the room. Led by the wedding party, a circle of people danced to the drum beat in the traditional manner that I well recalled. Soon, as more joined the circle, those at the front of the line had to move inwards, forming a second interior circle. I, too, was soon dancing, once again caught up in the hypnotic spell of the pulsating sounds of drums and high-pitched voices.

It was extremely warm in the confined space and before long everyone was perspiring profusely, especially the wedding party, who were now far too overdressed, but they hung in for more than an hour before departing, temporarily, to change into something cooler. The drummers, sweat pouring down their faces and arms, kept being replaced in turn by fresh new drummers, without any break to the sound or rhythm of the dance.

I was introduced to new dances, new only to me as they had all been around for hundreds of years but weren't danced in the sixties: the T-dance, which I had since read about, where everyone danced sideways in a large circle; the mountain dance, transported from the Mackenzie Mountains west of the Dehcho, which had a fast tempo, almost like that of galloping horses; and then other dance variations where pairs danced side by side around in a circle, or, in pairs opposite each other, but not touching. Although I joined in many of the dances, I sat out most of those unfamiliar to me, preferring to watch the dancers, the drummers and the crowd. Everyone seemed so vibrant and full of the enjoyment of life, just as they had been in the sixties. Déline, as a place, might have changed a great deal, but the people still seemed the same, despite all of the concerns they were beginning to share with me. And how good it was to see the participation of many young adolescents and children who had learned some of these dances in school. Some of the drummers, too, were young men, a change from thirty years ago when only middle-aged and older men were allowed to drum.

Several people came up to talk to me at various times in the evening and they echoed my thoughts about how good it was to see young people participating. They explained how important it was for younger people to continue this tradition and to feel they belonged in the community. There weren't many events that brought people of all ages together and allowed for such community solidarity, so drum dances were held at every important occasion. It was one of the few means they had of bridging the gap between the generations, and between traditional and modern ways.

All too soon the dancing and the drumming came to an end. It was simply too hot to continue. The drummers were drained to the point of exhaustion. The dancers had taken to spending increasing amounts of time outside the hall where the evening breezes wafted off the lake, moderating, to some extent, the heat of the low sun, at around 11:00 PM. In response to a "Hey, Miss Morris, jump aboard and come and join our party!" I clambered on to a pick-up truck and headed off for one of the many parties to be held that night. A large bonfire was lit beside Leon's home and before long about thirty people had gathered and were either sitting on picnic tables or just standing around. As usual, at this time of night, the mosquitoes were quite horrific, but thanks to the smoke from the blazing fire and the fact that I had already sprayed myself, I soon forgot about them. Perhaps they moved on to someone else's party.

Music blared through a window from the high-powered speakers and an expensive stereo system inside the house, and it was good to hear some old country and western favourites by George Jones and Buck Owens, mixed in with more contemporary songs. Someone collected ten dollars from each of us and beer was produced, courtesy of the hotel, with their staff keeping tabs and doling it out.

Many former students were present and I felt sure that by now I must have met all of those currently living in Déline. Somewhat polite and deferential with me at first, as the night wore on, we all relaxed. Miss Morris became Miggs—which they pronounced "Mix"—as we recalled and had many laughs about incidents from the past. Didn't I have my guitar with me so that they could sing some of the old songs I had taught them? I couldn't even remember which songs they were but they reminded me of several including "Michael, Row the Boat Ashore," "The Sloop John B," and "Clementine." We tried singing without the guitar, but soon, after gales of laughter, gave up on that.

Again, questions about my present life followed—where did I live? was I still teaching? why wasn't I married?—but, mostly they talked about their student days and, in answer to my prompting, about their present families and what they were doing, since most held jobs in the community. Gina Neyelle was the head chef at the hotel restaurant. Both Alina and Merine were teaching assistants at the school. Raymond Tutcho, from the 1967 trip south, greeted me with a big hug before explaining that he was now married with seven children and worked for the territorial government's Department of Public Works. George Dolphus and Walter Modeste—and everyone laughed with delight when I remembered to call them "Bikwi" and "Bia"—were busy carpenters, as there was always a demand for newly built or renovated houses. I was so pleased to hear that many of my former students were doing so well.

At one point Isadore Yukon, who was now in his seventies, came up to speak to me. Did I know that Francis and Agnes had both died young? I knew something of the circumstances of Francis' untimely death but hadn't known about Agnes. I expressed my sorrow but he seemed reluctant to talk more that evening. Instead, he told me how very proud he was to have gone to Ottawa with his wife Lucy, a few years before she died, to receive the Order of Canada from the governor general. What a thrill that had been for them. Now, long since retired from working on the barges with NTCL, he lived in the seniors' home and enjoyed driving a four-wheeler ATV around the village.

Then the forty ouncers of vodka began to emerge. Under the territorial permit system, larger quantities of alcohol are permitted at weddings. By now I was beginning to flag badly and decided to head for home; after all it was around 3:00 AM, or 5:00 AM my time. When had I last stayed up all night? I left basking in the attention and friendship shown to me during the day, in the warmth of my former students' memories across all those years, as well as a little warmth from the glow I felt from having enjoyed three beers.

It was the next morning and I could clearly hear male voices through my bedroom window.

"Hey, you shit-head. Come here. Come back here!"

"Leave him alone. Let him go."

"Fuck you. He slept with my wife last night."

By now I had risen from my bed and opened the window a little further to observe the scene below. My watch showed 8:30 AM. I recognized three of the four men from the party I had left several hours before. The response was inaudible, but the angry husband continued.

"Yes you did. I saw you leave with her." He staggered closer to the offending man but the other two grabbed his arms and pulled him away. His young wife stood off to one side, ignored by the others, and silently shaking her head. The husband's anger and frustration kept mounting and he clearly wanted to attack the other man. "Yes you did," he yelled again with abandonment. "You fucked my wife. She's a no-good bitch but she's my wife. I'm going to kill you," at which point he broke away from the others. With his arms flailing wildly as he struggled to maintain his balance, he lurched towards the apparent offender, clearly intent on assaulting him. Instead, he stumbled and fell to the dirt road where he lay pounding the ground and sobbing loudly.

Then I heard the other man's words. "You're full of shit. I didn't sleep with your wife. She was mad because you were yelling at her, so we went and sat inside Leon's house and talked." And he turned and walked away.

The husband's two friends picked him up and dragged him down the road as his legs gave way and his speech became even more incoherent. His occasional bursts of swearing could still be heard in the distance for several more minutes. His wife followed slowly, some distance behind the others, dragging her husband's jacket, and sobbing quietly.

A few hours earlier, before the vodka had done its damage, I had shared some good memories with both husband and wife.

CHAPTER SIXTEEN

CHANGES IN DÉLINE

Let me introduce you to a "shore lunch."

I had been asked to put on a slide show for the community on Sunday evening. Having made arrangements at the wedding feast the previous day to borrow a projector and a couple of carousel trays from Fred Tutcho, one of the two custodians, I was now, at noon, heading towards the school. I was also looking forward to exploring the large new edifice that had replaced our old four-roomed building, long since torn down.

"Hey Miss Morris. Remember me?" I stopped and looked towards a man of about 5' 9", dressed in dark clothes, emerging from a nearby shed. I turned off the road and went up to him. He looked familiar but I still couldn't place him. "I used to be your student," he added in a deep voice.

"I'm sorry," I said, shaking my head. "Perhaps if you were to take off your sunglasses."

Then I recognized him, but he beat me to it. "Morris Modeste." Of course it was Morris, and he hadn't changed much from the handsome young man he used to be when he was in the same class with Francis, Walter and Jimmy, just more weather-beaten and rugged, with a moustache that seemed to enhance his good looks.

After a few minutes of chatting, Morris said that he and Jimmy wanted to take me fishing and for a shore lunch that day, if I didn't have anything else planned. I explained about the slide show that evening, that I was on my way to meet Fred to pick up the projector at the school, and that I would have to be back around 4:30 to get the slides ready in the carousels in time for the show. He assured me that we could be back by then.

"We won't go far. Would you prefer lake trout or grayling?"

"Either one's fine, but I would prefer trout," I replied.

"OK I'll meet you by my boat shed on the lake shore at about one," as he pointed towards its location, "and don't worry if you need more time, we'll wait."

I was there shortly after one, but since Jimmy and Morris didn't appear for another ten minutes I had time to take in the beauty of the lake now that the smoke had disappeared. What a glorious day, with the sunlight shimmering and sparkling on the lake's blue waters, rippling slightly in a light breeze. And, finally, there in the distance, stood my mountain with the overhead sun shining down on its face. I smiled and told it how pleased I was to see it again. Now all seemed well with the world.

Former students, Morris Modeste and Jimmy Tutcho, cook up a delicious meal of trout for me at our shore lunch on Great Bear Lake.

Sitting on a large boulder and basking in the warmth of the midday sun, my shirt and jeans were adequate, but I had brought a thick sweater, jacket and scarf with me, knowing how much colder it would get as we moved at speed across the waters.

"I have to go to my house first to pick up some supplies," said Morris, as Jimmy and I clambered aboard his eighteen-foot aluminum boat with its 45-hp outboard motor. Both of them looked good, and other than aging—and hadn't we all?—they really had changed very little. When I told them this they laughed and said that perhaps it was due to the fact they were both still single—quite uncommon in men of their age in Déline.

Morris' log cabin, located at the extreme eastern end of the village, was surrounded by blazing fireweed and small Indian paintbrush plants and grasses. "It's absolutely beautiful," I exclaimed, entering into the combined kitchen, living room, dining room, no more than five by three metres, and spotlessly maintained.

"We built it for my mother after my father died, but now that she has passed away too, I live here. It's too small for my brothers and sisters and their families." A small bedroom and bathroom took up the back half of the cabin.

It was the kind of charming little cottage that people would have drooled over had it been located on a small island in the Muskokas of Ontario. The view, too, was spectacular, especially on such a glorious day, as you looked across a blaze of fireweed toward the azure waters of the lake just beyond, with not another dwelling in sight. A small, spruce log deck protruded from the front of the cabin with a small flagstone patio at the base of the steps, all built by Morris. But we could not linger. My two young bachelor friends and I were off for a shore lunch.

As we raced across the lake towards Sahtu De at breathtaking speed I now needed my thick sweater and jacket. "Not like boating with those five- and ten-horsepower kickers we used to have, is it?" Morris yelled from the stern. No, it certainly wasn't. Jimmy and Morris conferred then we pulled in closer towards the shore about a kilometre short of the river. Morris reduced the engine to a low purr. Handing me a fishing rod he said, "Now you can fish for our lunch."

"But I haven't fished in ages," I protested. "You'll need to help me." Morris kept the engine running slowly so that I could cast and trawl the waters with my rod and lure. I felt several tugs on the line but was too slow in snagging whatever nibbled at it. After what seemed like ages with no results, I said, "Hey guys. I'm hungry and I'm no good at this. You fish."

They both laughed and Jimmy, as if echoing my classroom words from thirty years before, said, "You just have to be more patient. Keep trying."

Morris added, "You'll catch one in a few minutes. It hasn't been that long and you're doing fine." And sure enough, several minutes later I felt the tug on my line, jerked my rod as Morris had shown me, and reeled in a good-looking trout. Must be at least fifteen pounds I thought to myself, pleased both with my accomplishment and the fact that we could now eat.

"A good size," said Morris. "About eight or nine pounds. So we'll need another one for our shore lunch."

Somewhat disappointed, though how could anything be disappointing on such a beautiful day, I continued my trawling and within five minutes had caught a second trout of a similar size.

"OK. Time for lunch!" exclaimed Jimmy from the bow, as Morris powered up the engine and we whizzed towards a stretch of golden sand on the west side of Keith Arm half way between Déline and Sahtu De. We carried our supplies beyond the sand on to the stubbly grass and I remembered that this was where the Sahtuot'ine in the past had gathered in the summer months and set up their tipis. Morris cleaned and filleted the fish with a few deft cuts, throwing the leftover skin and bones into the edge of the water. "The seagulls need to eat, too," he remarked. And then, just as others had in the past, Jimmy and I went to collect dry wood for our fire.

We returned with armloads of twigs and fallen branches. Adding a handful of dried lichen and moss from the muskeg to the underside of the wood, Morris had the fire blazing within minutes. Then he placed a large metal grill on top, propped up by stones. Jimmy had already filled a pot with water and it was soon boiling, ready for making tea. Despite his one paralyzed arm Jimmy was clearly adept at many tasks. Out of the picnic box emerged a small plastic tablecloth that Morris spread on the ground and on which were placed mugs, knives and forks, sliced bread, butter, pepper and salt, a lemon, and, wonders of wonders, here in the wilds of the North, tartar sauce.

As he cooked, Morris demonstrated and explained, just like an experienced TV cooking host, how he cut up the pieces of fresh trout, dipped them into a plastic bag containing flour, and placed them into a frying pan already sizzling with lard. "Butter is fine for one frying, but it burns with a second batch," advised the chef. Tea bags, not the handful of loose strong tea that I had become accustomed to in the past, were dropped into the pot of boiling water, and an opened can of baked beans and another of baby carrots were placed on the side of the grill. It all seemed incredibly elegant, I thought with a smile, far more so than when I went camping.

Morris had told me on the way over that he was going into the tourist business. He had been given the village outfitting license. Now he could conduct his own fishing excursions for southerners, camping and fishing further down the lake. He already owned two eighteen-foot boats with outboard motors. He had also purchased his tents and all necessary camping gear as well as an expensive, but very essential, high-powered short wave emergency radio.

"The fishermen will only need to bring their clothes, sleeping bags and fishing tackle," Morris said. As he explained each step in cooking the trout and then went on to describe other ways of cooking the various fresh fish that his tourists would get, it dawned on me. "So that's why you invited me along, Morris. You just wanted to practise on me before trying this out on your visitors."

With a broad grin on his face he replied, "No, that's not why we invited you. But, I would like to hear what you think."

By now, reclining back against a log in my rolled up shirt sleeves, sipping on the hot tea, eating one of the best trout meals I have ever had—cooked to golden perfection—and listening to Morris talking with enthusiasm about his new business, I thought about his demonstrated sense of organization and all his years of experience as a highly respected guide at the fishing lodges located around Sahtu. I assured him, with the utmost sincerity, that Modeste Outfitters would most certainly have my recommendation.

We then talked and shared our pasts. Jimmy had taken courses in accounting and computers. He had held several jobs over the years with Esso Canada, Air Sahtu, Native Courtworker Association of the NWT, as well as a variety of government positions in Déline. He was currently the executive assistant to the Déline Financial and Land Corporations. Morris preferred not to have a regular job as he still loved to go out hunting and fishing. Instead, he assured me that there was always plenty of work around the community, contract positions, that came his way. This was corroborated by the fact that he had already paid for his boats, outboard engines, snowmobile, and other equipment. Unlike most of us, Morris carried no debt on all these items. He was also very active with the Hunters and Trappers Association of Déline and was the current president. The HTA is a body that regulates hunting and trapping activities and is also very conscious of the need for environmental protection.

Glancing at my watch, I regretfully had to bring our reminiscing and their amusing stories to an end. How I would have liked to linger a little longer but my slide show called. We sped across the lake at what, again, seemed like supersonic speed and I loved it—all that wind blowing through my hair and the tang of lake water on my lips. We passed at least a dozen other groups dotted around the lake enjoying their shore lunches, too. This was obviously a popular way of spending a beautiful mid-summer Sunday afternoon.

The boat trip also gave me my first real look at Déline in its entirety. How it had grown from the very small village of thirty years ago. It seemed so attractive and welcoming from this distance. Then I realized that, since meeting many people who had made me feel welcome, I hadn't once thought again about how depressing it had seemed during my first few hours only two days before. It was indeed good to be back.

I arrived at the Culture Hall shortly before six only to discover that the room was far too light for a slide show, so with the help of the few people who had arrived early, we set to finding ways of covering the windows. By the time it was sufficiently dark some sixty to seventy people had arrived, sitting on the chairs left over from last night's drum dance, as well as on the floor.

After a few words of welcome I explained that the slides would be shown in order from 1965 to 1968, and that, other than an occasional comment, I wasn't going to say much. After all, these were slides of them and their families and friends. Instead I encouraged them to talk and ask questions among themselves. I felt this comment necessary because they were already sitting quietly and behaving rather like the well-mannered students they used to be. At that, they smiled, relaxed and were soon chatting away in Slavey and laughing uproariously at seeing themselves and others on screen. I just sat on the floor clicking the control button, answering the occasional question, and shared in their enjoyment. Once in a while someone appeared that the audience couldn't put a name to: "*Amii ote?*"—"Who is that?"—they would ask, and most times I could provide a name. After all I had seen these slides many times by now, and had had time to recall who people were.

John Tetso, the chief, arrived a little into the show and assisted with naming people on the screen. John had been in Joe Matters' grade seven and eight class in 1965. After the slide show he asked if I could get prints made of the slides so that they could be put in albums, then people could make their own copies from those. He assured me that the council would pay if I could arrange it. I willingly agreed to. Judging by their clapping and comments at the end it seemed that everyone had enjoyed the slides, but I knew it for sure the next day when many people stopped me on the road and asked if I would show the slides again another night, preferably a little later in the evening, since most adults were working until 5:00 PM. After consulting several people the decisions of time and location were made. The local radio station announced the repeat performance several times during the week and I took delight in hearing the words "...teacher Miss Morris ... slides ... eight o'clock Thursday ... school gym..." embedded in a stream of Slavey.

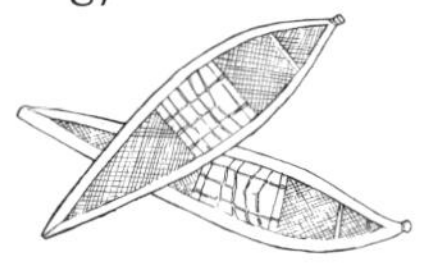

The next day I began the routine I was to follow for the next two weeks. Each morning, after updating my notes from the previous day, I made a list of those topics I needed to pursue and the people I needed to talk to. Although my primary reason for being here was to fulfil my dream of returning to Déline I also wondered, now that I had concluded my manuscript of the 1965-1968 years, if I should perhaps continue the story of the Sahtuot'ine into the present. I would take notes and then make that decision after leaving. I even brought a tape recorder with me but soon discarded it. I had come, first of all, to talk to people not to interview them. So, although I made plans to cover certain topics, I let the conversations flow freely, and then wrote up any information I felt might be relevant as soon as possible afterwards.

As with any such plan it frequently changed when I met someone else or became aware of some other event in the village and I would temporarily follow that fortuitous direction. As a result, I talked, and perhaps more importantly, listened, to many, many people, Dene and *mola*, from early morning until late at night, and sometimes even later, as I became more and more intrigued with the present Déline. Although my days were enjoyable and enlightening, yet at times, I felt overwhelmed by the amount of information shared with me. Virtually everyone I talked to willingly answered my questions and shared their views with me, sometimes reinforcing what others had articulated but, as was to be expected, often expressing contradictory views. I became increasingly aware that two and a half weeks was far too short a time to obtain a thorough understanding of the complex issues that existed in Déline in the mid-nineties. I would only be able to skim the surface. But I would do what I could.

How had the Déline of 1995 changed from the Fort Franklin of 1965? It took me very little time to realize that the village hadn't just gone through thirty years of changes; it had, to use space-age parlance, gone through thirty "light" years, when compared to the kind of changes people in southern Canadian and European societies had experienced in the same short time span. When I had left Fort Franklin/Déline in the late sixties these people were, to a large extent, just emerging from the age of hunters and gatherers. Within the short space of three decades—less than half a life span—they had travelled all the way from an Age that had changed very little over thousands of years, missed much of the Industrial Age, and were now already into the Technological and Information Age, a time that most of us in the South are also struggling to come to grips with.

As proof of that great distance travelled, vestiges of all three ages could be seen lying side by side, and often fitting together very comfortably: people who still believe in the power of the prophets to predict the future and heal people think nothing of operating fax machines, computers and laptops; those who still crave and eat boiled caribou right off the bone also fill their fridges with fast-frozen foods for microwaving; many who love the traditional drum dances also enjoy modern rock music; children who genuinely fear the Bushman talk knowledgeably about players on the Toronto Maple Leafs' team. Such apparent incongruities often fascinated me.

Most of these two-storey log houses in Déline were built by their owners and friends.

CHAPTER SEVENTEEN

A WALK THROUGH THE VILLAGE

Now for a tour of the village.

Before describing the Déline of today I must first say that no northern community looks as attractive in its summer nakedness, with all its warts exposed, as it will look during the nine months of winter when buried under a forgiving blanket of snow. When I think back to Déline in the sixties, I rarely conjure up summer pictures but instead visualize the clean, crisp, glittering snow and spirals of smoke emerging from the small log cabins. Only the lake has its own charm and ever-changing beauty at every season.

In 1995 Déline has a population of close to six hundred. It is a very youthful population with less than seventy people over the age of fifty and more than three hundred under the age of twenty-four.

The village extends about two kilometres in length and is shaped rather like a croissant—wider in the middle and narrower at both ends. As you approach the western end of the village the land begins to rise markedly above the lake. This, in my estimation, is the most attractive part of the village, an area where small pines rise from the fields of fireweed and berry bushes, and where most of the houses comprise sizeable yet attractive log cabins. This is the ridge, then located far west of the village, where Claire, Helen and I had walked up on my first day in 1965, and although it was now all built up it still gave me a good view of the new Déline.

The single dirt road meandering its way through the middle of the village has long since disappeared. Instead, several straight dusty-red roads, lying mainly in an east-west direction, and crossed by a few north-south roads in the fatter part of the croissant, the core of the village, dominate the village landscape.

To my left, as I look towards the east, stands the new nursing station, a formidable fortress, with its austere beige exterior and small windows, lacking the warmth of the former large pink building, which it replaced. None of the locals understood why the old nursing station had been replaced or why it had been rebuilt so far from one end of the village. Even though the nurses are very conscientious and provide a variety of health services, including neo- and prenatal classes, all of which are of vital importance to the community, I found few people who spoke highly of this facility. Was its importance diminished because, as one person suggested, the nurses were too aware of signs of abuse, of drunkenness and other human frailties that caused people to feel embarrassed? Or was it, as others suggested, because the nurses rarely joined in any village activities?

Nearby were several corrugated steel buildings where most of the hamlet's government trucks were housed and repaired. Just off the main road I spied an attractive, newly constructed, three-part log cabin. Beneath the picture of a large polar bear standing inside a blue circle—the government of the NWT logo—were the words, *Dept. of Renewable Resources, Main Office, Déline,* NWT. Next to another sign clearly stating Today's Forest Fire Hazard, with the word HIGH printed on a green band, stood a pick-up truck filled with rolled up sleeping bags and tents.

"Another bunch of young people are just off to do some more fire-fighting at Grizzly Bear Mountain," said a man dressed in a khaki uniform, peaked cap and dark glasses who approached me. "Hello, Miss Morris," he added.

"Walter?" I enquired, and he nodded as he took off his large work gloves and, with a nice smile, shook my hand. Although now a quite tall, powerfully-built man, Walter Beyha was one of the few people instantly recognizable to me. He had changed so little from the stocky kid called "Garw." Perhaps it had something to do with the fact that he had merely replaced the Hudson's Bay "army cap" that he always wore in the sixties with that of the territorial government department he now worked for!

"This is what I do," he said nodding towards the main office. "I'm the renewable resource chief and one of my jobs is to put out fires in the surrounding areas. This one at Grizzly Point is proving to be very stubborn, so we keep rotating the crews every ten days. There are about seventy young people out there at a time. We're trying to protect the few cabins and trap-lines located there." One team had just returned and the other would be flying out shortly. Grizzly Bear Mountain was on the other side of the lake about eighty-kilometres to the east and, after Walter had pointed out its general direction, I could see a faint pillar of smoke.

We talked more about his work, the training he had taken, and his family, including his brother Peter—and I could instantly hear across the years his "Oh you mean shit, Miss!"—who worked in the government offices in Déline. Then, after inviting me to drop by another day when he was less busy, he left and I returned to the main road.

I walked a little further down the hill, past the hotel, and came to the Northern store. Look carefully behind the brown corrugated steel walls and you will find the three remaining small buildings of the familiar white and red Hudson's Bay complex, tucked away out of sight, looking rather sad and dilapidated and used only for storage for their much larger successor.

Not far away and closer to the lake lies the grey-coloured corrugated steel Co-op store, affiliated with Arctic Cooperatives Ltd. Those who purchase shares at ten dollars each receive dividends according to the amount each family spends at the store during the year. The purpose of these local Co-ops has remained constant through the years: that is, to develop leadership within the community and to offer people the opportunity to participate in a business that is theirs, while also providing goods at prices that keep the Northern stores competitive.

Since the 1960s when Father Fumoleau helped the Dene start a Co-op in Déline, with a view to assisting the people, it has gone through both good and very rough times. But in more recent years, according to Tim Heins who had been the Co-op manager in Déline for the past ten years, "While still not being totally a part of the fabric of the community, it is more so now than at any other time. People are finally beginning to understand the concept and value of a Co-op store." More than ninety thousand dollars cash as dividends was returned to the Déline members in 1994.

Both stores devote about half of their space to food, kitchen and bathroom products, but also carry clothing, and general household items. A large Buffalo airplane flies in twice a week to Déline and the surrounding communities, bringing fresh food items, as well as other products to both the Northern and Co-op stores. In fact, everything is now brought into the community either by plane or by the winter road that is operable from Yellowknife, via Tulit'a on the Dehcho, for about three months of the year. The summer barges have long since become a thing of the past.

Recalling only too well the dearth of items available in the old Bay store, I was amazed to find such a variety of products available on these shelves and in their freezers, similar to what you could purchase in any small town in southern Ontario. Fast foods, such as pre-made pizzas, frozen dinners, pre-cooked chicken legs, pre-packaged lunches were all in high demand.

The variety of fresh produce was limited, but I could have indulged in pears, grapes, bananas, watermelons, tomatoes, even avocados—at a high price: $0.85 cents for a pear, $2.20 for two large bananas, $7.35 for a three kilogram bag of potatoes, $4.35 for a kilogram of apples, $5.99 for one cauliflower, and a six-pack of pop cost $6.00. Shopping for a houseful of people was certainly not cheap.

I was also delighted to discover that the electronic age had also reached the stores—just days before my arrival—so that I could use my credit or bank card to purchase groceries and other items. The Northern store also hosts the village post office and mail is flown in on the daily flights from Yellowknife—a far cry from our once a month mail delivery in 1965, weather permitting!

I returned to walking the dirt roads on which travelled a variety of government and private vehicles, most of which have been purchased in the past five years. Families tend to prefer extended cab trucks, and a favourite evening pastime, especially on summer weekends, is to take the family for a drive around town in the truck. There are also cars of all makes, panel wagons, one Suzuki jeep—owned by Peter Beyha—and increasingly, four-wheel ATVs. Bicycles have also become very popular with children in the past couple of years. Of course, snowmobiles have long since replaced dog teams for winter transportation and many families also own an eighteen-foot canoe with a powerful outboard motor.

Just a short distance from the Northern store stands the RCMP building, staffed by two officers who currently maintain a good relationship with the

Sahtuot'ine. But there have been times in the past when this was not so, when officers with little understanding of community strengths and concerns reacted strongly to every incident, however trivial. As mentioned to me, "The more hostile the officers were to the people of Déline, the more antagonism and violence that seemed to foster in the community. Things are much better now. These guys are not so uptight and they only get tough when there is a real need for them to do so."

Across the road from the Northern store and RCMP building stands a two-metre-wide satellite dish close to a large traditional tipi covered in canvas, now ripped in many places by the battering of winds. What a contrast between the old and the new—the age of hunting in juxtaposition with the age of technology. Many of the older people still enjoy eating some of their meals cooked on a fire inside the tipi, or just gathering there to meet and talk with friends on a warm summer's evening, sheltered from the lake's cool breezes.

Television arrived in the early eighties and is considered by many to have made the single greatest instantaneous difference to the community. For several years after its arrival, older people bemoaned the fact that adults who used to frequently visit each other now stayed at home and watched TV, especially soap operas. Two CBC channels, received via the central satellite dish, are distributed into most homes.[1]

Much could be said about the impact of television and videos on the Dene, just as much has been written about the impact of these media on children, adolescents and adults in the South. However, the impact of this new medium, arriving so suddenly in the eighties, on a people whose lives were so vastly different from those depicted on their screens—literally, worlds apart—was initially devastating.

Now, almost twenty years later, it has become a normal part of daily life. Understandably, the number of people watching television increases substantially during the long, dark winter months. Some said it helped alleviate the boredom of having too little else to do and assisted them in reducing the need for drinking. Others expressed their frustrations at being continually bombarded with examples of lifestyles that are, for many, entirely unattainable. Yet, in contrast, some mentioned that seeing a different way of life gave them a goal to strive and work for, to have what other Canadians take for granted.

In recent years, VCRs and video tapes have overtaken TV in popularity for many, just as CDs have replaced tapes and records. A wide assortment of very current videos and CDs are available either for purchase or rent in both the Northern and Co-op stores.

As I continued my walk through the village towards the east, I passed a large field of wispy grass on my left, presumably used, according to the tall backstop, as a baseball field. However, I never did see anyone play on it, and instead only saw people walking across the field on well-developed pathways leading to a group of newer buildings comprising the government offices, new school, hockey rink and community hall where the wedding feast had been held. But I left exploring these for another day.

Instead, I walked past the black building of the Basic Awareness Program where Sarah Cleary worked, and came to the senior citizens home, built a couple of years ago for those elderly people who had become infirm and could no longer look after themselves. The one-storey, long building was rather like a motel in that it contained about a dozen bright and cheerful, spotlessly clean, separate rooms, with a communal leisure room, dining room, kitchen and offices, at one end. Although government money funded the small staff, the building had been built by the Band Council with their newly acquired land claim money.

I couldn't help recalling how in the past these people would all have stayed with their relatives. Did they, in these changing times, feel rather rejected having to stay here? The few people I talked to told me they enjoyed staying where they had peace and quiet and were able to be with other friends of their own generation. They added that the children and young people of today, to use their words, "behave badly and are too noisy." No doubt it would be difficult for them to accept behaviour that to me didn't seem much different from that of children and youth in Ontario. These grandparents had very different memories of how children should behave as they recalled their own obedient children who demonstrated respect for the elders and their traditions.

Before heading for home, I passed the church and the deserted old mission, and cut down towards the lake, the shoreline now dotted with small fishing sheds, jetties, boats and outboard motors. I glanced back across the bay towards the log houses located on the distant esker, where my walk had begun this morning. It was indeed a very attractive view. Beyond, I could see the distant graveyard, perched on an even higher hill. Before much longer I would head that way, towards the Little Lake and the ski hill of old.

Bicycles come to Déline.

CHAPTER EIGHTEEN

GOVERNMENT AND POLITICS

"Did you really teach my mother?" asked Mike (not his real name), a young lad of about ten. I was on my way to accept Jimmy's offer to show me around the administrative offices when I came across a small group of children and their bikes down by the lake.

"Yes I did," I replied to my audience of kids dressed in jeans and T-shirts.

"Was she a good student?"

"Very good."

Mike paused, his running shoe carving semicircles in the red dust. "Could she read when she was my age?" I thought back. His mother had been one of my best students, a quiet little girl who rarely said much in class, but who consistently demonstrated a good grasp of all subjects.

"Yes, Mike, she could read well."

Still looking down at the red dust he responded. "I don't read good and I'm not smart like my mother." Before I could reply another little boy spoke.

"What was my father like in school?"

"How about my mother? Was she good at math? I am," said another child.

And so we continued for another five minutes as I answered their questions, mostly in the affirmative. Then, laughing and chattering away in Slavey, they hopped on their bikes and waved back at me. I headed across the abandoned baseball field towards the cluster of buildings that included the administrative offices.

The village had officially changed its name from Fort Franklin to Déline in 1992. Déline was the name long since given to this location "where the waters flow" and where Sahtuot'ine families had, in traditional times, come together during the warm summer months. A village council of eight members oversees municipal government affairs funded by the government of the NWT (GNWT), as well as the federally funded band business. Each government is housed in a separate wing of the new administration building.

Between the offices of the municipal government, headed by a local senior administrator, and the band council and its chief, almost all aspects of life in Déline are administered through a number of departments, as well as by the development corporations that give out contracts to operate the hotel, airport, sewage, water delivery, etc. In many ways, these roles and responsibilities are similar to those performed by any municipal level of government, with the addition of several unique facets that pertain to Déline's historical association with the federal and territorial governments.

In 1995 almost all employees, including those in leadership positions, were local Sahtuot'ine, most of whom have taken advanced courses in the South in business management, resource development, computers or accounting. This is all so different from the way things were during the late 1970s and early 1980s when Déline went through what the people described to me as their worst period. Several factors played a significant role in bringing about a situation that changed life in Déline forever.

In the 1970s, in order to establish an administrative infrastructure in each community, the government of the NWT (GNWT), now transferred from Ottawa to Yellowknife, believed it necessary to employ primarily experienced southern Canadians in the communities. In keeping with Commissioner Stuart Hodgson's devolution plan of giving more authority to the communities, part of their mandate was to train local people to eventually replace them. For some villages this plan worked well, but sometimes these southerners replaced Dene who had already demonstrated their proficiency in certain positions. Such was the case in Déline.

At the same time, the slump in fur prices continued and trapping ceased to be a viable means of earning a living. It no longer seemed worthwhile to spend a winter trapping in the bush only to return to the village several weeks later to discover that fur prices had dropped to the point when even a trapper's outfitting expenses could not be covered let alone enable him to provide for his family. Furthermore, as the prices of commodities and food brought from the South kept escalating, more and more cash was required to survive in the community. In time, the trappers discovered that they were financially better off staying at home and collecting Social Assistance.

Stripped of their pride and dignity, their sense of purpose and usefulness, many men began to drink excessively. Families became dysfunctional, traditional values were forgotten, drunkenness was accompanied by violence—especially violence towards women. The children, victims of these circumstances, also came under considerable abuse, physically, emotionally and sexually. Many women, too, turned increasingly towards alcohol in their pain.

Then came the expansion in the production of oil and gas at nearby Norman Wells that suddenly provided employment opportunities for several young men from Déline. At first this appeared fortuitous. However, there were no opportunities available for the older men. There was no place for them in this new economy. For the younger men, employment brought high wages but it also provided them easy access to alcohol, much of which made its way back to Déline, to exacerbate an already volatile situation. Many children were born during those years with no men claiming responsibility for them, and this generation of fatherless children grew up virtually without any parental guidance or support.

Such abrupt changes are difficult enough for most people to cope with when jobs or loved ones are lost, families break up, or sickness strikes, resulting in financial hardship and emotional turmoil. But how much more devastating and insidious are the results when a whole community suffers the consequences of such destructive changes. Déline, like countless other aboriginal communities across Canada, was caught in the grips of a culture of crisis.

Gradually the Sahtuot'ine of Déline began to turn things around by regaining control of many community functions. Employment opportunities opened up for those who had obtained the necessary education and training. People began returning to their traditional and spiritual values, and renewed their relationship with the land. Support structures were developed in the community for those who needed assistance or who were too old or infirm to make the necessary changes.

Despite periodic setbacks, and despite the considerable problems that still face them, the Sahtuot'ine are, by now, back in charge of their community and have the confidence and skills to deal with most of their concerns while fully recognizing that the road ahead will be long and difficult.

There is little doubt that much of this renewed optimism and pride in themselves was strengthened by the signing of the Sahtu Dene and Métis Comprehensive Land Claim Agreement with the federal and territorial governments in September 1993, under the leadership of George Cleary, president of the Sahtu Dene Council. When I talked about the Agreement with Raymond Taniton during the summer, he expained that although he was immensely proud to have represented Déline as their chief negotiator, he had found the whole process frustrating because the Dene from the five communities and the governments disagreed on so many matters. When I asked him about the apparently thorny issue of giving up their rights, Raymond explained that most had been regained within the terms of the agreement.

The primary objectives to be met by the land claim are summarized as follows:[1]

> This Agreement provides rights to the ownership and use of 41,437 square kilometres of land and resources, including sub-surface rights to 1813 square kilometres, within the Sahtu settlement area. It also recognizes the Dene way of life which is based on the cultural and economic relationship between the people and the land.
>
> The terms of the Agreement encourages the Dene's self-sufficiency and enhances their ability to participate fully in all aspects of the economy as well as providing them with specific financial, land, and other economic benefits, including resource royalties.

> It also provides the right, and guarantees a minimum of fifty percent participation, in decision making concerning wildlife harvesting and management as well as the use, management and conservation of land, water and resources. It further provides the right to protect and conserve the wildlife and environment of the Sahtu settlement area for present and future generations and includes extensive and exclusive hunting, fishing and trapping rights within this settlement area.

As part of the package, the Sahtu Dene and Métis obtained a cash compensation of $75 million to be paid over fifteen years minus the repayment of the costs of negotiations, loaned to the Sahtu Dene by the federal government. Additional implementation moneys were also received. The Agreement also ensures the Sahtu Dene and Métis the opportunity to negotiate self-government agreements. Déline then established two corporations to ensure that all land and financial transactions would be implemented successfully.

Sitting in Raymond Taniton's office for more than two hours, I listened in awe as he patiently explained the intricacies of the comprehensive land claim and implementation plan while I struggled to understand it. He walked me through the various manuals and maps, highlighting the most significant points and answering my frequent questions, while I frantically wrote copious notes. If I am still somewhat unsure about the details of this agreement, it is no fault of Raymond's.

Here was a young man who spoke no English when he began school in Claire Barnabe's class in 1965. He completed his grade eight by correspondence course and then left school to join his father as a hunter and trapper. He built his own house in the community and then used his carpentry skills to assist others. In 1986 he became a band councillor and then a sub-chief, lead land claim negotiator for Déline, ending up as the chief of Déline from 1991 to 1995.

When I asked him where his determination had come from he said it resulted from a combination of hunting with the elders for many years and listening to their advice, as well as from a near-death experience a few years ago when he went through the ice and survived.

That evening I reflected on my discussions with Raymond, Morris and Jimmy, and earlier ones with George and several other former students. It seemed that many of our conversations revolved around the intricacies of political decisions—federal, territorial and local, and I constantly found myself scrambling to keep up with them and make sense of what they shared. The teacher had indeed become the student.

The Dene know their lives will continue to be, to a large extent, at the mercy of decisions made primarily for the benefit of others—Canadians in general, and the requirements of industrial and business corporations—and that matters that are of significance to them will continue to be shunted aside. Only when they have obtained their right to self-government within Canada will they truly be able to restore the kind of autonomy and ability to control their lives they once had. Achieving self-government will be the Sahtuot'ine's next political goal.[2]

For the people of Déline and for many others in the North, political action—whether at the macro or micro level—has become a way of life, a way of ensuring the survival of their people, and of ensuring that young Mike and his friends will be able, in the future, to participate fully and productively in Déline or wherever else they choose to live.

The *Radium Gilbert*, so innocent looking and yet so lethal. It carried radium and uranium ore across Great Bear Lake between 1930 and 1960.

CHAPTER NINETEEN

DISTURBING EVENTS

After several days of visiting with people it was time for a change of pace. With lunch items purchased at the Northern store and the sun shining warmly on my back, I headed for the old ski hill by the Little Lake, via the graveyard.

Even from a distance it was clear that the graveyard had grown considerably in thirty years. Perched on a hill about a quarter of a mile beyond the western end of the village, the mass of graves, enclosed in the traditional manner by small, white, picket fences, dominated the landscape. A few larger, more ornate structures, painted light blue or pink, stood out above the forest of white.

I wandered around searching for the names of people I used to know. Many small graves, babies lost at childbirth or soon after, were tucked between those of their parents. Among the graves of young people were several of my former students. I paused beside those of Maurice and Jack Kodakin, brothers of Irene, drowned in a boating accident with two of their friends as they had tried to cross the rough waters of the lake in an overloaded boat. Maurice had been a rather serious young man, a good student with a kindly disposition, and I remembered Jack in Claire's class as a cute little boy with a mischievous smile. Nearby were the graves of several young men who had drowned when caught in a blinding snowstorm when they had snowmobiled too close to open waters.

Then I came upon the grave of Francis Yukon, next to that of his sister Agnes and their mother Lucy. Francis, dead at the young age of twenty-two. I knew about Francis's death. Claire had written to tell me many years ago. But everyone I talked to in Déline seemed to have a slightly different version of the details surrounding his death back in the summer of 1974. Apparently, a group of young people had gone to the north shore on a community caribou hunt. Later on, as the drinking became more serious, some people left and returned to Déline. The drinking continued to escalate and voices grew louder and more belligerent. Somewhere, in the heat of an argument, Francis pointed his .303 at Arsene Betsidea and threatened to shoot him. Arsene told Francis to put the gun down. When he refused, Arsene grabbed the barrel and, in the ensuing struggle, the gun went off and Arsene was killed. When Francis saw his friend lying dead on the ground he ran into the bush. He was never seen alive again.

Some people thought Francis must have become disoriented and got lost. Others claimed to have heard another gunshot in the distance and they believe Francis shot himself. The truth of what really happened that day seems to be as lost as Francis was. So are the details about the death of a woman, Margie Elemie, who was also killed that day.

Walter Beyha (Garw), who worked for a while in Yellowknife, recalls seeing a large photo of Francis in *News/North* under the headlines "Armed and Dangerous Killer headed for Yellowknife." The article created a state of panic among local residents, an idea that Walter stated was totally preposterous. According to the article both killings were attributed to Francis, yet as Walter explained, Margie Elemie had been shot by a .22 rifle, proving that it couldn't have been Francis. According to others, she was killed accidentally when a bullet ricocheted off a tree. Francis, Arsene, Margie—three needless deaths, sad symbols of the turmoil that existed in Déline in the 1970s.

The following summer someone came across Francis's wallet, boots, rifle, some bones, and a few pieces of clothing lying in a heap, perhaps giving credence to those who thought he had killed himself. His skull was found on a ridge overlooking the area, presumably carried there by wolves or a bear. In time, his skull, bones and personal articles were returned to Déline and buried in the graveyard. What a sad end for my Francis and his beautiful smile—a troubled end for a troubled young man.

As I meandered between the graves, I saw the names of many older people who were once familiar to me. I searched especially for the grave of Granny Zaul, whose funeral had moved me so much all those years ago, but I never found her. Perhaps the wind and snow had erased her name from her wooden cross. Instead I saw rosaries hanging from crosses, words of grief written on small plaques, an occasional photograph, a few coins lying on top of the picket fence rails, and artificial flowers still wrapped in plastic, flowers that would last for many years despite the harsh winters. All spoke eloquently of deep feelings at the loss of loved ones and that death was never far away from any family. On that sunny day, I found it fitting to see the fireweed and wild roses, and even an occasional pine tree, growing up through the graves as if nature, too, dignified the loss of loved ones and claimed them back to her earthly bosom.

After a while, as I leaned against a large rock, the smoky tang of lichen in the air, I turned my face toward the warmth of the sun. Across the bay the *Raduim Gilbert* lay silent in the waters close to the shore. How well I remembered waiting in anticipation, during the short summer season, for the arrival of these NTCL tug boats and barges that carried our annual supplies from the South. But, during these past few days I had been shocked and saddened to learn from the people of Déline of a more insidious use for them.[1]

Between 1932 and 1960, these same barges transported thousands of tonnes of radium and uranium ore across Great Bear Lake from Echo Bay to southern Canada. The people of Déline now suspect that the high incidence of deaths due to cancer in recent years among the older men in the village dates back to that time when they were employed by the mines to carry sacks of radioactive ores on and off the barges.

In 1900 Dr. James Macintosh Bell, a federal geologist working for the

Geological Survey of Canada, reported that "the steep rocky shores which here present themselves to the lake are often stained with cobalt bloom and copper green." When geologist Gilbert LaBine came across this report, he recognized the possibility that copper, silver and perhaps even gold might be present on the eastern shores of Great Bear Lake, near Echo Bay. He flew there in 1930 but what he discovered was even more valuable. LaBine discovered deposits of pitchblende, an ore rich in radium and uranium. He named his find Eldorado. Radium, selling for the astonishing price of seventy thousand dollars a gram, was considered enormously valuable in medicine for use in X-rays and cancer treatment. It was even used in a variety of other products such as luminous watch dials.

LaBine's Eldorado, located in 1932 at what became known as Port Radium, was the first major mining concern in the Northwest Territories and the first uranium mine in Canada. LaBine also established a refinery at Port Hope in Ontario. The raw ores were shipped westwards on barges across Great Bear Lake, down Bear River, and up the Mackenzie River to Fort McMurray in Alberta, and then by train all the way to Port Hope where they were refined into radium.

The eastern end of the lake had always been a favourite location for the Sahtuot'ine to await the arrival of the migrating caribou both in the spring and fall. So when Eldorado was established it brought about the Dene's first venture into paid employment. Many of the Sahtuot'ine men camped there were hired to cut timber for propping up the interior mine shafts and for building the miners' cabins, supplying the new settlement with firewood, and hauling the ore.

Sahtuot'ine men were employed each summer to carry the heavy uranium ores on and off the barges. Packed only in gunny sacks and weighing around forty-five kilograms, the ore had to be physically handled at least eight times. First the ore sacks were loaded on to large barges for shipment across Great Bear Lake, then on to smaller barges on the Bear River, to trucks for the journey around the St. Charles Rapids, and on to large barges for the remainder of the trip. Over the years the men hauled tens of thousands of sacks which often ripped and had to be refilled by hand or shovels. During the long barge journeys, the men frequently sat or even slept on top of the highly radioactive radium sacks.

In 1941 the Canadian government quietly purchased the mine. World War II was raging and Canada joined the United States to work cooperatively in building atomic weapons of mass destruction. Since the US had no uranium sources of its own, it purchased the Port Radium stockpiles at the Port Hope refinery and placed an order for a further sixty tonnes of uranium oxide. It was this uranium source that was used to unleash the horrific power in the atomic bombs that demolished Hiroshima in a single blast in 1945.

Unaware of the dangers to themselves and unaware of the use for the ore, Sahtuot'ine men continued to haul radioactive sacks on and off the barges until Port Radium finally closed in 1960 when there was no uranium left. During these thirty or so years, more than seven thousand tonnes of radioactive material were shipped south for refining. But it is estimated that some 1.7 million tonnes of material from the remaining waste products was dumped on the land surface as well as into Great Bear Lake and other small lakes around Port Radium. Even efficient extraction processes cannot capture all the radium and uranium from the original ores, and reports indicate that Port Radium was far from efficient; it is estimated that more than ten percent of radium and uranium elements remain within the non-radioactive pulverized rock materials. A variety of uranium by-products such as thorium, radioactive lead and polonium as well as by metals such as arsenic, cadmium and mercury are also included in these tailings.

While the men worked at the mines or on the barges, their families pitched their tents nearby, not realizing that the tailings were toxic and radioactive. Children played on the rocks and sand; in fact, they often played in the contaminated sand as one might at a beach. Women made clothing from torn gunny sacks still covered with yellow ore dust. The people were allowed to use broken planks from wooden docks saturated with spilled ore dust for fires on which they cooked their food. Some can still recall the strange green flames of the burning wood. They fished, drank water and washed themselves and their clothes in the surrounding contaminated lakes and pools.

During one of our discussions in the summer of 1995, Morris Modeste told me that his father, who died of lung cancer in the late 1980s, had been an ore carrier. Morris and others recalled seeing their fathers returning to their tents in the evenings, their hair, mouths and clothes covered in yellow dust from carrying the sacks. They had no idea that the dust they breathed and carried home was so dangerous to their health and that of their families. Only in recent years, sparked by the high incidence of cancer among people who were involved with transporting these ores in earlier years, have the people of Déline begun to suspect a connection.

However, Canada's federal government and the mine operators knew all along about the dangers of exposure to radioactive materials. As early as 1931, Canada's Department of Mines published a report that stated:

> The hazards involved in the handling of high-grade radioactive materials make necessary the adoption of certain precautions.... The ingestion of small amounts of radioactive dust or emanation over a long period of time will cause a building up of radioactive material in the body, which will eventually have serious consequences. Lung cancer, bone necrosis, and rapid anaemia are possible diseases due to the deposition of radioactive substances in the cell tissue or bone structure of the body....
>
> The fact, however, that radium or radioactive substances once deposited in the bone structure of the body are impossible to eliminate makes the taking of every precaution a most necessary factor....

The following year the Department of Mines Annual Report, referring to Port Radium, stated, "During the year under review, all those engaged in the radium work were subjected to regular examination each week for the presence of radon in the lungs, and to a blood test every month." No examinations were carried out on any of the Sahtuot'ine workers.

Many similar reports have been written over the years, but the Sahtuot'ine were never warned of the extreme dangers exposure to these ores posed to their health. They received no medical examinations, they were not encouraged to take precautions, they were afforded no protective clothing, nor were they offered the use of showers on the tug boats, showers that were made available to the non-Native men who worked on the barges.

After the mine closed in 1960, these same NTCL barges were then used to transport annual supplies into many communities along the Mackenzie River as well as to Fort Franklin. In the late 1980s, when supplies from Yellowknife and the south were transported to the smaller communities by airplane or on trucks using the winter roads, the barges were no longer required and were put up for sale. The Déline band, hoping to use it locally, and, of course, unaware of its dangerous history, purchased the *Radium Gilbert* for one dollar.

As more information came to light about the hazardous cargoes carried by these barges, the Déline band requested that the government perform tests on their newly acquired tug boat. The report indicated that the radioactive levels, though present, were within "acceptable limits," but people wonder and worry if they have been told the truth.[2] They have tried selling the barge for scrap but, so far, with no takers.

Further serious areas of concern remain. As the people of Déline begin to learn more about the effects of radioactive contamination, they worry about its impact on their food and water supply. Their only source of water for drinking and washing is from the lake, making it necessary to keep monitoring the lake.

Lake fish near Port Radium might also be affected by the absorption of radioactive contaminants into their bodies and into the plants and plankton on which they feed. Will supplies of fish and their ability to reproduce decline over time? More immediately, how will the people know if the fish are safe to eat?

The area around Port Radium has always been one of the traditional pathways for the seasonal migrations of caribou. Lichen is an important component of the caribou diet but it collects a great deal of radioactive dust from the air that can then be ingested by the animals. It is also feared that polonium gas, a very poisonous element created from the decay of radon gas and dispersed by wind, might accumulate in the caribou's edible tissues. How will this affect those Dene who continue to eat caribou and moose?

The people of Déline have so many unanswered questions and considerable suspicion about the answers already received. The more they learn of the government's past concealment of the truth, the less trust they have with the present government's replies. As a part of the Land Claim Agreement of 1993 the Dene were required to "select" lands within those the federal government had indicated were available around Great Bear Lake. To this end, the elders and community leaders "selected" a number of land areas that would ensure the economic, cultural and spiritual survival of the people, areas that were important because of their traditional significance, places where they had always gathered for spiritual purposes, or special locations for hunting and fishing, such as around the area that became Port Radium. During this selection process the Dene had to rely on the federal government not to withhold any information that might prove detrimental. Yet the government did not see fit to share their knowledge of the areas of contamination with the Sahtuot'ine. As the leaders have since said, "Had we known about radioactive contamination on those lands and what that meant we would never have selected them as designated areas. We would have selected other locations."

In the meantime, many of Déline's elders who once worked on the barges continue to die of bone, lung, throat and other forms of cancer. There is also much suspicion about the deaths and ill health of women and children who once camped on these tailings. Successive generations have been deprived of fathers and grandparents who should have been their foremost teachers of Sahtuot'ine traditions and values. Some young people have expressed not only fear for themselves but also for the health of future generations. Others have expressed a sense of hopelessness and rage, and even suicidal feelings.

In 1996 the Déline Dene Band Uranium Committee was formed. One of the committee's first actions was to produce a comprehensive research document titled "They Never Told Us These Things."[3] They have also pressed the federal government into accepting its responsibilities for having the tailings at Port Radium and other "hot spots" cleaned up, so that future damage may be minimized. The task would be huge yet the survival of this community may depend upon it.[4]

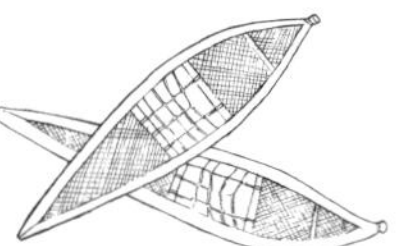

After a while, I walked on towards the ski hill, along the shores of Little Lake on which we had depended for plane arrivals in the 1960s during the main lake's freeze up and break up. This smaller lake is still used periodically for the float planes that have remained a common sight in the North. But by 1995 Little Lake's importance had decreased since the nearby airport runway handled more than two hundred and fifty flights a month in the summer and some one hundred fifty to two hundred a month in the winter, a far cry from the less than half a dozen planes a month we experienced in the mid-sixties.

I thought back with fond memories to those times when we would race from the village by dog team or snowmobile to catch or meet a plane arriving on Little

Lake. I also recalled, with less fondness, those times of waiting patiently in the freezing temperatures and bone-chilling wind, while the pilot lit his Herman Nelson heater to soften the oil in the engine so that the propellers of his Cessna or Beaver could swing freely and we would be able to leave.

Since there was no clear path along the lake, I had to force my way through a mass of small bushes. It proved tiring and before long I began to wonder if the ski hill still existed, although people had assured me it did. Finally, I came upon a sizeable gash in the woods on my right. This straight, wide clearing leading to the top of the hill bore no resemblance to the narrow winding path down which Pete, Liz, Claire, Helen and I used to hurl ourselves on our cross-country skis. Was this really the same place? I made my way slowly up the hill, stopping frequently to eat the delicious wild strawberries growing low to the ground. Yes, this indeed was our ski hill. There, incredibly, near the crest, was a familiar rectangle of the interwoven spruce covering, now turned brown, that had once lined the floor of our lean-to, where we would rest and drink hot chocolate or strong tea at the end of a hard day of skiing.

I sat on a nearby tree stump and ate my lunch, and contemplated how different life had become for the people of Déline in these intervening thirty years. Most of the old, so-called traditional ways of earning a living had virtually disappeared. Many people still participate in some hunting, primarily of caribou and the occasional moose, but with snowmobiles and stronger outboard motors on their boats, the men are able to travel quickly over long distances to the old familiar locations favoured by their ancestors, and they are now only gone for a few days to a couple of weeks at any one time.

Fishing with nets and rods is still popular, but since dogs have been replaced by snowmobiles, the demand for fish is much less. As a result, there has been a marked increase in the availability and size of trout, whitefish, herring and grayling in Keith Arm.

Few people are still engaged in making crafts. With the decline in moose hunting, hides used for making articles of clothing are in short supply and expensive to purchase from elsewhere. Women also complained that even when they made slippers they received little in return for their time and costs from the retailers in Yellowknife and elsewhere. Perhaps of greater significance, few young people want to learn these skills and, as an elderly women explained, "Now that we are older our eyes and our fingers are not so good any more."

Among the men, only Johnny Neyelle remains active in making crafts. One evening, as I strolled along the lakeshore, I came across Johnny, now in his late seventies but changed remarkably little. He was fixing the septic tank near his house. We talked for a few minutes but since the odour was not too pleasant I continued on my walk! Returning the same way about an hour later, Johnny, who had now corrected his tank problems, called me over and asked if I would like to see his workshop. We had already had a good chuckle about snowshoes made "for the feet and for the wall" and I had told him how I had a pair of his snowshoes, still in perfect condition, on the wall of my home in southern Ontario. He showed me a dozen traditional caribou-skin drums that he had made on consignment for the Dene drum dances at Wrigley (Kwedzehk'o). The order was ready for shipping. I wanted to purchase one from him but didn't want him to feel obliged to sell me one of these. So we just chatted as I admired his work. He also talked sadly about the dearth of craft production and how none of the young people were interested in learning these skills, skills that were dying out with the elders.

Most elderly people said their lives were now easier and for that they were grateful, but many also expressed a sense of aimlessness. Although visiting with relatives and friends remains important, many seemed to regret having little to do but fill their empty days watching a great deal of television. Perhaps the greatest disappointment of all for them is the realization that the traditional ways and many of the values that meant so much to them are now rapidly disappearing.

People between the ages of thirty to fifty felt quite differently about their lives. These are the people who are proficient in English, received sufficient schooling, including advanced education and training, and who are now employed in a variety of occupations provided by the federal and territorial governments, the local council and the two stores. These are the people who, to all intents and purposes, run the community. They repeatedly told me that life was much better now than in the old days, and that they were happy with what their jobs provided them: their comfortable houses, cars and trucks, TVs and VCRs, household appliances, faster motor boats, Ski-doos, occasional trips to Yellowknife and the South. However, there was almost always an aura of wistfulness for the past. Most people still enjoy camping on the land or visiting their cabins dotted around the lake on weekends during the long sunlit hours of summer. There they can fish, pick berries, and with luck, shoot a moose or a stray caribou. Several men also stated that they looked forward to participating in the annual caribou hunts to provide additional food for the community. Despite all the changes, their hearts are never far from the land.

Although there was much more to ponder, it would have to wait until another day. With one last look at Little Lake and the ski hill, I rose from my tree stump and decided to head back to the village by following the path upwards through unknown territory. In the distance I could hear the hum of large power saws cutting down trees. Perhaps it was Morris Modeste and his work crew clearing the bush for the new, soon to be extended, airstrip.

My path led me along the crest of the hill before eventually turning back towards the lake. Suddenly, I was standing in the middle of the garbage dump. I was appalled. What an eyesore. There was so much waste here: broken fridges, washing machines, trucks, tires, cable, even two crashed airplanes. Then I realized that most of the items were arranged quite neatly in specific areas. This wasn't just a garbage dump, it was, in fact, a huge recycling plant. Where else was a person to get spare parts without having them flown in at considerable expense? If you needed a new door for your fridge, well maybe there was one here, or a new tire for your kid's bicycle, or some additional wiring. And how else could you get rid of the accoutrements of modern society, for there was little hope of them decaying quickly in these cold climes? So, by organizing the dump, the people had turned a liability into something productive and much needed.

As had happened to me several times since returning to Déline, my initial judgement had, upon further reflection, proven to be too hasty. What seemed to be a negative aspect of something on the surface often turned out to be quite different and far more positive once I looked at the situation more closely.

ʔEhtseo Ayha School, Déline. The new school was built in 1986. By 1996 all grades, from kindergarten to grade twelve, were available to students.

CHAPTER TWENTY

EDUCATION

Déline's large modern school is named ?Ehtseo Ayha School, after a former much-respected Sahtuot'ine prophet. In 1995, classes ran from kindergarten to grade ten, with the eleventh and twelfth grades added in September of 1995 and 1996, respectively. Although Judi Tutcho, the principal, had already given me permission to visit the school, I also checked with Dolphus Baton, one of the two custodians busy at work cleaning the school, to ensure that he was agreeable to my wandering around.

The facility has a pleasant appearance. Large, bright classrooms are located on both sides of a single long corridor; there is a large well-stocked library, a teaching and learning centre and, much to my surprise, a lab with some twenty Apple computers, complete with what were then state-of-the-art Pentium processors and accompanying software. A full-sized gym is also used for community events. Several stock rooms are well supplied with all the paraphernalia teachers always need to assist them in doing a good job of educating young minds. Other than the students' artwork displayed in the hallway and the twenty or so photographs of community elders hanging in the foyer, I could almost have been standing in a modern school anywhere in Canada.

How very different from our little four-room building. No one shared such a magnificent view as mine, for classrooms in this school, built on a slight incline at the northwest corner of the village, looked out either onto the playground or the end of the airstrip. No longer was it possible for a teacher to glance out of the window and catch a glimpse of an elderly woman returning from the bush, hunched under her bundle of kindling, or see a man, .410 at the ready in his hand, off to hunt for ptarmigan, or watch others going fishing across the lake by dog team or canoe depending on whether it was a lake of ice or water.

During my stay in Déline that summer, no topic generated more discussion and more concern than education. Invariably, the discussion focused on three interconnected areas: programming in the school, the attitude and behaviour of young people, and fears for their future. No matter whom I talked to, Native or non-Native, everyone had strong and often conflicting views on these subjects.

The territorial government provides funds for all aspects of education. The move towards teaching Native languages in schools in the Western Arctic began around 1980 when the territorial government finally accepted the Dene's arguments that the preservation of their culture and language through instruction at school was essential. At that time George Cleary was principal of the Déline school and he began emphasizing Slavey language instruction. John Tetso, the

1995 chief, and another local person were asked to help by producing books in Slavey for young children. Soon after, Jane Modeste, Morris' sister, was hired full-time to take over the production of books and other teaching materials in Slavey. Initially, these materials were just for use in the Déline school. However, before long, Jane was hired as a regional consultant and visited many communities along the Dehcho, sharing Déline's materials and assisting others to produce their own.

Unlike several other Western Arctic communities, almost everyone in Déline in 1995, except for the elderly, was fluent in English and Slavey. A few parents stated that they wanted their children to learn only English in school, recognizing that the best jobs in Déline and elsewhere go to those with a good command of English. Most parents, however, were adamant that they wanted their children educated in both languages. But delivery of such has not always been easy. The strength of the school's Slavey language program has depended primarily on the commitment and initiative demonstrated by each principal, a commitment that has varied considerably over the years.

During our reunion in Ottawa, Judi had also mentioned that the teachers hired for Déline by the education department were crucial in making adequate language instruction possible. Most are still recruited from the South as there are insufficient numbers of trained Dene teachers available and some of those who are qualified don't always want to return to these small, relatively isolated communities of their youth.

The territorial Department of Education provides Native language and cultural curriculum programs both at the elementary and secondary level. But it is both difficult and expensive to produce such materials for all schools in eight northern languages. It has, therefore, fallen to the teaching and learning centres of individual schools to supplement materials from Yellowknife with locally developed products. It was clear from my discussions that Déline's centre, presently operating with a staff of two, is very important in the teaching of the Slavey language in the school.

Many people in the community also wanted the school to provide some traditional cultural learning so that young people might develop a greater sense of familiarity and appreciation for the former life of their parents and grandparents. Few young people today seem interested in knowing anything about the traditional ways of life. Their points of reference are what they now see and hear on television, videos and CDs. However, the school in Déline has, as have schools in other northern communities, provided a variety of activities to support parents' requests.

Walter Beyha and Morris Modeste took groups of students out to the bush for ten-day periods to give them a sense of what living on the land had been like in the past. Another time, John Baton took a group of students out on the land. After shooting a moose he then demonstrated how to skin and butcher it, as well as how every part of the animal could be used. By all accounts the students enjoy such ventures and no doubt do gain a better appreciation of their grandparents' skills. Many people in the village would like to see their frequency increased, but such ventures are expensive for the school, which receives little additional funding from the government.

Aside from the school's efforts, the elements of cultural transmission occur incidentally and informally when children and youth participate in drum dances, the stick gamble and other daily community activities, and when they accompany their families out on the land, even if only on weekends or for brief trips.

For years the Sahtuot'ine had been requesting that secondary as well as elementary schooling be provided in their own community so that their children would not have to move away. Now Déline, like an increasing number of other northern communities, has its own secondary school. But it appears that what was a good idea ten to fifteen years ago is not necessarily quite so viable in these rapidly changing times.

Many parents in Déline are pleased that their children have access to higher-grade levels in the village. Others are not—at least not pleased that now their children *have* to attend in Déline. As one mother, who spoke for many, explained it: "The parents should have a choice where their kids go. It wasn't right that the kids had to go to Yellowknife in the past. It isn't right that the kids have to stay here in Déline now to finish their schooling. There should be a choice. For some kids it is better that they stay here. For other kids they need to go to school in Yellowknife or Fort Smith." Many believe that educational standards in Yellowknife are higher, thus making it easier for students to apply for college or university. Some also consider that students educated in Yellowknife benefit from their interaction with students from other places as well as from an awareness of life beyond Déline. However, while recognizing these advantages, some parents acknowledged it also meant their sons and daughters might no longer want to return to Déline on a full-time basis.

"When we went to school you made us behave and you made us work hard," was the view expressed by many of my former students. "That doesn't happen in school now. Some of the teachers can't discipline the students and even when they do, all the kids have to do is complain to their parents who then get angry with the teachers. That makes it difficult for everyone to learn."

A 1996 report conducted by the NWT Teachers' Association and the NWT Department of Education indicated that abusive language, insults, obscene gestures and physical attacks are common to many NWT schools, especially at the junior and senior high school levels.[1] The study was initiated because of the growing concern for the safety of both teachers and students, where one-third of the incidents involved physical abuse, with almost ten percent directed at teachers, and it is on the increase.

The following words by Johnny Washie, a Dogrib who frequently writes for Yellowknife's *News/North* and is an ardent proponent of the need for young people to be well educated, hold particular significance when one realizes that the drop-out rate from schools among aboriginal students in the NWT continues to hover at or above eighty percent.

> We all know our world is changing quickly and many of our young Dene people will have to adapt to changing times.... Education is the key to opening doors, to challenging our world and enabling us to adapt to changing times.... Without an education we will be left far behind. With a good education we will be able to handle our own affairs and have greater control of our lives in the communities....
>
> We need to encourage our young aboriginals to stay in school if we want them to be somebody in their own field in this modern world.... Education is just like a snowshoe—it breaks the trail.... Life without school will be difficult indeed.[2]

Educational issues have become much more complex since the sixties. Our students were well behaved and worked hard, often struggling to do so. But those were different times. It was a simpler time when children obeyed their parents and their teachers. Our students did not suffer from the same social problems that children and youth face today, and consequently we had few discipline problems to deal with.

I recalled my dissatisfaction with many of the materials used and topics taught unless we made copious adaptations, and how irrelevant much of it must have seemed as we ignored their language and culture in the school. And yet, despite all my apprehensions, many of my former students repeatedly expressed, during the summer of 1995, their satisfaction with the education we had provided them. Perhaps my fellow teachers and I can take some credit for that, but I believe far more was attributable to the strength of families with their traditional beliefs about child rearing, as well as the community support the children then had. It gave them strong roots and a confidence to try new things. That support was also extended to the teachers as we did our best to help their children bridge both worlds.

However concerned parents now were about their children's education, they were equally, if not more worried about the behaviour and attitude of young people in the community. This is a modern-day dilemma: parents who were brought up by traditional methods are in conflict with the youth who see nothing relevant in the "old ways" to help them cope with their new world.

Young children were certainly allowed a great deal of freedom and apparently had few constraints put on them. No doubt those children, frequently left to their own devices, found it difficult to obey school rules and tended to rebel in class. However, most of the children and adolescents I met that summer seemed to behave much like children in the South. I only came across a handful who took delight in bullying others or vandalizing property, again, not so different from elsewhere.

During the summer holidays, the recreation department organized daily activities for children—mostly sporting activities. In the winter there is a strong hockey program for boys and girls as well as many other organized sporting activities.

Many of the adolescents who had jobs around the community during the summer appeared pleasant and responsible. Those with whom I talked seemed to share the same kinds of anxieties, dreams, insecurities and confusion that all teenagers demonstrate. But the degree of boredom and frustration expressed here was more pervasive and they listed some of the reasons for me: too little to do in Déline, excessive drinking among their peers, too much time spent on card playing by their parents, awareness of an immense gap between them and their parents and especially their grandparents. Several expressed the futility of continuing their education if, in the end, there were no jobs here for them to return to—jobs that would pay them enough money to acquire all they had come to expect. Yet, at the same time, because of their strong ties to family and community, many expressed further apprehensions about having to leave Déline in order to find employment. A few had decided that life on Social Assistance was preferable and had already dropped out of school and out of life.

"In the past our parents would teach us how to behave," explained Jimmy Tutcho,[3] who summarized the views of many adults with whom I spoke. "They taught us our values through stories. We were loved by all members of our family when we were very young. We learned what was required of us by working alongside our parents and doing our share of tasks around the house or the camp. We never thought of disobeying our parents, and if we did, we would have to face the quiet anger of an elder or even the chief who would be brought in to speak to us. Very soon, even as children, we were given considerable freedom and independence, but by then we knew what was expected of us.

"Now, too often, parents don't spend enough time with their young children, and they either just yell at them, or give in to their wants. There are too few grandfathers left and, anyway, none of the younger children want to listen to the elders anymore. In fact they often laugh at them. Instead they prefer to watch television. So they are growing up with too much freedom and none of the values that they need to know to be responsible people. This is not good. So even though things are good here now, we worry a lot about the future for our kids."

One of the Sahtuot'ine's most sacred traditions was the practice of noninterference and it is still respected to a large extent today. People believed they should be free to make their own decisions and learn from their own mistakes without interference from others. This also applied to children. So parents are now caught in the dilemma of wanting their children to behave without interfering with their freedom.

In his excellent book, *Return to the Teachings*, Rupert Ross, although talking generally about Aboriginal people across Canada, explains that in traditional times children were taught things at almost every instant and in a wide variety of ways through their daily participation in their parents' lives and through stories and ceremonies.[4] That teaching did not focus on teaching each person exactly what to say, think, or do, which is how most of us non-Natives were brought up, instead, it focused on two other elements.

First, it taught that life was a matter of responsibility that all people had to bear at all times. Second, it taught children how to develop the personal qualities they would need to be able to carry out those responsibilities. What people actually did in the fulfilment of their duties, however, was largely a matter of free choice.

Ross then goes on to use an analogy:

> I have come to see traditional child rearing as a three-legged stool, where two of the legs (teaching children responsibilities and developing their personal attributes and skills) made it possible to allow for a third leg of almost complete freedom to make particular choices. The first two legs, however, were cut away (as the old ways have disappeared).... The only leg remaining was the habit of noninterference. All by itself, that *habit* does indeed promise chaos."
>
> The problem in many Aboriginal communities, I now suspect, lies not in noninterference but in the fact that this approach is no longer accompanied by teaching about responsibilities or by any guidance in developing essential personal capacities."[5]

Is that not what Jimmy meant when he said, "So they are growing up with too much freedom and none of the values that they need to know to be responsible people"?

Perhaps the answer lies in re-teaching the two other legs of the stool and focusing again on teaching children responsibilities and developing their personal attributes and skills to handle such responsibilities. As Ross points out, many Aboriginal communities across Canada are making strong efforts to return to this more traditional way of rearing their children.

Or perhaps parents will instead choose to learn new child-rearing skills to meet the ways of the new world. But who will teach them how to provide the needed structure for firm guidance to go with the caring that already exists? Where are the models for modern-day parenting? Surely not from the TV sitcoms that blare into their houses. And in the meantime, what about the present generations of children and youth who have grown up without such guidance?

Bringing up children is seldom easy for any parent especially in these days of rapid change. For most of us the gaps between one generation and the next have been relatively small. But for the people of Déline, as is true for many Aboriginal people, the gaps are immense—and so are the choices and solutions for dealing with them. Yet, recognizing that unruly children suffer in the long run, an increasing number of parents in Déline are trying to find ways to raise their children to be responsible adults. Many are succeeding, often by using a combination of traditional and more modern ways.

Furthermore, the bonds that exist between family members and especially their children and grandchildren still remain strong and are a positive force in the community. When a child is fearful of returning home because of his parents' excessive drinking or gambling, he knows that he is always welcome to bunk down and eat at another relative's house for a few days. Even though an occasional grandparent complained to me that grandchildren, neglected by their parents, ended up spending too much time with them, they would not dream of turning these children away. No child is left out in the cold.

Despite all the frustration of adolescents and parents, the fact that there have been so few suicides among young people in Déline in the past ten years—below the Canadian average and much below the higher NWT average—has to be yet another indication of the strength that still exists within families and in the community of Déline as a whole. And this, too, bodes well for the future.

With a rapidly increasing young population, parents wonder if there will be jobs in and around Déline for their children when they grow up.

CHAPTER TWENTY-ONE

JOBS

BWHAAA! BWHAAA! I leapt to one side of the dirt road as the deep-throated air horn belonging to a huge white dump truck blasted at me—BWHAAA! Its thick tires were as high as my head. Glancing up into the cab I caught the large grin on Ronald Beyonnie's face as he slowly, but very proudly, drove past me. I waved back as a convoy of several more brand new trucks passed by and continued on their practice circuits around the village.

These drivers represented half of the eighteen men who had just completed the theory component of their Heavy Equipment Operator On-the-Job Training Program and who were now into the more enjoyable part of putting theory into practice. The other nine were familiarizing themselves with driving heavy-duty Caterpillar bulldozers.

This six-week course, run under the auspices of Arctic College, had been arranged by Chief John Tetso and the band members, as well as by Dave Speakman, the community adult educator. The band, using some of their land claim money, paid the men seven dollars an hour to attend the course of ninety-six class hours with another two hundred hours in the field. Once the men—no women on this course, yet!—receive their certificate and class three driver's licences, they will make good money. Their first job will be to clear the land and build a road to the relocated and enlarged airport and airstrip, scheduled for completion in the summer of 1998.

"Where are the jobs needed for all our young people going to come from?" I frequently heard this lament from people in Déline. It is a concern felt throughout the North where the birth rate is growing at twice the national rate. In keeping with the trends depicted in the last NWT census, within the 1995 Déline population of some 570 residents, 307 (fifty-four percent) were under the age of twenty-five, and of those, almost a half were under the age of ten. Such an increasingly young population puts tremendous strains on any community. Unless there are drastic changes in the economic opportunities available in the vicinity over the next few years many, if not most, will be unable to find future employment in the village and will either suffer the accompanying social malaise, or else will have to leave.

This out-migration of individuals and families to larger communities such as Inuvik, Norman Wells and Yellowknife is already happening and is the main reason why Déline's total population has remained somewhat static for several years despite a large increase in births. Unfortunately, as is often the case, some of the best-educated and most capable people tend to be the ones most likely to leave. Most find this decision difficult and painful as family and community ties are strong. They are torn between a sense of community responsibility and meeting their own personal and family needs elsewhere. But out-migration has not solved the unemployment problem. In fact, with the continued escalating growth of a younger population, the time bomb is ticking.

According to "The Human Resource and Training Strategy for the Community of Déline, 1995 to 2000,"[1] between 1984 and 1994 the number of people in Déline with jobs had declined, whereas those seeking employment had grown by more than sixty-six percent. Of those unemployed, more than sixty percent were aged between fifteen and twenty-four. The report goes on to outline a sizeable number of employment opportunities that could be made available to the people of Déline over these next few years, but it is abundantly clear that these jobs will only be attainable if many more young people obtain further education and training.

Much of the talk in the NWT over the past few years has centred around the enormously rich discovery of diamonds in the area located north-east of Yellowknife, between Great Slave Lake and Great Bear Lake. Ekati Mines, owned by Broken Hill Proprietary (BHP) Diamonds Inc. and partners, was given approval to begin construction by the federal and territorial governments, as well as by the Dogrib people on whose traditional lands these discoveries were made, only after months of serious discussion by all parties in a series of formal hearings, with specific emphasis on environmental concerns.

The Dene recognize and welcome the significant economic opportunities that BHP, the first major diamond mine in North America, will bring, both directly through the mine operation and through the many secondary support businesses that will also create jobs. BHP has guaranteed that 72 percent of the jobs will go to NWT residents and of those, at least half will go to Aboriginal people. The labour demands are large and will create about a thousand jobs per year over the next twenty-five years. To put that in perspective, the total number of jobs in the entire mining and oil industries in the NWT in 1996 was around fifteen hundred. A small percentage of the jobs will require advanced degrees and specialized experience, but about three-quarters of them will employ people with training and experience in heavy equipment, mechanical trades, mill and shop trades, and construction trades, as well as in a variety of support services. Some of Déline's recently trained heavy-duty truck and bulldozer operators are already working at the mine.

Diavik, a second major diamond mine located in the same general area, is also in the final stages of obtaining environmental and other permits from the federal and territorial governments, after extensive discussion with the Dogribs and others.

Additional mining exploration for gold and diamonds is occurring within the

Sahtu Claims Area. Government geologists believe this region also has considerable potential for the discovery of minerals and they state that it is only a matter of time before other exploration companies turn their attention to this area.

With land claims settled in much of the western portions of the NWT, land previously unavailable is now open for exploration. This is good news for the Sahtu Dene. It is expected that the Mackenzie Valley/Dehcho, including the Sahtu region, will boom over the next ten years because of renewed oil and gas exploration and drilling in the Norman Wells area. If this holds true, again a number of job opportunities in a variety of areas will become available to the people of Déline as well as a share in financial remuneration

The development of infrastructure within Déline itself offers considerable opportunity for training and employment. Funding from the GNWT has recently supported the relocation and enlargement of the airport as well as many smaller community projects, including more village housing. Ongoing maintenance of these facilities and local roads will also be required.

Almost one third of the working people of the NWT are employed by the three levels of government—federal, territorial, and municipal or band councils. This holds true for Déline where the business and administration of the community provides many stable jobs. Qualified and trained people in Déline, mostly those between thirty-five and fifty, currently hold these positions, and they will eventually need to be replaced as they retire. Skills in administration, computers, accounting, clerical and office management, and social services are paramount in these positions. As already mentioned, the Déline Band Council also contracts out many businesses to local people. And one must not forget the jobs associated with both the Northern and Co-op stores. In addition, the implementation and administration of the land claim agreement will also create some jobs there.

Northern tourism presents further employment opportunities. In 1995, forty-eight thousand people visited the NWT providing for about $51 million worth of economic activity. That same year the Déline Development Corporation entered into a partnership with two other corporations and tourism operator Chummy Plummer. Together they now control four of the five tourist lodges frequented by Canadian and US sports fishermen on Great Bear Lake. The arrangement allows for cost sharing and creates jobs for local people in the area. Other tourism ventures are also being explored in Déline, such as Modeste Outfitters. The community has also purchased a thirty-foot cabin vessel that can carry tourists and fishing parties to locations around the lake. At other times it is contracted out to the government for various projects, such as environmental work. The band also built a large new hotel in the community in 1998.

During the past five years there has been a substantial increase in the number of people running their own small businesses in the NWT in such ventures as small engine repair shops, hairdressing and barber shops, bakeries, moccasin and snowshoe factories, and local gift stores, to mention a few. Furthermore, the Inuit in particular have demonstrated that, in addition to the sale of their highly regarded prints and carvings, there is an increasingly lucrative market among tourists and export to the South for such items as craft work, jewellery and unique clothing for the fashion industry.[2] Generous grants are available from the territorial government to assist people to get started in these new ventures. So there is much room for exploring similar activities for enterprising persons in Déline.[3]

One of the main impediments to mounting full-scale economic development in many Western Arctic communities is the high cost of purchasing and shipping materials from the South and the subsequent delivery of finished goods to southern markets, since, for most of the year, air transportation has to be used. Advocates for a year-round road along the Dehcho to Inuvik present a good case when they say that such a road would substantially reduce the cost of materials and food items as well as make tourist attractions and other business ventures more accessible in the Western Arctic. Given the immense cost incurred annually to construct and maintain the major winter roads, which are only operable for three to four months of the year, it is perplexing that there has not been more progress made on the expansion of a permanent highway north from Wrigley, despite its considerable expense. Furthermore, construction of the road would provide on-the-job training and employment for many people in the Sahtu and other adjacent areas.

I can't help recalling the substantial opposition to road and resource development along the Dehcho by the Dene in the days of the Berger Commission's enquiry. But more than twenty years have passed and lives have changed immensely. The Dene still insist on the right to be involved in all stages of development but people are no longer afraid of these technological changes. In fact, many people in Déline and other communities welcome the training and employment opportunities they bring as well as the financial remuneration to be gained from such increased economic activity.

Opportunities for education and training, as well as substantial financial assistance, are abundant in the NWT through a whole variety of programmes operated by the GNWT, often in conjunction with industry. Two major institutions, Arctic and Aurora colleges, which play such an integral role across the NWT. Main campuses in the Western Arctic are based in Inuvik, Yellowknife and Fort Smith. In addition, more than a dozen community learning centres are located in smaller villages such as Déline. Currently, many young people from Déline are involved in post-secondary school education and training. However, encouraging more young people to complete their schooling and take advantage of the courses available to them will remain one of the major challenges for the parents and community leaders. So will getting young people off chronic social assistance dependency.

The chief and village band council, only too aware of these future employment concerns, are also committed to spending land claim money to provide more local job training opportunities, as well as looking for ways to create employment opportunities in Déline.

Enormous challenges face the people of Déline—challenges of educating the young both at school and beyond, challenges of ensuring employment opportunities for those educated young people to return to, and challenges of dealing with the consequences of social disintegration if sufficient jobs are not available. It is a daunting task and many difficult years lie ahead. Yet, when I recall talking to many of the community's leaders about these challenges, I was encouraged by their optimism tempered by their sense of realism about what they face, as well as their determination to do all they can to ensure a better future for their children.

CHAPTER TWENTY-TWO

BINGO, FISHING AND JUSTICE

Bingo night, Déline style.

After dinner and washing the dishes, Cec spread several Bingo sheets across the dining table. My curiosity was aroused. She explained that every Friday night, with the help of the local radio station, she played Bingo at home. Ten sheets for ten dollars—three boards a sheet—with which to play the first ten games, could be purchased earlier in the week at the administrative offices. You could also buy additional sheets of six boards for two dollars with which to play the final whole board game, accompanied by a list of forty-five numbers. Providing these in advance saved radio time later on. It sounded interesting although I was sure there would no longer be any "Legs Eleven" or "Kelly's Eye," as I recalled fondly from my days of running Bingo in the old school.

Tonight's Bingo caller, Ronald Beyonnie, interrupted the CBC northern programming promptly at 7:00 PM. Although most of the discussion was in Slavey, Ronald called the numbers in English. The first game was for any two lines or four corners. Purple daubs from Cec's big marker started to fill her boards as the numbers were called. With only a handful announced, we heard the phone ringing on the radio—someone had already called in a Bingo. "There will be a two-minute break before we start the next game," said Ronald, and we rejoined CBC's country and western music program as the called-in card was verified. "The winner of game one is Jane B," and Jane B was now one-hundred dollars richer.

The evening progressed through the other nine games as I assisted Cec with the number daubing. This was Bingo without crowds and dense smoke. How much more pleasant it was to play in the comfort of your own home, chatting about other things between games. Cec was the local head of the social services department and she had already shared with me how depressing it could be at times dealing constantly with social assistance issues. But, this Friday evening was not a time for such serious talk—just a bit of friendly gossip.

Finally, with all ten games played and no winner in this household, it was time for the whole board game. Cec had already daubed all of her numbers from the list of forty-five, leaving her with only a few blanks to fill on each board. If she completed a board before seven more numbers were read she would win $1000. Apparently that rarely happened. More usual was for the first winner to

Stella (Betsidea) McKeinzo cleans several lake trout for her family's use in 1966. By 1995, "shore lunches" were very popular and fish were caught, cooked over an open fire and eaten immediately.

receive $500, the second $300 and the third $200. Although she came close, she was out of luck this time. However, I decided to try my luck the next Friday—but to no avail. In 1994 Bingos raised almost $140,000 for the band council to use on local projects.

In addition to the Bingo evenings, the local radio operated for about an hour twice a day, mostly to make announcements and respond to musical requests. These programs are almost entirely in Slavey. Several times during my stay I again heard my slide show announced as I continued to be asked to put on more shows. The slides were clearly a big hit and I had noticed some people attending more than once. I, too, enjoyed watching and listening to the people's reactions.

One Sunday evening, as Cec and I were in the middle of a crib game, I received a phone call asking if I would show my slides at the senior citizen's home that evening. I agreed to even though I didn't receive the request until 10:30 PM. And I thought old folks went to bed early, I said to myself. Not so when daylight is almost continuous. It was almost 1:00 AM by the time I finished but their enjoyment made it all worthwhile.

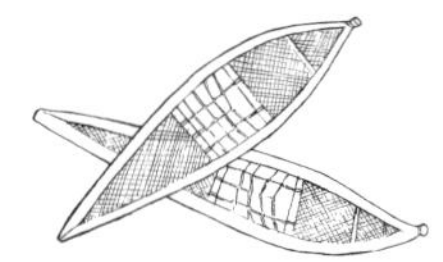

John and Cec had said that, weather permitting, and if John had fixed his outboard motor, we would be going for a shore lunch down the river on Sunday. Much to my delight the day turned out to be sunny and warm. We packed all the gear into the eighteen-foot boat, and, after church, headed across the lake for Sahtu De. I love travelling at speed but my heart was in my mouth at the rate with which John navigated the turns of the river. I had to keep reassuring myself that he had done this dozens of times before and obviously knew every rock and shallow area. My self-talk must have worked, for after a while of zooming down river I began to relax and enjoy the ride. All too soon John cut the engine and we came ashore along a small spur on the left bank. John jumped out, grabbed the rope in one hand and fishing rod in the other, tied the boat to a branch, and within minutes had caught our first grayling. Cec and I were left to unload with help from Atanda and Janine, a seven-year-old friend of Atanda's.

Once we had unpacked the foodstuff onto the shore, Atanda and I were sent fishing while John got the fire going. Cec and Janine went off to pick berries before starting to prepare lunch. I didn't catch anything for a while although Atanda had four good-sized grayling. Then John suggested I move closer to the boat where there was a nice eddy, and sure enough, I soon had caught a half-dozen ugly-looking things, not at all like trout. (My opinion appears to be in the minority as many people consider grayling to be very beautiful, especially their dorsal fin.)

Because I still wasn't at ease with the backward and forward motion of casting, I kept a watchful eye on Atanda to make sure she wasn't behind me. We kept fishing successfully for quite a while. Then, all of a sudden, I heard a piercing scream from behind. I knew it wasn't from Atanda because I could still see her about fifteen metres to my left. I quickly turned around and was horrified. My line had wrapped itself around Janine's head and I could see the three-pronged hook either in or close to her left eye.

Janine was terrified and so was I. She kept jumping up and down, her screams shattering the quiet. Just don't let it be in her eye, I pleaded as I ran towards her. I gently put my hands on her shoulders and told her to keep still so that I could unwind the line. Then I went for the hook, and thank goodness, it was not in her eye, but not more than a millimetre away. With the line loosened and Janine standing very still it came out easily, having only just nicked the skin. I gave her a big hug and apologized to her as she received hugs from everyone who had now joined us. I couldn't believe how close I had come to causing a serious disaster and several times during the afternoon bouts of shivers went through me as I realized how easily Janine's eye could have been damaged or even lost.

The rest of the day was very enjoyable. The grayling, skinned, dipped in flour and fried, tasted much better than they looked, in fact, they were very good eating. As we had caught close to twenty fish John said that he would drop off the remainder, gutted and cleaned, to the senior citizens home that evening. Then we spent a leisurely time with our pots picking *jie nezo* (nice-looking, juicy, wild blueberries) and a few blackberries, although it was still early for them. Janine spent the whole time by my side, chatting away and teaching me lots of Slavey words. I again wondered why I had made so little effort to learn any Slavey in the past. It wouldn't have been that difficult to pick up a few phrases and words. But it was even easier to get the drift of a conversation now since many English words were interjected in Slavey sentences.

All too soon it was time to leave and, again, we passed several other groups of people enjoying their shore lunches on both sides of the river and around the lake. Speeding up river at a good clip, though not as fast as earlier on—or was that just my impression now that I felt more comfortable on the river—I thought about the jet boats with their draft of only six inches. Several had made the trip from Tulit'a to Déline that summer, covering the distance of some one hundred forty kilometres in less than ninety minutes. I couldn't imagine travelling the river at those speeds.

"Hey Miggs. Are you going up to the court?" A young woman approached me as I walked towards the administrative buildings.

I knew nothing about this and so asked, "Where is it being held, and can anyone attend?"

"Yes, anyone can go. It's at the hall in the arena. Come with me." So I did.

I entered the room where the wedding feast had been held. The furniture had been rearranged with tables placed on three sides of a rectangle in the middle of the room and several rows of chairs to the side nearest the door. I sat down nearer the back where I would have a better view of the proceedings, and eventually discovered that Cathy McKeinzo, the young lady who had invited me to accompany her, was the probation officer. Little happened for almost an hour, during which time I talked to various people, who drifted in and out.

The circuit judge, accompanied by lawyers and others of his retinue, spends a day each month in Déline. Before the formal proceedings began, the lawyers and their newly-found clients huddled in separate corners of the room briefly discussing the circumstances of each case. As I watched, I found myself wondering how effective a lawyer could be in defending his client in this setting.

The first case involved a Déline youth of about eighteen, who had, while staying in Norman Wells, stolen a snowmobile for a few hours and gone joy-riding. It was later found abandoned but intact. What particularly interested me in this case was that after listening to all the arguments from the defendant and prosecutor, the judge, before sentencing the young man who was proven guilty of the offence, read out the submission from the Déline Justice Committee. They recommended to the court that, since this was his first offence, he be put on probation for nine months, perform thirty hours of community service and participate in any counselling programs as directed by the probation officer. This would also include a period of time out on the land with an elder. After considerable deliberation the judge sentenced him according to the committee's recommendations, then added one day in jail to be served in the local Déline RCMP detachment.

The second case involved three adolescent males who were charged with beating a local middle-aged man on December 24, 1994. These were the people whom I had earlier seen talking to their lawyers. It was clear from the photos of the wounds and bruises inflicted on the victim, now entered into evidence, that he had been badly beaten.

I listened intently as the victim and the first witness on his behalf provided their accounts of what had transpired. After the cross-examination, the defendants had their turn. What struck me most was the timidity, almost reticence, of both accused and victim, to want to answer any questions put to them. Such reluctance made sense for the defendants but less so for the victim. This man had fallen asleep in a friend's bedroom after a bout of drinking. The adolescents had entered the bedroom and viciously attacked him and, it seemed to me, he had every right to feel angry, but I saw no anger. Only a reluctance to incriminate his offenders.

Was this a normal response to the present situation of having to speak out in court in the presence of these rather intimidating legal personnel? Or were there other dynamics at play here that had little to do with the judicial proceedings but everything to do with getting along with each other, a prime ingredient for survival in any small community. The beating had occurred seven months before. During those months both the victim and the accused had lived in close proximity to each other, as had their relatives and friends and, for all I knew, these men could have remained good friends too. Having to wait seven months to testify seemed to add another wrinkle to the provision of justice in the North.

The accused were found guilty and because this was not their first incident of violence they were given four months each in the jail in Yellowknife. Afterwards I talked to the mother of two of the adolescents, a former student of mine with whom I had spent some time during this visit. I had also met one of her sons before knowing about the court case, a pleasant, well-spoken grade eleven student who was doing well at school.

"This must all have been very difficult for you," I said.

"In some ways, yes. But I am glad they are only going to Yellowknife and they will be home in two months. I was afraid that this time they might get sent to a southern jail and that would be much worse as they would be with really bad criminals there," the mother replied.

"This kind of thing has happened before then?"

"Unfortunately, yes. You know, Miggs, you couldn't wish for nicer boys when they are sober but once they get drinking they always end up in fights. My husband and I have talked and talked to them about it and they always promise to stay out of trouble. But it keeps happening. I'm not excusing them but it's very hard for them to stay away from drinking when all their friends do it. Still, I just don't understand why they have to beat up people like this, and they always feel so badly about it afterwards."

The following Sunday, the older of the two sons sat close to me at the back of the church but he did not participate in the service. He merely sat with his hands clasped and his head bent the entire time.

The muskeg near Déline.

CHAPTER TWENTY-THREE

SUBSTANCE ABUSE

"Hey, Miss Morris. It's really good to see you again." Slurring his words, the nearly fifty-year-old man grabbed my hand and shook it, then, brandishing a Coke can in his other hand, he staggered towards a chair. I was sitting in Cec's kitchen, drinking coffee and talking to Lloyd, a southerner who had spent many summers in Déline assisting with adult education, when Rick (not his real name) dropped in. We chatted for a while. I enquired about his family and his job and then, with some gentle persuasion from Lloyd, he was on his way.

"Coke laced with hair spray," said Lloyd. "It's an easy, cheap way to get high if you can't get any booze."

"How do people get their hands on alcohol here?" I enquired. "Isn't Déline a dry town—except for the special permits at weddings? And the RCMP seemed very thorough at searching our bags when I arrived," I added.

Lloyd explained, "You can have a bottle—even a bottle of 150 proof—sent by mail. Or you can have a friend bring it by boat from The Wells. Boats can zip unseen past Déline when they leave Bear River and then approach from the east. The RCMP can't possibly check every boat docking here. It really is very easy for those who want it and have the money to pay for it. There's far less drinking than there used to be, especially among older people. Many have stopped drinking altogether. But there's a lot of drinking among the adolescents, especially on weekends."

"How about drugs?" I enquired.

"Not much, except for lacing Cokes like Rick did. There's also much less sniffing here than in some other communities. Alcohol is the big thing in Déline."

I thought about the young kids I had heard of who stayed with friends or relatives for a few nights when their parents were drinking heavily. I thought about the young men who had just been convicted of beating up an older man. I recalled seeing a woman during my stay who appeared with a large bruises on her face. I remembered the words of an adolescent who had told me, "They think it's cool. Their parents drink, their friends drink and so they do too." And then I thought about Francis and all the other young people who had died "accidentally" many years ago during heavy bouts of drinking.

I also thought back to my conversation with Morris Neyelle a few days earlier at the hotel restaurant.[1]

"May I join you?" I looked up from my heaped plate of delicious golden French fries and saw Morris, coffee and sandwich in hand, smiling at me.

"Of course, Morris." We chatted for a while about the wedding and drum dance of a week ago, his community sewage contract, my visit to the graveyard and the many people whom I had known before who had since died, especially former students. I also told him how pleased I was to have met his father Johnny again and to see him looking so well. "He doesn't seem to have aged at all in these thirty years, Morris. And there he is still making snowshoes and drums and other artifacts. His eyes and fingers must still be in great shape."

"Yes, my father is a very special man who has stayed true to the old ways while coping with all the changes around him. I've always learned a lot from him and he gave me a great deal of support when I stopped drinking more than four years ago."

Morris went on to explain that after his brother Ted's death due to alcoholism he had taken stock of his own life. "It's very difficult to give up drinking when you've been doing it for a long time but when I looked at my life I didn't like what I saw. I didn't like what was happening to me and my family, especially my children. I realized I was setting them a bad example and that I could be ruining their lives too. So I stopped drinking. I also quit smoking two years ago.

"You have to make up your own mind to quit. It's your own choice. No one else can decide for you. You have to look at the price you will pay if you continue drinking or go back to it. You have to look it squarely and face up to it. I looked at the truth of my life and that truth made me strong.

"Addiction centres can help but they're not going to solve our problems. If you want to change you must decide for yourself and you have to stay strong and have faith in yourself. But it's not easy. I talked it over with my father and he always supported me, but a few of my friends would no longer have anything to do with me. I just had to accept that some friends are like that. But maybe one day they will come to me for help and I'll be glad to support them in giving up drinking."

He said that many people in Déline had turned to alcohol in the troubled times of the seventies and eighties, but now, more and more people were quitting. "But there are still lots of adults who keep drinking and so do their kids. It's very destructive for everyone. But they have to make their own decisions."

I thought about what Morris had said and could only imagine how difficult such a struggle must have been, especially when his friends turned away from him. It must indeed have taken a great deal of commitment and strength from him and from the many others in the village who have also reclaimed their lives.

Why is substance abuse so endemic among Aboriginal people in the North? Why have so many lives already been ruined and there appears to be little relief in sight from this cycle of human destruction, for such addictions are both the result and the cause of further problems and addictions? The answers to these questions are extremely complex but Rupert Ross' insightful book, *Dancing With a Ghost: Exploring Indian Reality*, provides an excellent analogy that might help us understand what happens when two cultures collide and especially when one culture assumes dominance over the other:

> A culture is, in its vulnerability, much like a house of uniquely shaped cards. Take away one card and the entire structure is threatened with collapse. Insert another person's card, shaped to fit his unique house, and it may well displace more than it supports, further weakening an already shaky structure. That outsider's card may have been designed to perform the same function as the missing one, but it is so uniquely tailored to fit with its complementary cards that it may prove counterproductive when jammed into another structure.
>
> If that outsider's card is to prove useful at all, it must be substantially reshaped, a task which can only be done by its new owner, for only that person (or culture) is fully aware of the fit that must be found. Just as importantly, that reshaping can only take place if there is adequate time for reflection and experimentation. In the North, the time has been so short and full of other stresses that one can only look on in amazement that anything remains standing at all.[2]

For thousands of years the Dene, living in a very demanding physical environment, had coped successfully with all the tribulations of life. They had long since developed, within their unique culture, their own complex strategies for coping with the inevitable stresses and sorrows of daily life. A system of beliefs and traditions provided them with a code for living, and a set of social and spiritual resources enabled them to cope with life's eventualities. Then they came into contact with people from an entirely different European culture, with its own traditions and beliefs, people who denigrated Native ways at the very time when widespread sickness was already causing immense emotional turmoil on these northern people.

After this initial period of dislocation and confusion, most of the Sahtuot'ine were left almost entirely on their own for several decades. This allowed them to integrate the changes into their lives to create a somewhat different culture, one that came to meet their needs and provided them with the ability to cope with life's stresses with a high degree of success. In other words, according to Rupert Ross's theory, there had been adequate time for the Sahtuot'ine to experiment and alter the newly introduced "cards" to fit their own "cultural structure."

The changes of the last forty years, however, have been sudden and drastic and have caused major tears in the fabric of their lives. The new outsiders' "cards" arrived too quickly and there was no time or opportunity for reshaping them. They were jammed in to the previous structure where there was very little "fit." With memories of the recent past still alive and no clear vision for the future, confusion and a feeling of helplessness to control their lives have taken over. Many of the social and religious beliefs—both a mixture of traditional and Catholic—that had strengthened them in the past, no longer seem relevant, especially to the younger generations.

A further dynamic must also be mentioned. In the past, when Dene survival on the land depended on a high degree of family and group cooperation, there was considerable antipathy towards displaying emotions such as fear, anger, sorrow or hate. Keeping one's emotions hidden was valued. This is a tradition that many still espouse. As a result the Sahtuot'ine were compelled to cope with overwhelming social disintegration by keeping all their emotions locked up inside.

Speaking about Aboriginal people in general, Ross further conjectures:

> I suspect that Native people use alcohol in exactly the same way many of us do: to blow off steam. Unfortunately, two unique factors come into play where Natives are concerned. The first is the obvious fact that their "steam" has reached a point of pressure that's hard for us to imagine, given all the losses and confusion described so far. The second factor, however, may be the most critical, for it involves the fact that Native people may have been left with no other culturally sanctioned way to vent that steam. Quite clearly, their sources of sorrow, anger and personal desperation regularly exceed anything most of us are ever likely to experience. When, at the same time, traditional ethics forbid even expressing those sentiments and traditional methods of spiritual healing have all but been eradicated, the bottle remains almost the only avenue available to pursue release. Alcohol "permits" the saying and doing of things that would otherwise not be tolerated, for it permits the individual and his community the comfort of being able to say, "It wasn't really me who broke all those traditional rules and did all those immoral things; I was just drunk."[3]

Multiply this scenario from family to family and it leads to catastrophe in a small community.

Several Native communities across Canada in recent years are coming to grips with the pain and suffering of their people by establishing healing centres or healing circles. The Alkali Lake Band in British Columbia is a recognized leader in this field of community healing where the people there have consciously chosen to end burying their grief and anger.[4] They have come to realize that if their people and their children are to survive and grow up to be healthy individuals, then it is up to them—Native people helping Native people.

Two common factors are usually present in these healing centres. People are encouraged to talk and share their feelings and concerns even though this is contrary to earlier traditions. As the chief of Alkali Lake said, "Speak from your heart to one another … open up your hearts and share your troubles … Silence is the first enemy."[5] This is a tremendously difficult and courageous step for people to take, acknowledging to those in the healing circles, including family and friends, not only their anger and fears but also admitting to the wrongs they have committed. But there is a strong conviction that healing and forgiveness can only be achieved if one is completely honest with oneself and others.

Along with this open sharing is a return to, or a revival of, traditional ways that have been so important in the past—a return to the sweat lodge and pipe ceremonies for some, as well as a return to the drum for healing songs, prayers and drum dances. Elders are encouraged to share their wisdom with the focus on healing for the future, and others are encouraged to listen. Counselling emphazises respect—respect for yourself and for others—and a belief that each person is capable of healing him- or herself.[6]

As more evidence emerges of the physical, emotional and sexual abuse of children and youth in residential schools across the North, as well as the South, those who have been abused are being encouraged to speak out. After decades of feeling shame and assuming guilt to themselves, never sharing their feelings with others, not even to close family members, healing is beginning.

Similarly, more Aboriginal people are getting involved with judicial issues in the healing circles. They know that the jails of Canada are filled with a hugely disproportionate number of Aboriginal people. They see their people, especially their young, returning with the same hate and anger they left with, the same predilection to alcohol and other substance abuses, the same reasons to commit further acts of violence in their communities.[7]

Aboriginal people increasingly feel the need to incorporate a Native voice into the justice process, as their view of "the criminal" is different from that of southern society where the emphasis is primarily on punishment. An elder whom Ross quotes stated at a northern healing conference, "We know you have a *legal* system; we're just not sure it's a *justice* system."[8]

Native communities focus not so much on the criminal acts but rather on what prompted them to perpetrate such acts. Just as alcoholism and other substance abuse is viewed as a disease, a symptom of a much deeper malaise, so too are criminal acts seen more as wrongdoings by people with an illness which require healing rather than punishment, although retribution and restitution may also be necessary.

In the healing circles, victims and abusers alike concentrate on honesty, forgiveness and treatment. This process of disclosure to family, friends and victims, is often far more difficult for the "criminal" to deal with than a period of incarceration. However, with strong community support, the abuser comes to face the effects of his actions on his own life and that of his family and can begin to work towards a healthier future. It is about making things better for everyone.[9]

This combination of the non-Native way of vocalizing one's anger and shame, whatever the cause, along with a return to more traditional mechanisms, is proving to be very effective in many Aboriginal communities. It takes considerable time and energy and is often very difficult and demanding on all who participate, not just those with the greatest needs. But those involved in the healing circles believe that every individual bears responsibility for the health of the group, so that although individuals must decide for themselves to take this journey, others in the community who have already done so must be there to help, a philosophy that reflects the traditional belief in the interconnectedness of all things.

Not all communities have healing circles. However, strong people such as Morris Neyelle and others in Déline, are taking stock of their lives and are coming to grips with their own problems and those of their communities. They are finding the determination and courage it takes to go through a long and difficult healing process, for their own sakes and for the sake of their children. Some are also turning to the many governmental and community support services that exist across the North, such as Déline's own Basic Awareness Program. But support groups require adequate funding from government and other sources, along with many committed professionals and volunteers, to operate effectively. Unfortunately, government cutbacks in recent years have caused the closure or downsizing of many programmes that provided strong support for people in the NWT in the past. This has placed more pressure on individual communities, such as Déline, to do what they can to develop their own programmes, not an easy task, given the enormity of their challenge. In the meantime, communities are also finding ways of dealing with root causes such as boredom, lack of job opportunities, apathy towards pursuing an education, and the need for intergenerational communication.

> "I tell you—to sober up ain't easy. You get tested left and right but if you believe in yourself and the good Lord nothing is impossible. That choice is still yours to make … and sobering up opens doors to a new life."
>
> —Morris Neyelle[10]

CHAPTER TWENTY-FOUR

RELIGION

It was becoming increasingly clear to me that in the 1990s traditional spirituality had come to play a larger role in the lives of the Sahtuot'ine. My first hint came after the drum dance following the wedding. Then I was told about the prophet's house located at the eastern edge of the village, not far from Morris Modeste's cabin. Erected in honour of a highly regarded former prophet named Ayha, for whom the new school was also named, this small log cabin was built in 1989 with the help of people from Whati (Lac La Martre), an area where Ayha frequently visited and preached.[1] An altar stands at one end of the small chapel, decorated with linens, candles, rosaries, religious pictures and flowers. It is a place where people come, as individuals or as groups, to pray and find peace and tranquillity.

?Ehtseo Ereya Ayha, a Dogrib from north of Tucho (Great Slave Lake), was born in 1858.[2] Ayha is considered to have been one of the greatest prophets in the histories of both the Dogrib and Satuot'ine and he apparently had more influence on the people than any of the later prophets. He and a band of Dogrib followers moved to the Déline area around 1914 because of a trading dispute in Behcho Ko (Fort Rae). He travelled extensively around Sahtu and south to Tucho, but in his later years when he settled near Déline people came from far away for his answers, his blessings, his teachings about life, as well as his visions and prophecies for the future. Many miracles have also been ascribed to him. In one of his prophecies Ayha warned his people, long before uranium was ever discovered, that the waters of Sahtu would one day be poisoned and would turn yellow as a result of white man's activities at the eastern end of the lake. He added that much sickness and death would accompany these changes.[3] Because people in Déline today have no doubt that he was referring to the radioactive contamination that they have only recently become aware of, many visit Ayha's House to, once again, ask for his guidance. Ayha died in 1940 at the age of eighty-two and is buried at Déline. Several of his descendants still live in the village.

Prophets, or *nakwenare?e*, are considered to be very important healers and preachers by the Dene and have existed in the Sahtu region for as long as people can remember. Father Emile Petitot first wrote about *nakwenare?e* during his years of travelling around Sahtu in the mid-1800s, and he and the priests that followed

The inside of the former tipi-shaped church in Fort Franklin/Déline in 1968. Father René Fumoleau, assisted by altar boys Peter Beyha and George Cleary, officiates at one of the multiple wedding ceremonies.

ridiculed their practices.[4] However, despite the antagonism that existed between the Catholic priests and the prophets in earlier times, by the 1960s Christianity, and more specifically Catholicism, had been incorporated into their prophetic beliefs. They believed they were divinely inspired to bring the word of Christianity's God to the people, stressing that through self-discipline and by keeping God's word, a person would save his or her soul.[5]

This was also the message of Naedzo, the most influential prophet in Déline in the 1960s. Naedzo, or Old Man Naedzo as my students called him, was a rather distinguished, white-haired, blind man with a sunken closed eyelid that covered his sightless right eye. He was considered by the people to be a holy man and a divinely inspired preacher who offered spiritual nourishment and salvation to those who followed his teachings. Although he sometimes preached about the dangers of drinking and gambling at cards, most of his messages tended to be more affirmative, as he emphasized the need for people to be actively involved in good spiritual and social behaviour, and to live according to the will of God.[6]

The priests who lived in Déline from the 1950s to 1970s, such as fathers Brown, Fumoleau and Denis, felt no threat to their religious authority from prophets such as Naedzo; I remember Father Fumoleau referring to him as "a truly holy man." Since the priests remained in Déline for many years, spending their lives in daily interaction with their parishioners and becoming fluent in Slavey, they were much respected. They became accepted as authorities in all religious matters and were pivotal in the validation of the prophets.[7] They also welcomed the prophets' attacks on drinking and their earnest advice to reflect on one's spiritual condition and to pray to God for help and guidance.

Naedzo, as an inspirational teacher, was still held in high regard in Déline in the summer of 1995. But Ayha, with his ability to predict the future, appears to have been unique among the prophets, especially since several of his predictions have since come true, including his apparent warnings of the dangers of radioactivity. Thus his influence has increased over the years and his prophecies are still widely accepted.

There has also been an increased interest in the potency of Lac Ste. Anne near Edmonton, and an annual four-day pilgrimage to the holy curative waters has become customary for many of the Sahtuot'ine. One man told me how he had taken his dying wife and immersed her in the holy waters a few years ago, and although she has since died, he believes that the curative waters lengthened her life. He was one of two dozen other middle-aged and older people who flew to Lac Ste. Anne while I was at Déline.

A further impetus in the return to traditional spirituality has centred around the large gatherings held each August at Whisky Jack Point, east of Déline. Here, an encampment of about forty tipis, housing close to two hundred people, is erected for three days. A prayer tent, also referred to as a "healing tent," is also set up. Everyone with whom I talked claimed that being there together in a spiritual, harmonious environment, with no drinking and no fighting, was a wonderful, renewing force on their lives. It enabled them, once again, to feel proud to be Dene.[8]

Out of curiosity, I attended church one Sunday morning to see how the community managed since there was no priest in Déline. At 10:30 AM the bell tolled and the service began shortly after eleven. About sixty people attended that day, mostly middle-aged and older, although there were also a few younger couples and adolescents. Cec had informed me that she was a member of a small church committee that organized the services, both the daily sayings of the Rosary and the Sunday service. The service comprised several hymns sung in English, Latin (*Kyrie eleison*) and Slavey, accompanied on the organ by Louis Taniton, an elder. In addition, members of the congregation read excerpts from the Bible in English. Then Charlie Neyelle, considered to be a modern-day prophet, gave a sermon in Slavey based on one of the Bible passages read earlier. Charlie, Johnny's oldest son, is a man in his early fifties who still carries on some hunting and trapping, alongside his job at the Co-op. He is considered to be an excellent preacher, a spiritual healer and keeper of the songs, and is held in very high regard both in this community and throughout Denendeh where he also preaches.

I also made some enquiries about the prevalence of *ik'o*, the medicine power. *Ik'o* remains an important belief among the older people, and several men and women in the village are reputed to have *ik'o*, but since it can be used for good or evil, there is still much secrecy surrounding its presence. A former student, now in his mid-forties, told me that he used to be quite skeptical in his youth until he personally witnessed episodes where people were cured by healers through the use of medicine power. He had also witnessed incidences when medicine power was used to achieve success in hunting.

There is little doubt that this heightened and renewed interest in traditional spiritual values is very significant in the lives of many adults in Déline. Perhaps, in these times of immense change, it provides the older people with an anchor, a source of strength, a link to the familiar past. For some, it has also been an instrumental force in their battle against alcoholism. And, as the older generations recognize the cultural gap that has grown between themselves and their children, there is an increasing belief in the community in the need to involve people of all ages in traditional events whenever possible, thus enabling the youth to share in and draw strength from traditional values. Such events almost always include the drum.

Even though the importance of traditional spirituality is clearly evident in Déline in the 1990s, yet, everywhere one looks, in the church, the Prophet's House, the graveyard and in many people's homes, the Virgin Mary and the rosary are held in high esteem. Pictures and statues of Jesus are also evident. Christianity, with a decidedly Catholic flavour, still provides a bulwark for the Dene's beliefs alongside the more traditional spiritual ways. There appears to be no conflict in holding what might seem to be two sets of beliefs. Rather, as has been the Dene way for so long, there has been a blending, a fusion of both, a kind of synchronicity that provides a basis for their strength and beliefs, and a support for them in their struggles with modern life.

Receiving my drum from Victor Beyonnie (*left*) and Johnny Neyelle at Victor and Elizabeth's fiftieth wedding anniversary, July 1995. Afterwards, the inside of my drum was signed by many people.

CHAPTER TWENTY-FIVE

THE END OF A JOURNEY

I had moved to the house next door and was folding laundry. Forty-one pairs of socks and several more without partners, nine teenager T-shirts, an assortment of underwear, two pairs of sheets, eight bath towels, three tea towels, a bath mat, face cloth, and the top and bottom of a sweat suit.

Cec's daughter, Pat, who was married to David, Morris Modeste's brother, had asked me to house sit for them on the weekend, my last weekend in Déline. They were afraid of their house being broken into if it was left empty. Pat, David and two of their children, like many other people from Déline, were off camping down the lake for the August 1 long-weekend holiday. A couple of families had invited me to accompany them and I would dearly have loved to go, but bringing me back for my early Monday morning flight would curtail their long weekend. Furthermore, if another storm blew in I might be stranded eighty to a hundred kilometres away and miss all my flights. So stay I must. With little for me to do, it now looked as if my last couple of days would be a real letdown, so I continued to fold the laundry Pat had brought in off the clothesline and placed it neatly on one of the beds.

Although Pat and David's home looked identical to Cec and John's from the outside, the interior placement of walls and the decor were quite different. The pine log walls gleamed under their coat of Varathane. The small kitchen was well supplied and neatly organized. As I sat on their recently purchased spacious couch I enjoyed listening to some of their CDs on a quality stereo unit and glanced at the several professionally-taken family photos on display. The children shared two bedrooms, one of which I was occupying. This house, like so many others in Déline, was so unlike those sparsely furnished, drafty cabins of the sixties. Only the several pieces of dried fish hanging on a line strung up in the kitchen reminded me of the past.

After a while I dropped by to say goodbye to Helena who had just returned from a few days in Tulit'a.

"You look glum," she said. "Sad to be leaving?"

"Very much so," I replied. "I just feel so flat. I suppose it's partly because I'm disappointed that I couldn't go out on the land this weekend. Nor will I be here for the big back-to-the-land gathering next week."

"You're not sorry you came?" Helena interjected.

"No, far from it. I've loved meeting so many of my former students and those adults whom I was friends with thirty years ago. They've made me feel very special by remembering me and reminding me of the times we shared together.

Everyone should have this kind of heart-warming experience at least once in a lifetime."

Helena was baking muffins. In fact, each time I visited her I found her baking something or other. Lucky for John and their son, Ian.

"I've harboured this dream of returning to Déline for a long time, Helena, and I'm so glad I did, but now that there is so little time left I just don't want to let go. No one likes a good holiday to end but it's more than that. This place and these people have always had an immense hold on me. I'm not sure I quite understand the strength of my fascination or, one could even say, my obsession, but it's there. I know I can't stay here and yet I don't want to leave.

"It's partly because I am really fond of many individuals and now that I have reconnected with them I don't want to lose them again. I want to continue our friendships and can only hope they will too. What a fool I was to sever my ties with them all those years ago but now I feel I've been forgiven, rather like a prodigal daughter.

"It's also partly to do with the tremendous admiration I feel for the people. I felt this in the sixties when I knew something of the struggles in their lives. It was their attitude towards life, their strength of character—a quiet, sincere strength as they dealt so capably with daily life in this harsh climate, their sense of humour, their love for their children, the respect and appreciation they showed us Outsiders, and their overriding quiet pride and dignity. I didn't know much about spirituality then, but now I would say that these were very spiritual people, rooted in their deep feelings for the land that has nourished them in so many ways."

Helena, realizing I was on a roll and needed to think things through, just sat and listened, occasionally plying me with more instant decaffeinated coffee. I continued.

"Life in Déline has changed considerably since I was last here and I am deeply saddened by much of what I see and what I have been told. And yet, Helena, that same strength of character seems to have endured in most of the people I have met again. Despite the cultural and social upheaval that has dominated their lives in recent years, most adults have preserved the essence of their former traditional ways of thinking, fortified and nourished by their maintenance of the Slavey language. Everything has changed and yet little has changed. The 'everything' includes those things that are visible on the surface, those areas where they have grown closer to modern society, but the core of their existence still seems alive and well.

"I would be overwhelmed by the magnitude of the challenges they face, and I'm sure there are many times when they must feel so too. And yet, I believe they will keep working diligently at finding ways to overcome them. For every person who has expressed fear and pessimism about the future, I have met as many or more who conveyed a real sense of optimism, a sense that, as long as they can maintain adequate autonomy over their own destiny, they will be able to deal with their concerns—the way their parents and grandparents used to in earlier days.

"It's as if they were saying, 'As a people we have always faced challenges. When we lived on the land every day was a struggle just to survive: being on the edge of starvation when the caribou could not be found for food, clothing, and shelter; times when the fish or rabbits were scarce; times when our families were decimated by death and disease; the intrusion of strangers who changed our lives in so many ways; and always the endless bitter, biting cold, except for a few brief summer months. Dealing with those hardships was our way of life and ultimately we overcame them and survived and believed that life was good. Now we have new hardships and challenges and we shall overcome these too, and even though some will not be able to make the journey, we will survive as a people.'"

I sipped more coffee and ate another of the excellent buns Helena had baked previously. The muffins were not yet ready.

"Perhaps I'm just a foolish idealist or, perhaps, I've been back for too short a time to really understand the complexity of the situation, Helena, but that's how I see things. So why am I feeling so morose? Maybe it really is nothing more than a feeling of sadness at leaving good friends, especially since I probably won't see them again for quite a while, if ever."

I doubt whether Helena agreed with all I had said but she chose to say nothing, so we talked about other things for a while longer and then I left.

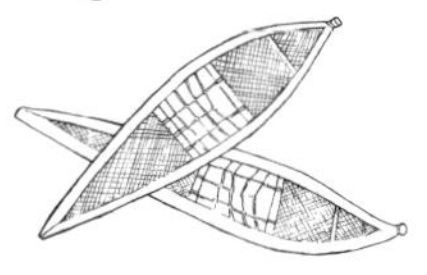

The warmth of the late morning sun led the way as I took a last walk, beyond the village, out onto the muskeg. I needed to think more about what I had said to Helena. What a beautiful day to be walking over the springy turf, a slight breeze wafting through my hair, the sun warm on my face and hands, the soft sounds of small waves lapping on the nearby lake shore, and from the village, occasional sounds of children playing and a dog barking. A seagull swoops low over my head and screeches at me. I stop to take in a deep breath of clean, crisp air and the familiar acrid muskeg and lichen odour I've always loved. Oh, to be out camping on the land!

I headed back to my new home for lunch and indulged in some of the dry fish hanging in the kitchen. Later on I walked back to the village and bumped into Jane Kenny and her daughter Kaylene. Jane invited me over for coffee. I was so pleased she had returned from Edmonton a few days earlier as it appeared at one time that she wouldn't be back until after I had left. She thanked me again for the photos I had given her earlier on then brought out albums with photos of her parents and other family members. Her mother was still alive but her father, whom I well recalled, had died of cancer several years ago. He too had carried uranium ore onto the NTCL barges for many years.

Sunday morning. I was very aware of my impending departure and decided to attend the church service once again. I sat in a pew at the back of the congregation of about sixty and realized that this is where I felt the closest to the old Déline, the Fort Franklin of my days, as I looked around and recognized so many of the older people, as well as many of my students, now adults with families of their own. Kerchiefs still covered the long dark or greying hair of the older women. Their calf-length dresses, jackets, ankle socks and shoes or boots had changed little. Similarly, many older men still wore plaid shirts, dark pants and jackets, rubber overshoes, and when outside, dark-coloured caps. On the other hand, most of the younger women wore skirts or pants and lighter-coloured jackets, and no kerchiefs. Many had long hair, but equally as many now had short, sometimes curly, hair. The children could have passed for kids in the South in their T-shirts, sweaters and jeans.

As before, several people took part in the service with Bible readings in English. Again, old Louis Taniton accompanied the English, Latin and Slavey hymns on the organ, but as I sat back and gazed around the church my mind was seldom on the service. Instead I thought about the people sitting in front of me and was carried back to the 1960s.

Louis didn't play the organ then—none of the villagers did—but he was always present, usually with his wife, at all important functions. He must surely now be in his mid-eighties but he looked as sprightly as ever. Near the front sat Victor Beyonnie with his wife Elizabeth. Victor had been such a fine chief and an orator who could keep me spellbound even though I understood few of his Slavey words. I also recalled snippets of our conversations during the construction of the old log community hall and especially the time he came to school to berate the kids—in Slavey—for breaking the fluorescent lights in the hall. And there was Johnny Neyelle and his wife, Jane, who had stayed up all night to build a coffin for Granny Zaul and cover it with a blue blanket dotted with tiny white crosses. Johnny, as skilled a craftsman as ever, still makes round, caribou skin drums for the dances, and meticulously woven snowshoes, both for the feet and the wall! Over to my left sat William Sewi and his wife Rosie. William, our school janitor, who not only kept the school clean and warm, but was always cheerful when called upon to help us teachers with our various plumbing, water and sewage problems, regardless of the hour. And Rosie who never missed a Bingo or a movie and who invariably greeted me with a smile and couple of words in English.

Though there was no Father Fumoleau or Father Denis or, in fact, any priest present, and even though this wasn't a Latin Mass or even a Mass of any recognizable description, yet, as I sat there that morning, I sensed the sincerity of the people's faith, especially during the familiar nasal singing of hymns in Slavey. But I couldn't help wondering about the considerable pain and suffering, and, yes, the occasional joy and laughter, they must have experienced during these past thirty years. My world had changed considerably in this time span, but nothing like theirs had.

The service was coming to a close. Charlie Neyelle had already given his sermon and distributed communion to these devout people. I was overcome with an immense feeling of affection, of love, of admiration, of connectedness towards these people with whom I had once spent some of the happiest years of my life and again briefly these past few days. Almost involuntarily, I suddenly knew what I had to do and before I had time to change my mind I was out of my seat and found myself walking quietly towards Walter Beyha who sat with his family close to the front.

"Walter," I whispered. "I want to say a few words to the people. Will you translate for me?"

If he was surprised he didn't show it but just replied, "Of course. Just wait here until Charlie finishes." He moved over to let me squeeze into his pew. A few minutes later we were both standing at the front of the altar. Walter said something to Charlie and then told me I could begin.

My palms wet and my mouth dry, I felt as nervous as if I was addressing a huge gathering in a high-powered meeting. I had given no thought to the specifics of what I had wanted to say. I was just filled with an overwhelming need to say something to these people before I left. I began, speaking a few sentences at a time, to give Walter a chance to translate.

"As some of you know, I shall be leaving Déline tomorrow. Even though almost thirty years have gone by since I lived here I want you to know that during all those years, even though I didn't return, I alway kept many, many fond memories of the time I spent here. Déline, or Fort Franklin as I knew it then, has always been a very special place for me. You treated me kindly, taught me much, and you gave me your friendship. I'm just sorry that it took me so long to return.

"However, I'm very glad that I did come back and I have enjoyed my time here this summer. It's been good to meet and speak with many of you again. But the time has gone by too quickly and so before I leave tomorrow, I want to tell you again that the people of Déline will always have a very special place in my heart. *Mahsi cho*."

When I had finished and looked at Walter he asked, "Is that it?" I nodded and went back to my seat virtually in tears.

Was that it? I suppose by Déline standards of making a speech mine wasn't very long nor was I very articulate. Yes, I could have said more, much more—

about how strongly I admired my former neighbours, people who have had their lives torn asunder, their families ripped apart, their friends lost in oblivion, or lost in the confusion that has turned their world up-side-down. Yet they carry on and struggle to overcome things they don't understand and changes they never asked for, with pride and determination and a sense of humour of old, which, despite everything, was so evident in most with whom I had talked these past days. The service had ended. As I sat at the back of the church collecting myself, a few elderly people passing by took my hands and nodded at me. Eventually, I left and walked down the stairs and again, when I reached the bottom, several older people came over and, accompanied by a few words, hugged me. I did not need to speak Slavey to understand the warmth and kindness expressed in their faces and I was glad that I had spoken.

After visiting a couple of people I returned to Pat's. The phone was ringing.

"Miss Morris?"

"Yes," I replied with surprise.

"I'm glad I got you. I called a couple of times before." I didn't recognize her voice. "Stay there and Chief John Tetso will be over in a minute. He wants to talk to you."

"OK." I put the phone down and John arrived within a very few minutes.

"Victor and Elizabeth are having their fiftieth wedding anniversary feast and they want you to come," he said.

"They do? When?"

"Right now." No time to change and anyway John wasn't dressed up.

The feast was at Dolphus and Mary Baton's house. About a dozen mostly elderly people sat on the floor around a piece of clear plastic on which had been placed a white embroidered tablecloth. The turkey that I had seen Victor buy at the Co-op two days before was carved into slices and chunks. Around it were dishes of mashed potatoes, several kinds of vegetables, bannock, bread, cranberry sauce, creamed salad, stuffing and a jug of gravy. Most people's plates were already laden with food and it didn't take long for mine to be too.

"I'm glad John found you," said Mary leaning over my shoulder as she put another plateful of potatoes in the centre. "As you can see, we moved all the furniture to the hallway so that we could have an old-fashioned feast with everyone sitting on the floor." I looked around the square of people. Other than John and his wife Irene, most of the guests were elders. I felt immensely honoured to have been invited to join in such a special occasion. Few of this generation had learned any English and most of the talk was in Slavey but I didn't mind. I was just delighted to be there. Occasionally John would translate an amusing anecdote or a brief comment by one of the elders as they recollected, with enjoyment, some event we had shared in the sixties.

I had brought my camera and asked Victor and Elizabeth if they would like me to take some photos. The nods and smiles on everyone's faces gave me my answer. I took a few shots of all the guests as the leftover food and plates were cleared. Then Mary placed a large, decorated, iced cake on the tablecloth. On it, in blue icing, were the words: "Happy 50th Anniversary, Victor and Elizabeth." Everyone beamed and I took more photos, which I would later send them.

After pieces of the cake had been distributed to everyone, Victor and Johnny Neyelle stood up and asked me to join them. Victor said he was happy I had returned to Déline and thanked me for coming to his special anniversary feast. Then Johnny handed me one of his drums. He explained that the people of Déline wanted to give me this drum to thank me for returning and to help me remember them when I left.

I was overwhelmed by such a tribute. My eyes welled up with tears as my face beamed with joy and gratitude. We hugged each other, then someone grabbed my camera and took a couple of photos of Victor, Johnny and me. I thanked Johnny for giving me one of his precious drums, which I assured him I would always treasure, and I thanked Victor and Elizabeth for inviting me to share in their golden anniversary feast. Then I repeated some of what I had said earlier that morning in church, with John translating, even though I knew many of them had been there. But I needed to share again how much my earlier years in Déline had meant to me and how happy I was to have returned, and now to receive this special honour.

It wasn't that any gift was necessary but of all the things they could have given me, nothing could have meant more than a drum. Over the years, I had increasingly come to realize its importance to the people of Déline—to all Aboriginal people in our country. Just as the beating of the drum gives life and purpose to a drum dance, so, the drum represents and encompasses the heartbeat of the Sahtuot'ine and gives life to them too. The drum has been their one tangible link to their past, to their life on the land, to their culture and spirituality that flowed through it, to a time before the coming of the Europeans—the explorers, traders and the missionaries who brought with them new ways and a new religion, and, most especially, the successive governments who had so often ignored their interests and needs.

Clearly the drum has remained central to the lives of these people of Déline as they have coped with all the rapid societal changes. It has remained central to their drum dances, their stick games, their weddings, and to the revival of spirituality in the community, and is an ongoing symbol of the circle of life. I found myself believing that as long as the drum remained integral to their lives, the people of Déline would continue to overcome all the obstacles they faced.

I will always cherish my drum, their gift to me, probably far more than

Victor or Johnny or anyone else could realize. Somehow, this drum made me feel included, in a small but special way, in their lives. Several times during my stay former students had asked if I would come back and live in Déline. But I couldn't. I couldn't for many reasons—partly for health reasons, especially in such a smoky environment, and partly because my roots were now established in southern Ontario. But Déline had been my home—a very special home—for a brief but memorable part of my life. Although I could no longer live there, I saw the drum as an invitation, a kind of permission from the people to always regard Déline as "my home," full of people I care about, as I follow the struggles and the joys of their lives even if from afar.

We sat down to finish our anniversary cake. Soon after, some of the women began clearing away the dirty dishes and adding more food on the tablecloth as a new group of people took their places and began to eat. Many of these were the family members of those who had just eaten, the next generation. Many other people also dropped by to wish Victor and Elizabeth well and were given a piece of cake. Then we went out onto the smallish deck and steps and stood around chatting.

As I basked in the glorious sun, and the warmth I felt from receiving my drum and being invited to this special lunch, Merine Takazo suggested, "We should sign the inside of your drum," and soon everyone was signing it. Even some of the elderly men and women placed their X's, while Jane or Merine or Albert or Morris or some other former student wrote the person's name alongside the X. Some people added comments such as, "Hope to see you again in the future" (Violet Beyonnie); "Will be thinking of you. Take care" (Bernice Neyelle); "Good Luck (Fred and Chris Kenny); and my favourite, "Our land is your land" (Morris Neyelle). But after realizing that there wouldn't be enough room if everyone wrote comments, people just signed their names.

How wrong I had been yesterday to think this weekend was going to be an anticlimax to the rest of my stay. And the day had not yet ended. I was informed that following the feast, a group of people would begin to play cards on Mary and Dolphus' kitchen floor.

Card playing and gambling had existed in the sixties, but its occurrence had escalated since then. Many were openly critical of those addicted to gambling who frequently neglected their children. So when they asked me to join them, I hesitated for just a moment, then accepted their invitation and agreed to come back soon. My camera had ceased to function properly so I needed to check it out. I returned to find the game already in progress with about a dozen people sitting in a circle on the floor. I stood and watched for a while as Bernice Neyelle explained the rules of Poker Bingo to me. I used to love playing cards during the years I lived up North but I was unfamiliar with this game and it was played with such speed that I had difficulty catching on despite Bernice's patient explanations.

However, by the time someone dropped out and I was invited to join in, I was ready. My main concern was the five-dollar ante for each game, with the winner taking the whole pot. This was a far cry from our five-cent antes of the sixties—even accounting for inflation! More importantly, I only had twenty dollars cash left. Just enough to pay for my cab from the airport in Yellowknife the next day, should George or Doreen not be able to meet me. That meant just four games. Sure enough it was soon gone. But I was hooked and wanted to play more—hooked on the game itself and hooked on being with this group of adults with whom I had become reacquainted. This was my last evening in Déline and I didn't want to leave.

Would they accept a cheque from me? No problem. Elizabeth Kodakin reached for my cheque and gave me the equivalent in cash. I was back in the game for a while, at least. We played game after game in rapid succession and I began to win. As soon as someone left his or her place, now broke, someone else from the outside circle joined in. At some time Helena arrived with her camera. I had been unable to fix mine and didn't want to fiddle with it too much in case I lost the photos I had taken in the afternoon at Victor's feast. Since Helena had only come to watch she agreed to take some photos for me. Mary Baton and friends brewed new pots of tea in rapid succession, though I mostly stuck to water.

The evening sped by and when my watch told me it was past 11:00 PM I realized I should leave as I needed to pack and tidy up Pat and David's place. But how could I leave for by now I had won a sizeable chunk of money? I had long since regained my Yellowknife taxi fare and replaced the cost of my cheque and still had more than a hundred dollars. I tried not announcing that I had a winning hand, but someone, leaning over my shoulder, would blurt out a "Miss Morris. You won again." It was getting embarrassing. I didn't come here to win all this money. I didn't keep playing for that. I only wanted to be with these people on my last evening. Then I announced that I was quitting but before doing so I would pay for everyone's ante into the next game. After some protesting, they finally agreed and thus I managed to unload sixty dollars, which made me feel somewhat less guilty about walking away with my winnings.

I said my goodbyes and thanked everyone for a great end to my visit. In fact it had been a wonderful day. Morris and Bernice Neyelle drove me home in their truck and as I climbed out Morris handed me a tape of the Déline Drummers, "for you to take home with you and think of us when you play it."

It didn't take me long to pack and tidy up before going to bed. But even though I was very tired, my mind continued to revel in the events of the day, a permanent smile on my face. It had been a perfect ending to a memorable visit.

The next day, as prearranged, Lloyd came to pick me up. The early morning sun already shone with warmth and there was not a cloud to be seen. What a difference from the dense, overhanging smoke during my arrival just seventeen days before. I would have no difficulty seeing Déline from the air this time but I was unsure about my camera. I had fiddled some more with it and found how to advance the film manually, with difficulty. I just hoped it would work. It didn't.

A number of people came to see me off at the airport, among them Jimmy, Helena, Jane and Kaylene, and Tim the Co-op manager.

"Are you going straight back to Ontario?" Jimmy asked.

"No, I'm spending a couple of days in Yellowknife with George and Doreen and their family." It seemed ages since I had left Yellowknife and I was looking forward to seeing them again. And despite my reluctance to leave I was also eager to return home to share tales of my trip with Alison and friends.

The Beechcraft was on time and I was greeted by the same pilot who had flown me in to Déline two and a half weeks ago. We smiled in recognition as I clambered aboard.

"Had a good time?" he enquired.

"Great," I replied. One word that conveyed so very much. "Which way will you be flying?" I asked.

Seeing the camera slung around my neck he replied, "Normally we leave directly east and then head south, but I'll do a swing around the village if you like." My head nodded in appreciation.

Off we went, flying upwards over the deep blue waters of the lake and along the length of the village with its criss-crossing red roads. I could see everything so clearly: the graveyard's white picket fences, the sombre beige nursing station, Walter Beyha's forestry cabins, the dominant cluster of ?Ehtseo Ayha School, community hall, skating rink and administrative offices where people had just arrived for work, the ugly little hotel which had the best golden French fries, the RCMP detachment, the seniors' home close to the Basic Awareness Centre, the Co-op store, and the Northern store with its three, dwarfed red and white buildings, all that remained of the former HBC. It was still too early for the usual small groups of people gathered at the entrances of the stores. In fact, the streets were almost deserted. But wasn't that lonely vehicle Peter Beyha's Suzuki speeding to work?

Now we were over the rarely used old mission where I had once spent many hours talking to Father Fumoleau[1] and running the post office when he was away. The new church with its reddish roof still could not dim my memories of the beautiful old white church and its silver roof, a beacon from afar.

Higher and higher we climbed into the cloudless sky. Even though the buildings were now shrinking rapidly I was able to locate Cec and John's and Pat and David's log houses. And finally, at the edge of the vast expanse of muskeg and short evergreens, there stood Prophet Ayha's house close to Morris Modeste's beautiful little log cabin and stone patio.

All too soon we were heading across the lake towards the far eastern shore of Sahtu—Great Bear Lake. I kept my eyes on Déline as long as possible as it grew faint and shrivelled to a dot and then was no more. And still I kept looking back for a long time.

Through my tears I continued to scan the shoreline, bays, islands, lakes and inlets below as I tried to place where we were, places I had visited long ago by boat or airplane, places I desperately wanted to cling to.

With my drum by my side—clutched carefully, as it would be for my entire trip back to London, Ontario—and my head reeling with thoughts and glimpses of memories, my heart was already filled with *hiraeth*—a poignant Welsh word for which there is no exact translation in English—a kind of yearning for that which is no more.

I knew that I had, once again, left behind another large part of myself in the beautiful wilderness of this northern land and its proud people.

The songs of our ancestors' drums
The heartbeat of the land
Echo in the hooves of caribou
Travel on the wind

We hear their songs in our drums
Drums that will lead us through the mists of tomorrow
And we will survive.

Aerial view of the central area of Déline in 1996.
Photograph courtesy of C. Bloomquist

EPILOGUE

THE VILLAGE OF WIDOWS

For a while, beginning in May 1998, the people of Déline attained national prominence as their story was covered from coast to coast on radio and television by CBC, *Maclean's*, and many other media sources. All told of the immense feelings of despair in the village as a high percentage of the men—fathers and grandfathers—had died from various forms of cancer, especially bone cancer, over the past few years. Considerable evidence points to these deaths being attributable to radiation exposure from years of carrying sacks of radium and uranium ores from Port Radium across Great Bear Lake to southern Canada in the 1930s to 1960s, as well as from camping on the contaminated tailings. The community soon came to be known in the media as the "Village of Widows," and an hour-long documentary of that title was aired on Vision TV in the spring of 1999.[1] Included in this moving film were scenes of the small delegation who travelled in August 1998 from Déline to share their grief and sorrow with descendants of the atomic bomb that fell on Hiroshima in 1945—a bomb that contained uranium mined at Port Radium.[2]

Although their grief at having lost loved ones and their fears for the future are never far from the surface, daily life in Déline continues in a positive manner as the community takes important steps both within the community and on the national level. One area of some satisfaction comes from knowing that the federal government has recently made the commitment to clean up the tailings in and around Great Bear Lake, as well as studying the effects of the contamination on the peoples' health.

Closely associated with this initiative are the negotiations for self-government between the Déline band and the federal government. Although this will be a lengthy process, negotiations are proceeding well and the people of Déline are already planning and training for that time when they will manage their own affairs to an even greater extent.

Where are they now? An update on the people of Déline frequently mentioned in *Return to the Drum:*

Cec Baton	Retired from Social Services; received a "Wise Woman" award from the Status of Women Council of the NWT.

John Baton	Cec's husband; deceased (1998).
John (Mantla) Bekale	Senior Aboriginal Affairs Advisor, BHP Diamonds Inc., Yellowknife, NWT.
Peter Beyha	Senior administrative officer for the hamlet, he oversees all government business in Déline.
Walter Beyha	Chief of Renewable Resources; currently on a leave of absence to obtain his degree in Renewable Resources from Arctic College in Fort Smith.
Doreen Cleary	Teacher/counsellor for the Yellowknife District, working with students attached to a shelter for abused women and children from across the NWT and Nunavut.
George Cleary	Director, Indian and Inuit Services, Department of Indian and Northern Affairs Canada, Yellowknife, NWT. Also very involved in plans to prepare and train Déline residents for self-government.
Jane Kenny	Teaches grade one at ?Ehtseo Ayha school in Déline.
Morris Modeste	Self-employed, includes operating an outfitters camp; still actively involved with Hunters and Trappers Association.
Charlie Neyelle	Holds spiritual healing workshops throughout the North and is especially involved in helping those who have problems with alcohol.
Morris Neyelle	Band councillor and active in local politics; also involved in issues pertaining to alcohol abuse and recovery.
Bernice Neyelle	Manager of the new twelve bedroom hotel in Déline that opened in October 1999.
Raymond Taniton	Former chief of Déline (twice); now has a contract with Parks Canada to do environmental work at Grizzly Bear Mountain Park on Great Bear Lake.
John Tetso	Chief in 1995—deceased (1999).
Jimmy Tutcho	Band Manager—oversees the operations of the Band Council.
John Tutcho	President of the Déline Land and Financial Corporation.
Judi Tutcho	Former Languages Commissioner of the NWT, based in Yellowknife (1996-2000); is now studying for her Master's degree in BC.
Raymond Tutcho	Former chief of Déline (1996-1997). Is now working for the Housing Department in Déline.

Elders still in relatively good health: Johnny Neyelle, William Sewi, Rosie Sewi, Louis Taniton, Isadore Yukon.

René Fumoleau	Retired priest, living in Lutsel K'e, NWT; occasionally travels across Canada promoting his published books about the North.

NOTES

Chapter Three

[1] Father René Fumoleau donated the snowmobile to the Prince of Wales Northern Heritage Centre in Yellowknife, NWT.

[2] For additional information on earlier life in the bush see: G. Blondin's *When the World Was New* and *Yamoria the Lawmaker*.

Chapter Five

[1] G. Blondin, *When the World Was New*. Yellowknife: Outcrop Publishers, 1991, 58-9. Used by permission of the author.

Chapter Seven

[1] Sources of additional information for this chapter:

1.1 G. Blondin, *When the World Was New*.

1.2 ____. *Yamoria the Lawmaker*. Edmonton: NeWest Press, 1997.

1.3 J. Helm, *Prophecy and Power Among the Dogrib Indians*. Lincoln: University of Nebraska Press, 1994. Used by permission.

1.4 J. Franklin and J. Richardson, *Narrative of Second Expedition to the Shores of the Polar Sea in the Years 1825,1826, 1827*. London: J. Murray, 1828.

1.5 M. Morris, "Great Bear Lake Indians: A Historical Demography and Human Ecology." In *The Musk Ox*, Part 1, Vol II, 3-27 and Part 2, Vol 12, 28-80. Saskatoon, SK: Institute for Northern Studies, 1972-73.

[2] J. Franklin and J. Richardson, *Narrative of Second Expedition to the Shores of the Polar Sea in the Years 1825, 1826, 1827*.

[3] P. Duchaussois, *Mid Snow and Ice: The Apostles of the North West*, London: Burns, Oates and Wasbourne, 1923, 261.

[4] Ibid., 223.

Additional Recommended Reading

M. Asch, "The Slavey Indians: The Relevance of Ethnohistory to Development." In *Native People, The Canadian Experience*. Eds. R. Morrison, R. Bruce and C. Roderich Wilson. Toronto: McClelland & Stewart, 1989.

J. Helm, *The Handbook of North American Indians*, vol 6: The Sub Arctic. Washington: The Smithsonian Institute, 1981.

S. Rushforth, "Bear Lake Indians." In *Native People, The Canadian Experience*.

Chapter Eight

[1] A Nodwell is an enclosed, tracked vehicle capable of carrying several people.

Chapter Nine

[1] For additional reading on the transition of power from Ottawa to Yellowknife see: J. Hamilton, *Arctic Revolution—Social Changes in the Northwest Territories, 1935-94*. Toronto: Dundurn Press, 1994.

Chapter Ten

[1] Reprinted, with several modifications, from an article written by the author in *North*, July-Aug 1968.

Chapter Eleven

[1] My original discussion with Father Fumoleau has been supplemented here, with his permission, from his book *As Long As This Land Shall Last*. Toronto: McClelland & Stewart, 1975.

[2] R. Fumoleau, *As Long As This Land Shall Last*, 35.
[3] Ibid., 141.
[4] Ibid., 157.
[5] Ibid., 158.
[6] Ibid., 162.
[7] Ibid., 169.
[8] Ibid., 181.
[9] Ibid., 193.
[10] Ibid., 177.
[11] Upon later investigation, several of those whose names appear on the treaty documents denied signing (usually an X) any pieces of paper in 1921.
[12] R. Fumoleau, *As Long As This Land Shall Last*, 225.

Chapter Twelve

[1] A Mother Hubbard is a calf-length cotton print dress with a fur-trimmed hood, often worn as a "coat" by Inuit women and girls.
[2] It was only years later that I discovered that my chest problems were also due to an over-exposure to second-hand smoke.

Chapter Thirteen

[1] M. Hodgson, "Rebuilding the Community After the Residential School Experience." In *Nation to Nation*, Eds. Diane Engelstad and John Bird. Concord: Anasi Press, 1992, 103.
[2] K. Abel, *Drum Songs: Glimpses of Dene History*, Montréal & Kingston: Queen's University Press, 1993, 235-6.
[3] Ibid., 231.
[4] R. Fumoleau, *Denendeh, A Dene Celebration*, Yellowknife: The Dene Nation, 1984, 25. Used by permission.
[5] M. Angus, "Comprehensive Claims: One Step Forward, Two Steps Back." In *Nation to Nation*, 69-70.
[6] R. Fumoleau, *Denendeh, A Dene Celebration*, 26.
[7] Although the Court of Appeal and the Supreme Court of Canada later overturned the right to apply for a caveat on a legal technicality (caveats cannot be filed against unpatented crown lands), the decisions of Judge Morrow have never been challenged in court. His judgement forced the federal government to adopt a new policy toward Native peoples' rights.
[8] R. Fumoleau, *Denendeh, A Dene Celebration*, 27.
[9] Ibid.
[10] R. Fumoleau, *Denendeh, A Dene Celebration*, 28-9.
[11] K. Abel, *Drum Songs: Glimpses of Dene History*, 253.
[12] R. Fumoleau, *Denendeh, A Dene Celebration*, 32.
13 T. Berger, *Northern Frontier, Northern Homeland—The Report of the Mackenzie Valley Pipeline Inquiry*, Vol 1. Ottawa: Supply and Services, 1977.
[14] R. Fumoleau, *Denendeh, A Dene Celebration*, 32.
[15] M. Angus, "Comprehensive Claims: One Step Forward, Two Steps Back." In *Nation to Nation*, 71.
[16] K. Abel, *Drum Songs: Glimpses of Dene History*, 257.
[17] The Inuvialuit of the Beaufort Sea region had already arrived at a settlement with the government in 1984.
[18] Fort Good Hope Community Council, "Regaining Control at Fort Good Hope." In *Nation to Nation*, 135.
[19] *Sahtu Dene and Métis Comprehensive Land Claim Agreement*, vol.1. Ottawa: Indian and Northern Affairs, 1993, 9.
[20] K. Abel, *Drum Songs: Glimpses of History*, 258.
[21] B. Hammersmith, "Aboriginal Women and Self-Government." In *Nation to Nation*, 56-7.

Additional recommended reading

M. Asch, *Home and Native Land, Aboriginal Rights and the Canadian Constitution.*
"Political Self-Sufficiency." In *Nation to Nation.*
D. Engelstad and J. Bird, *Nation to Nation: Aboriginal Sovereignty and the Future of Canada.*
R. Fumoleau, "Are You Willing to Listen?" In *Nation to Nation.*

Chapter Seventeen

[1] Shortly after my visit, Déline received wide-open satellite television with a multitude of US and Canadian stations.

Chapter Eighteen

[1] *Sahtu Dene and Métis Comprehensive Land Claim Agreement*, Vol.1, 145.
[2] In October 1999 the Déline Dene Band signed an order in council that paves the way towards greater independence. Negotiations for self-government between the band and the federal government are proceeding well.

Chapter Nineteen

[1] Some of what I learned during my visit to Déline in 1995 has been supplemented by information provided by the Déline Uranium Committee report, "They Never Told Us These Things," which was published during the writing of these chapters. *A Record Analysis of the Deadly and Continuing Impacts of Radium and Uranium Mining on the Sahtu Dene of Great Bear Lake, Northwest Territories, Canada.* Déline: Déline Band Council, 1998. Used by permission.
[2] Independent tests performed in 1996 indicated that radioactive readings were still very high in the tugboat's showers.
[3] When the people of Déline discovered that the uranium mined at Port Radium, uranium ores that many of the men had helped load onto the barges, had been used as the primary source for the atomic bomb dropped on Hiroshima, Japan, on August 5, 1945, there was an immediate feeling of revulsion that they had been a part of that horrific destruction of life, even if inadvertently. The committee decided to send a small delegation of six people from Déline, in August 1998, to express their empathy and apologies to the people of Hiroshima. Author George Blondin, a former ore carrier and one of the delegates, wrote in *News/North* (August 24, 1998) of the warm welcome the Sahtuot'ine had received during their two-week stay and of the bond that was created between the two communities. Yellowknife: Jack Sigvaldason Publisher, Northern News Services, 1995-2000.
[4] In January 2000 the Minister of Indian Affairs and Northern Development met with the people of Déline and pledged the government's commitment to clean up or contain the uranium tailings at the Port Radium mine as well as several other hot spots in the area. The government will also begin an ongoing study on the effects of contamination on the health of the people.

Chapter Twenty

[1] *News/North*, August 26, 1996.
[2] Ibid., November 18, 1996. Used by permission.
[3] Quoted with permission from Jimmy Tutcho.
[4] R. Ross, *Returning to the Teachings: Exploring Aboriginal Justice.* Copyright © 1996 by Univeristy of Saskatchewan, 83-4. Used by permission of Penguin Books, Canada.
[5] Ibid., 84-5

Chapter Twenty-One

[1] Déline Lands Corporation. "The Human Resources and Training Strategy for the Community of Déline, 1995 to 2000," produced by Muskox Program Development, Yellowknife, NWT.
[2] In 1998 D'Arcy Moses opened Nats'enelu Ltd., a fashion and traditional arts business at

Fort Simpson. Having already made a name for himself among the fashion houses of Montreal, Paris and New York, Moses, whose mother is a Dene, decided to explore the Native roots he thought he had lost through adoption by an Albertan family.

[3] Since the writing of these chapters, Déline has experienced a substantial revival in the making of crafts and Dene-style clothing.

Chapter Twenty-Three

[1] Quoted with permission by Morris Neyelle.

[2] R. Ross, *Dancing With a Ghost: Exploring Indian Reality.* Markham, ON: Octopus, 1992, 148. Used by permission, McClelland & Stewart Ltd. *The Canadian Publisher.*

[3] Ibid., 149.

[4] Ibid., 153.

[5] Ibid., 152.

[6] Ibid., 143.

[7] Ibid.,170-74.

[8] Ibid., 170.

[9] Ibid., 167.

[10] Morris Neyelle of Déline in a Letter to the Editor, *News/ North*, November 1997.

Chapter Twenty-Four

[1] Sources of additional information for this chapter:

[1.1] G. Blondin, *When the World Was New.*

[1.2] — *Yamoria the Lawmaker.*

[1.3] Helm, *Prophecy and Power Among the Dogrib Indians.*

[2] G. Blondin. *Yamoria the Lawmaker*, 110.

[3] G. Blondin, *When the World Was New*, 78-9; 240-1.

[4] J. Helm, *Prophecy and Power Among the Dogrib Indians*, 62-4.

[5] Ibid., 28-29.

[6] Ibid., 28.

[7] Ibid., 56.

[8] Since 1995 spiritual gatherings have increased in frequency and winter gatherings are now held in the village. People from other communities have also been invited to participate including at least one visit from the Inuit of Kugluktuk (Coppermine) where youth suicide has become a serious concern.

Chapter Twenty-Five

[1] Bern Will Brown describes the years he spent as a priest in Déline, where he built the mission in 1950, in his book *Arctic Journal*. Ottawa: Novalis, Saint Paul University, 1998.

René Fumoleau has written two beautiful books of poetic stories about the Dene, including several on the people of Déline: *Here I Sit* (1995) and *The Secret* (1997). Ottawa: Novalis, Saint Paul University.

Epilogue

[1] Produced by Peter Blow, an independent filmmaker in Toronto.

[2] Dec 1999-April 2000. *Dats'i ?a (The Suffering)* was a millennium tribute to the Dene uranium ore carriers of Sahtu (Great Bear Lake). This exhibit, initiated and organized by Cindy Kenny-Gilday, was held in Yellowknife. Cindy, sister to Jane Kenny who now lives in Yellowknife, was also the chairperson of the Déline Uranium Committee report "They Never Told us These Things" referred to in this book. Buzz Hargrove, president of the Canadian Auto Workers, visited the exhibit in April and pledged additional funding to help finance a cross-Canada tour of the exhibit next Fall.

INDEX

D

E

F

G

H

I

O

P

Q

R

S

T

U

V

W

Y

Z